How to Listen to and Understand Opera

Robert Greenberg, Ph.D.

PUBLISHED BY:

THE GREAT COURSES
Corporate Headquarters
4840 Westfields Boulevard, Suite 500
Chantilly, Virginia 20151-2299
Phone: 1-800-832-2412
Fax: 703-378-3819
www.thegreatcourses.com

Copyright © The Teaching Company, 1997

Printed in the United States of America

This book is in copyright. All rights reserved.

Without limiting the rights under copyright reserved above,
no part of this publication may be reproduced, stored in
or introduced into a retrieval system, or transmitted,
in any form, or by any means
(electronic, mechanical, photocopying, recording, or otherwise),
without the prior written permission of
The Teaching Company.

Robert Greenberg, Ph.D.
Chairman, Department of Music History
and Literature
San Francisco Conservatory of Music

Professor Robert Greenberg has composed over 40 works for a wide variety of instrumental and vocal ensembles. Recent performances of Greenberg's work have taken place in New York, San Francisco, Los Angeles, Chicago, England, Ireland, Italy, Greece, and The Netherlands, where his "Child's Play" for String Quartet was performed at the Concertgebouw of Amsterdam in 1993.

Dr. Greenberg holds degrees from Princeton University and the University of California at Berkeley, where he received a Ph.D. in music composition in 1984. His principal teachers were Edward Cone, Claudio Spies, Andrew Imbrie, and Olly Wilson. His awards include three Nicola De Lorenzo Prizes in composition, three Meet the Composer grants, and commissions from the Koussevitzky Foundation of the Library of Congress, the Alexander String Quartet, XTET, and the Dancer's Stage Ballet Company.

He is on the faculty of the San Francisco Conservatory of Music, where he is chair of the Department of Music History and Literature and director of curriculum of the Adult Extension Division. He is creator, host, and lecturer for the San Francisco Symphony's "Discovery Series."

He has taught and lectured extensively across North America and Europe, speaking to such corporations and musical institutions as the Van Cliburn Foundation, Arthur Andersen, Bechtel Investments, the Shaklee Corporation, the University of California/Haas School of Business Executive Seminar, the Association of California Symphony Orchestras, the Texas Association of Symphony Orchestras, and the Commonwealth Club of San Francisco.

His work as a teacher and lecturer has been profiled in *The Wall Street Journal*, *Inc.* magazine, and the *San Francisco Chronicle*. He is an artistic co-director and board member of Composers, Inc. His music is published by Fallen Leaf Press and CPP/Belwin and is recorded on the Innova label. ∎

Table of Contents

INTRODUCTION

Professor Biography i
Course Scope 1

LECTURE GUIDES

LECTURES 1 AND 2
Introduction and Words and Music 5

LECTURES 3 AND 4
A Brief History of Vocal Expression in Music 35

LECTURES 5–8
The Invention of Opera and Monteverdi's *Orfeo* 69

LECTURES 9–12
The Growth of Opera, the Development of Italian Opera Seria,
and Mozart's *Idomeneo* 157

LECTURES 13–16
The Rise of Opera Buffa and Mozart's *The Marriage of Figaro* 219

SUPPLEMENTAL MATERIAL

Timeline 329
Glossary 334
Biographical Notes 339
Bibliography 344

How to Listen to and Understand Opera

Scope:

This course is designed as a methodology, a guide to listening and understanding opera. For this reason it does not provide a comprehensive overview of the entire operatic repertory. Armed with the knowledge of opera gained from this course, however, the listener will be able to explore in greater depth the extraordinary and compelling world of opera for himself or herself. The listener will come to appreciate how music has the power to reveal truths beyond the spoken word; how opera is a unique marriage of words and music in which the whole is far greater than its parts.

He or she will learn the reasons for opera's enduring popularity. The history of opera is traced from its beginning in the early seventeenth century to around 1924, with references to landmark operas, musical, cultural, and social developments, and historical events that influenced opera's growth. We learn how operatic style and form have changed continuously throughout the history of European music, as they were influenced by political, social and cultural developments, and how different national languages and cultures have shaped their own types of opera and operatic style.

The course opens with one of the most powerful moments in opera: the dramatically loaded aria "Nessun dorma" ("No one shall sleep") from Giacomo Puccini's *Turandot*. We are exposed to opera's unique incorporation of soliloquy, dialogue, scenery, action, and continuous music into an incredibly expressive and exciting whole that is far greater than the sum of its parts. This famous aria shows us the power of the composer in creating music that goes beyond the words of the libretto to evoke unspoken thoughts and feelings—that which cannot be said in words alone.

The study continues with a discussion of how music can flesh out a dramatic character and evoke the unconscious state. We are introduced to operatic archetypes such as Figaro and Carmen. We learn that the ancient Greeks revered music as a microcosm of all creation, believing music can change the face of nature and alter souls. The monophonic and, later, polyphonic music of the Middle Ages is examined. We see how the end of the absolute authority of the Roman Church encouraged the rise of secular and instrumental music. We examine the Renaissance, its rediscovery of ancient Greek and Roman culture and the evolution of the madrigal, ultimately rejected in favor of a more expressive vocal medium: early opera. The renaissance intermezzo is discussed as the precursor of modern opera. The reforms of the Florentine Camerata are examined as they relate to the earliest operas. Part I of the course concludes with an analysis of the first successful attempt to combine words and music into musical drama, Monteverdi's *Orfeo* of 1607.

In Part II we see how recitative, the essence of Monteverdi's style, made music subservient to words and how, because of its forward-driving nature, recitative cannot express personal reflection. We learn how the invention of aria gave opera composers a powerful tool to stop the dramatic action for moments of self-reflection. Gluck's reforms and his *Orfeo ed Euridice* of 1762 are addressed as the starting point for the modern opera repertory. The explosion of operas in the Golden Age/Dark Age of opera is discussed, along with the formulaic reforms of Pietro Metastasio (including his da capo structure for arias) and the vocal abuses that those reforms provoked. We learn how different voice types are assigned different roles. The rise of opera seria and its characteristics are discussed, along with an analysis of the second act of Mozart's *Idomeneo*—opera seria transcendent.

The second part of this study continues with the development of opera buffa, from its origins in the popular folklore of the commedia dell'arte to its eventual replacement of opera seria. The role of Enlightenment progressives in this development is addressed and Mozart's brilliant *The Marriage of Figaro* is discussed as one of the greatest contributions to the opera buffa genre.

Part III opens with a discussion of the bel canto style of opera. We see how the nature of the Italian language and culture gave rise to this type of opera, with its comic, predictable plots, one-dimensional characters, appealing melodies, and florid melodic embellishments. The highly pressurized business of opera in the 18th century is revealed, and we are introduced to Rossini's *The Barber of Seville* of 1816 as the quintessential bel canto opera.

Giuseppe Verdi is the focus of Lectures 19 through 22 of Part III. His career is summarized, and his operatic inheritance is reviewed. We learn how Verdi broke the bel canto mold; how he dominated Italian opera for over half a century by virtue of his lyricism, his emphasis on human emotions and psychological insight, and his use of the orchestra and parlante to drive the dramatic action and maintain musical continuity. Verdi's *Otello* is discussed as one of the greatest operas of all time.

Part III of this course concludes with an examination of French opera. We learn how it developed as a distinctly different genre from Italian opera, shaped as it was by the French language, culture and political history. We learn how Jean-Baptiste Lully set the foundation for a French language operatic tradition, and how his greatest contribution was the design of a recitative style suited to the French language. The reforms of Jean-Philippe Rameau are discussed, along with the influence of Enlightenment progressives such as Jean-Jacques Rousseau, who championed a more natural operatic style. Christoph Willibald von Gluck's position as the model for the next generation of French composers is reviewed. Finally, the subject of 19th-century French opera is addressed. Grand opera, opéra comique and lyric opera are examined as distinctive French genres and Act Two of Bizet's dramatically powerful *Carmen* is analyzed.

Part IV opens with an examination of the rise of German opera, with its roots in German folklore. We discover how German singspiel grew from humble origins as a lower class entertainment to high art with Wolfgang Amadeus Mozart's *The Rescue from the Harem* (1782) and *The Magic Flute* of 1791. We learn how 19th-century German opera grew out of the tradition of singspiel and how Carl Maria von Weber's *Der Freischütz* established 19th-century German opera.

The discussion of German opera continues with an examination of Richard Wagner: the man, his personal beliefs, musical theories, and operatic innovations. We see how Wagner went back to the ancient Greek ideal for inspiration and how he conceived the idea of an all-encompassing art work, or music drama, in which the role of the orchestra is that of a purveyor of unspoken truths. We are introduced to Wagner's concept of leitmotif and his revolutionary use of dissonance. Wagner's *Tristan und Isolde* is discussed as the most influential composition of the 19th century, aside from Beethoven's Ninth Symphony.

The subject of late romantic German opera is addressed and exemplified by Richard Strauss and his controversial opera *Salome*. We go on to an overview of Russian opera and the concept of nationalism. The late development of Russian opera is outlined from Mikhail Glinka's *Ruslan and Lyudmila* to Modest Mussorgsky's *Boris Godunov*. We see how the Russian language shaped the syllabic vocal style of Russian opera and how Russian rhythms, with their asymmetrical groupings of accents, are distinct from Italian, German and French rhythms.

The course draws to its conclusion with an overview of opera verismo, a 19th/20th century genre that favors depictions of the darker side of the human condition. The pivotal second act of Giacomo Puccini's *Tosca* is discussed as a transcendent example of opera verismo. Finally, we hear part of a scene from Richard Strauss's *Capriccio* in which the essence of opera is debated. Is it words or is it music? It is neither. It is an indefinable combination of both, with the whole greater than the parts. ■

Introduction and Words and Music
Lectures 1 and 2

Lectures 1 through 4 [of this course] are conceived of as a large introductory set, consisting of three separate parts. ... Part I ... is a general introduction to and definition of opera. ... Part II ... is a presentation I call "Words and Music." ... The third part ... is a brief but extremely intense history of expression in vocal music.

We will begin our consideration of opera by examining Giacomo Puccini's *Turandot* (1924). The scene is set in the city of Beijing in ancient China. Turandot, the daughter of the Chinese emperor, has promised to marry the man who can solve three riddles. So far no one has succeeded in answering these riddles. Calaf, the young Tartar prince, falls in love at first sight with Turandot and promptly announces his challenge to the riddles. He solves the riddles and then volunteers that if Turandot can discover his name before dawn, she will be freed from her vow to marry him and he will die. Turandot commands that no one shall sleep until the stranger's name and identity are discovered. Calaf sings a magnificent aria reflecting his love for Turandot and his confidence that his identity will remain a secret until morning. His aria, which begins with the phrase "Nessun dorma" ("No one shall sleep"), is one of opera's most dramatic and emotionally powerful moments.

Puccini could have set Calaf's aria in a variety of different ways. For dramatic reasons, he chose to set it as a love song. It is significant for its sense of joy and redemption not seen in the opera up until this point. Does this feeling come from the words or the music? This question forces us to examine the nature of opera.

First, we will look at some derivations and generalizations about opera. An opera is a drama that combines soliloquy, dialogue, scenery, action and continuous music, the whole greater than the parts. Literally, opera means musical work or composition.

The repertory we call opera is a diverse one. In its four hundred-year history opera has run the gamut from aristocratic to popular entertainment. Throughout its history, operatic singing style has changed constantly, depending upon the language being sung, the size of the room being sung in, the ability and taste of the singers, and the expectation of the audience. For most of its history, opera was the single greatest spectacle available to its audiences. It is the oldest continuously active musical genre.

> **For most of its history, opera was the single greatest spectacle available to its audiences. It is the oldest continuously active musical genre.**

To what might we attribute the popularity of opera? It is posited on the idea that music has the power to distill, crystallize, and intensify the meaning of words. Children at play, who sing-song their words to themselves and their toys, exemplify the operatic ideal.

The primary reason for opera's lasting popularity is the expressive power of the musical experience. T.S. Eliot said that music "evokes the fringe of indefinite feeling which we can only detect out of the corner of the eye." Music has the power to evoke the ineffable, moods and states of consciousness that other arts cannot.

In opera, the composer is a dramatist. He or she uses music to create the character. For example, Wolfgang Amadeus Mozart chills us with Electra's crazed fury as she sings "Of Orestes and Ajax" from *Idomeneo* (1780). Similarly, Gustav Mahler hits us off guard with the bittersweet feeling of lost love in "As I Walked through the Field this Morning" from his *Songs of a Wayfarer* (1884). Georges Bizet likewise intrigues us with his revelation of Carmen's power of sexual manipulation in the "Seguidilla" from *Carmen* (1875), and Gioacchino Antonio Rossini warms our hearts with Figaro's upbeat personality in the famous "Largo al factotum" from *The Barber of Seville* (1816).

These arias exemplify the reasons for the enduring popularity of opera. The sheer beauty of the vocal music, along with the excitement of the theater, is an irresistible force. Moreover, there is an incredible intensification of feeling and meaning when words and music are combined, and this is the essence of opera. The music rounds out the character. It begins where words leave off. The combination of the self-reflective nature of words with the emotionally reflective nature of music packs a powerful appeal.

Married to words, music has the ability to evoke symbolic meaning and universally appealing character archetypes. Bizet's Carmen is the archetypal, street-smart, seductress. Rossini's Figaro is a comic, clever, fast-talking servant archetype, whose predecessors date back to Roman comedy.

George Bizet's characters are strongly archetypal.

This course has several goals. First, we will review an outline of the history of opera from 1600 to 1924 or so. Second, we will observe the development of national schools of opera. Third, we will develop a methodology for listening to and understanding opera. And ultimately, we will celebrate the power of words joined to music! ■

Introduction and Words and Music, I
Lecture 1—Transcript

Welcome to "How to Listen to and Understand Opera." Lectures 1 through 4 are conceived of as a large introductory set, consisting of three separate parts, and I will tell you what they are now and then we will move on.

Part I of our introductory set is a general introduction to and definition of opera, and a discussion of opera's enduring popularity. Part II of our introductory set of lectures is a presentation I call "Words and Music," and I hope it will amuse you. The third part of our large introductory set of lectures is a brief but extremely intense history of expression in vocal music from the time of ancient Greece to the years around 1600. I trust I am not biting off a tad bit too much, but we will get through it, I guarantee.

First, my friends, I have a story to tell you, so please check it out. Our story takes place in China in ancient Beijing. The daughter of the Chinese emperor, the haughty and beautiful princess Turandot, has promised to marry any man of royal blood who can solve three riddles posed by her. If he should fail to come up with the proper answers, he will be beheaded. I would tell you that the walls of the city are already decorated with the heads of unsuccessful suitors. This is a whole new twist on the concept of the dating game: Bachelor Number 3? Wrong! Off comes that head. Yes, indeed. Clearly this sort of quiz-and-kill has put a major crimp in the princess's social life and, if you'll excuse me, has taken a rather large slice off the top of the local royal families.

Among the crowd at the latest execution, this one of the prince of Persia, is Timor—Timor is the old, blind Tartar king—and his son the prince, Calaf. Timor and Calaf are in disguise, because currently they are being pursued by enemies. So, rather than wearing the finery of their office, they are wearing the clothes of peasants. Calaf, the young prince, is sickened and horrified by the spectacle of the Prince of Persia's beheading. Just as he's about to spew the nastiest curses in the direction of the princess, he gets a clear look at her, and of course, he is utterly enraptured. He falls hopelessly and helplessly in love with this beautiful creature. He then mounts the platform, Calaf does, and he strikes the great gong three times, indicating that he is to be the next challenger wishing to solve the riddles. My friends, once again we are left to ponder the native intelligence of post-adolescent princes, Calaf's smarts in particular. All right; it's just a story, so let's continue.

I will make a long story short for our purposes right now. Calaf, indeed, manages to solve the riddles. Turandot is appalled, and she begs her father not to force her to honor the agreement. "Look—if nothing else, Dad, look at the way this guy is dressed, for goodness sake!" Calaf offers that if she can discover who he is and what his name is before dawn, she will be freed from her vow and he will allow himself to be beheaded. Again, one wonders about Calaf's intelligence, but he seems to know something that the rest of us do not. Her father, the emperor, agrees to this deal. Turandot commands that no one shall sleep until the stranger's name is discovered. By the way, she tells the palace staff that if they don't discover the stranger's name, they will instead be beheaded, thus adding a little work incentive to the issue at hand. Calaf himself, of course, is utterly certain that he will be victorious. This is what we call in the trade an "aria opportunity." Calaf can sing about his confidence, sing about his position, sing about his joy about having solved the riddles.

So, these are the words that the co-librettists—that is, the co-writers of this story, Giuseppe Adami and Renato Simoni—supplied to the composer, Giacomo Puccini, for this moment in the opera Turandot of 1924. Calaf sings "Nessun dorma! Nessun dorma! No one shall sleep! No one shall sleep! You too, Princess, in your cold room are watching the stars, which tremble with love and hope. But my secret lies hidden within me. No one will know my name! No, no, I will reveal it only on your lips when daylight breaks forth and my kiss will break the silence, which makes you mine!" Meanwhile, offstage, we hear the women of Beijing singing, "Nobody will know his name…And we will have to die, alas! Die!"Calaf sings again, "Depart, O night! Quickly set, stars! Quickly set, stars! At dawn I will win! I will win! I will win! Vincerò! Vincerò! Vincerò!" Thus ends the aria.

Now, here's the question we must ponder. How will Puccini set these words? It's up to Puccini to take these words and put them to music, so we say he's going to set the words. What words in the text will he use as his cue to create the mood of the following aria? For example, "Vincerò, vincerò" are strident, victorious words. Should this be a strident, victory march for Calaf? Well, it's a possibility, if he takes the cue from "vincerò." How about Calaf's line, "But my secret lies hidden within me." Well, if Puccini decides to use those words as his cue, this could be a sly, and mysterious, and quiet aria. Perhaps the offstage women have supplied the mood for this aria, filled with terror and fear and anxiety as they are—"We will have to die! We will have to die!" Will this be a nervous and heart-rending aria?

None of the above. Puccini's choice is as follows: He sets these words as a sublime and glorious serenade to the princess, to the stars and to the oncoming dawn. "Nessun dorma" becomes a transcendent love song, which finally explains the depth and power of the prince's infatuation with the princess, his willingness to risk everything and his conviction—"You, too, Princess, are watching the stars, which tremble with love and hope"—his conviction that the princess herself is desperate for love.

Please, let's listen to this aria. Let's contemplate this text and then talk a little more about the choices Puccini makes in writing this particular music.

"Nessun dorma." (musical example)

Well, wow, and double wow! If that doesn't grab at your heart and squeeze just hard enough to cause pain but not enough to stop it, then your heart's not working hard enough, my friends. Look, this aria, this serenade, this love song changes everything. Its sheer radiant beauty and passion change our perception of the prince, change our perception of the story. My goodness, this love song even offers redemption, the one thing we think is beyond her, to the princess herself. Now, here's the big question. Does this sense of redemption, this sense of sheer radiant beauty and joy, this story-changing aria—does this come from the words or does it come from the music? As the Italians would say, "le parole o la musica"—from the words or the music? Or is it from some combination of both, the whole greater than the parts? This forces us now, finally, to define and speak in generalizations about opera and its nature.

Opera defined for starters: An opera is a drama which combines soliloquy, dialogue, scenery, and action and continuous or nearly continuous music—

the whole always greater than the parts. This is going to be my mantra. I'm going to chant it constantly: the whole always greater than the parts. We can talk about all the silly aspects of opera and we will—indeed, we will. But, we always must look holistically. What are we aiming for dramatically? An opera is a drama, which combines soliloquy, dialogue, scenery, action and continuous or nearly continuous music, the whole always greater than the parts.

Literally, opera means simply musical work or musical composition. This huge repertorial world we call "opera" is an incredibly diverse and varied theatrical musical tradition. This thing we call "opera" is at least as varied as this thing we call "food." There's good and bad, light and heavy. Some of it is well cooked, properly prepared and imaginatively presented, while some is served, if you'll excuse me, pretty raw. Some meals are short and to the point and others can go on all evening. Like food, some opera is good for us, and some, frankly, is not. Although the opera that's not good for us doesn't mean it's not fun. I mean, nachos aren't good for us either, but there's times when we cannot resist their lure. So, let's understand that whether it's good or bad for us is not a reflection on whether we have a good time while we're there.

Like food, there are distinctly nationalistic schools of opera, each of which reflects the spirit of their time, their place and their audience. In its 400-year history, opera has been an intimate, aristocratic entertainment and a huge public spectacle. Operatic stories have run the gamut from great and profound drama to a level of stupidity and vacuity that would make a TV network programmer blush. At different times, opera has celebrated mythological creatures, kings and queens, the confrontation between the upper and the lower classes, common people, the supernatural and bizarre, and the everyday and commonplace. In its 400-year history, operatic singing style has changed constantly from era to era and even, my friends, from place to place depending upon: (1) the language being sung in, (2) the size of the rooms being sung in, (3) the ability and taste, or lack thereof, of the singers themselves, and (4) the expectations of the audience.

Please, please, please. We have got to remember that for most of its history opera was the Super Bowl half-time show, the wrap-around screen surround-sound theater, the computer-animated virtual-reality experience of its time. In a pre-electronic age, opera was the single most stimulating, extraordinary, sweep-the-audience-off-its-collective-derrière-into-another-world, special-effects-dominated, fantasy-entertainment environment known to Western humankind.

Opera as a musical genre is also the longest continuing running show around. For perspective, I'd like us to compare some other media genres, some notable inventions, births and events, so that we have a sense of this extraordinary time span that operatic history represents. So, indulge me.

Television as a medium is roughly 60 years old. Commercial radio is roughly 80 years old, motion pictures and recorded music, roughly 100 years old. Telephone service is roughly 120 years old. I would tell you that it was in 1860 that Fredrick Walton created linoleum out of linseed oil. In 1838, the Daguerre method of photography was presented to the Academy of Sciences in Paris. 1828, the first commercial railroad was built in the United States. 1824, our friend Ludwig van Beethoven completed his "Ninth Symphony."

In 1770, Beethoven was born. In 1756, Wolfgang Mozart was born. The genres of symphony and string quartet came into being around the year 1750. In 1732, Franz Joseph Haydn was born. In 1719, Leopold Mozart, Wolfgang's father, was born and Daniel Defoe wrote *Robinson Crusoe*. In 1709, the piano—this marvelous amalgam of wood and felt and steel—was invented.

In 1689, Peter the Great became the Czar of Russia. In 1685, and this was a very good year for composers, Johann Sebastian Bach, George Frederick Handel, and Domenico Scarlatti were all born. That's 1685. Mark that one in your calendars, please. In 1667, Jonathan Swift was born. In 1666, Antonio Stradivari labeled his first violin. In 1664, the British renamed New Amsterdam, New York. In 1648, the Peace of Westphalia concluded the horrific Thirty Years' War. In 1640, the first European café opens in Venice, and I can assure you it was not a Starbuck's. In 1633, Galileo recants.

In 1626, the Dutch colony of New Amsterdam is founded on the Hudson River. 1619, the first slaves are brought to North America, arriving in Virginia.

In 1613, fire destroys the Globe Theater in London. In 1612, Shakespeare completes *The Tempest*. 1607, the Jamestown, Virginia colony, the first English settlement on the American mainland, is founded. Also, in 1607, Monteverdi's *Orfeo* becomes the first operatic masterwork. It is composed and premiered in 1607. 1603, Queen Elizabeth I dies at 70, ostensibly still a virgin, and Sir Walter Raleigh is arrested and imprisoned. 1600, Shakespeare writes *Hamlet*, the Dutch opticians invent the telescope, Giordano Bruno is burned as a heretic in Rome, the future King Charles I of England is born, and Jacopo Peri composes *Euridice*, the earliest surviving opera.

The point of this brief chronological exercise is as follows: Opera is an old musical genre. It spans a tremendous amount of recent and not so recent historical time. Much has happened in the world since the invention of opera and the world has changed dramatically since opera was invented; yet opera endures. Can we say that about any other late sixteenth-century entertainment? We cannot.

So, to what do we attribute this astounding run of operatic popularity? In order to answer this question, we must get into the next body of information—a popularity and operatic repertoire that spans 400 years of Western history, which brings us to a presentation that I call "Words and Music." Please bear with me. Ultimately we will be listening to more operatic excerpts and talking about the essence of the words, and how those words are best translated into music to heighten and intensify those words. First, we must go back to the question I asked moments ago; to what do we attribute the astounding run of operatic popularity, indeed?

Let's start by quickly destroying that most typical operatic stereotype, that opera is essentially very large people, be-horned and be-breast-plated, singing, nay, screaming, nose-to-nose at a volume that would peel the chrome off your Chevy truck, thank you very much. No, that's not a good stereotype. It's just the Wagnerian one, and we will deal with that when we get to Richard Wagner. Opera, like any other vocal music, is posited on a simple idea—that music has the power to distill, to crystallize, and intensify the meaning of words. I am going to say that again because this is so important. Opera, like any other vocal music, is posited on a single idea, a simple idea—that music has the power to distill, crystallize, and intensify the meaning of words. This is, of course, what the essence of song is.

We have a tendency, and it's an ugly tendency sometimes (not "we", but some of the unwashed out there who don't know better) to call any piece of music a song, whether it's a symphony by Beethoven, an opera by Verdi, or indeed, a pop song. A song is generally thought of as something with a simple lyric—that is, a straightforward storyline set to a fairly simple accompaniment. Obviously, opera is neither simple nor simple. The words tend to be complicated and the music even more so. Yet, at its very essence, opera is song. At its very essence, opera is words intensified by music.

Many people say to me opera is the most unnatural possible thing—these big people yelling and screaming and singing all these silly things. On the surface the operatic experience might seem to be unnatural. But please, what I always tell these people and would say now, is observe children at play. Who's more natural than a child? They haven't learned to be embarrassed by anything yet. They haven't learned to feel foolish yet. Well, when children are at play, as often as not, they singsong their words to each other, to their toys, to themselves. They know that they can heighten their experience and intensify the emotional content of what they're doing if they sing it rather than just speak it. You see, kids are natural-born opera composers. We just kind of lose that as we get older, and we learn shame and embarrassment. What a terrible thing. Look, my friends; this is what opera is. It is the intensification of words with music. It is the institutionalization of the power of song.

Now, back to that stereotypical image of opera as looking and seeming funny, because sometimes opera does look and seem funny. W. H. Auden wrote this: "No good opera plot can be sensible, for people do not sing when they are feeling sensible." He's got a point. I'm sure we've all gone to musicals, for example, where someone starts singing and we say, "This looks really stupid. You shouldn't sing at a moment like this." We have to suspend our disbelief long enough to accept the singing as an intrinsic expression at that moment. But we must add the following to Mr. Auden's idea; people often do sing when they are feeling something powerful.

Reason number one, then, for the lasting popularity of opera: the expressive power of the musical experience. Again, I quote another writer, this one T. S. Elliot, from his essay "Poetry and Drama," and I quote,

> It is a function of all art to give us some perception of an order in life, by imposing order upon it. The painter works in selection, combination, and emphasis among the elements of the visible world, the composer in the world of sound. It seems to me that beyond the namable, classifiable emotions and motives of our conscious life when directed towards action—the parts of life which prose drama can adequately express—there is a fringe of indefinite extent, of feeling which we can only detect out of the corner of the eye and which we can never completely focus on; of feeling of which we are only aware in a kind of temporary detachment from action.

Just to cut in on Mr. Elliot for a moment. What he is talking about then, is there are certain feelings we have when we just pause in repose and reflect, not when we're actually active, but feelings we have when we pull back from action and reflect.

> This peculiar range of feeling can be expressed by dramatic poetry at its moments of greatest intensity. At such moments, we touch the border of those feelings which only music can truly express.

So what T. S. Elliot is saying, and I find this very brave, frankly, that a poet is admitting the weakness of his art and handing over to the composer the ultimate ability to transmit those feelings that words can't—those sublime, ineffable, unknowable, yet definite feelings we all get.

We all know this is true about music. We all know music can create a sensibility that nothing else can. How many times, for example, have we heard, let's say a song, something that we associate with our past. For a moment in time, for a brief moment in time, we are thrust backwards. We smell the smells, we see the sights, we feel the feelings of that moment in our past, which that particular piece of music—usually a song from our youth—represents to us. These are extraordinary and sometimes even bittersweet moments, reminding us often of lost youth, friends and innocence.

The next time this should happen to you, pull yourself back and ask yourself, "You know, what if I just heard those words? Would I still be feeling these feelings and sensing these sensibilities if I'd heard the words? Or, was it the music that brought back these memories and these feelings?" Well, the answer is, of course, that it's the music. It was, it is, it's always the music that, to paraphrase Elliot, evokes the fringe of indefinite feeling, which we can only detect out of the corner of the eye.

Another quote, because I can't resist. This is from E. T. A. Hoffman, composer, philosopher, novelist, librettist, gadfly. Hoffman wrote this about music in about the year 1830. Check it out, "Music is the most romantic of all the arts, as its subject is only the infinite, the secret Sanskrit of nature expressed in tones, which fill the human heart with endless longing, and only in music does one understand the songs of trees, of animals, stones, and floods."

Well, what he is saying is that music can evoke "stuff" that words can't. We'll feel feelings and experience things through pure music that words don't allow us to. This is exactly what we're talking about, and this is precisely what Hoffman is on to. Music, divorced from words, has the power to evoke feeling and experience beyond that of any other art, beyond that even of spoken language. Since opera combines words and music, it is the job of the music to heighten the meaning and emotional impact of the words to a level past, and I mean way past, that of which the words themselves are capable. This brings us to an incredibly important concept, and I'm glad we're getting to it right here, two-thirds of the way through our first lecture—and that concept is the composer as dramatist.

The composer as dramatist. In opera, my friends, it is the composer who is the dramatist, much more so than the writer of the play or libretto. I've been using that term promiscuously and I haven't defined it yet. Let me do so. *Libretto* means "little book," and a libretto is simply the play that is set to music. Writing a libretto is a specialized art, just like writing a screenplay might be. One has to be very brief and succinct and allow the composer to fill in all the gaps, just as, if one is writing a screenplay, one must be constantly aware of all the visual and other information that will add to the words that you're actually writing. So, libretto writing is not just a matter of writing a play, or writing a story, then handing it to a composer. It is a very advanced art on its own. When we talk about a librettist, we are talking about the writer of an operatic play. When I say *libretti*, I'm simply sticking to the Italian and using the Italian plural rather than saying "librettos," which sounds vaguely like potatoes to me. So, libretti would mean many libretto.

In any case, what I'm saying is the composer is the dramatist, much more than the person who wrote the libretto or the play. Case in point, and this will illustrate it better than anything I could say. We're going to listen to the climactic aria from Mozart's opera *Idomeneo*. This opera dates from 1780. This is Electra's bone-chilling exit aria "Of Orestes and Ajax." An exit aria is just what it sounds like. It's when a major character has one last shot to make their point before they walk up the stage. And, if they don't bring down the house with their exit aria, then the house is not going to come down for them. The composer has to be darned sure that he or she has supplied this featured character with music that is going to garner the maximum number of bravos and bravas, lest the singer be unhappy. My friends, aside from feral dogs, there's nothing quite worse than an unhappy singer.

Background: Electra is a princess in the family of Atreus, who rule in Mycenae over the kingdom of Argos. Again, Electra is a princess in the family of Atreus, who rule in Mycenae, in Greece, over the kingdom of Argos. Now, the House of Atreus is your quintessential, dysfunctional Greek royal family. The father is Agamemnon, the king of Argos. Mom is the unstable Clytemnestra. The brother is Orestes, and Electra has two sisters, Iphigenia and Chrysothemis.

The background to our story: Before leading his invasion force to Troy, Agamemnon went hunting and killed a stag sacred to the goddess, Artemis. He went hunting. He couldn't play poker. He couldn't go bowling. He couldn't do those chores around the house that he's not going to have a chance to do for the next decade or so. No, he's got to go out and kill a deer. And that's what he does. Artemis retaliates by becalming the sea beneath Agamemnon's fleet, until he, Agamemnon, sacrifices his daughter, Iphigenia, to the goddess. Now, this does not go over big at all with Clytemnestra, who is furious and, of course, cannot forgive her husband. We must also keep in mind that Agamemnon was the same person who killed Clytemnestra's first husband and child in order to marry her in the first place. While Agamemnon is at war with the boys, Clytemnestra takes as her lover Aegisthus. Together, she and Aegisthus kill Agamemnon after his return. They bop him over the head with a double-headed ax while he's taking a bath.

Orestes, of course, is beside himself and he avenges his father's death by murdering Clytemnestra and Aegisthus, after which the Furies hound him into madness for his matricide. It is one of these basic days in Greece, right? In one of the versions of this story, Electra, already nearly insane herself, dies from joy at the news of her mother's murder. In another version of the story, Electra leaves Argos and wanders all around the Mediterranean, crazed with rage and grief.

This brings us, at last, to Mozart's version of the story of the opera *Idomeneo, Re di Creta*, "Idomeneo, King of Crete," 1780. Mozart wrote the music. Giambattista Varesco wrote the libretto. The action takes place, as you would guess, on Crete following the conclusion of the Trojan War. Electra is there in Crete, mourning her father's death and her brother's madness. She is unbalanced but not, not at least yet, off her rocker. Electra has fallen in love with the heir to the Cretan throne, Prince Idomante. Electra's rival for Idomante is the kind and sweet and beautiful Ilia. Don't you just hate her already? She's the kind of person that makes everybody crazy. She's a Trojan princess who's been brought to Crete initially as a prisoner, but now that the war is over, she is free. Needless to say, Electra loses out in this particular triangle, and near the very end of the opera the announcement of Ilia and Idomante's betrothal is made. I would tell you that the already bitchy, vindictive, and unstable Electra absolutely loses it. She goes bonkers, nuts, ballistic.

This is the moment that we join the opera and these are the words Mozart's librettist, Giambattista Varesco, supplies for this key dramatic moment. Electra: "I feel the torments of Orestes and Ajax in my breast. The image of Allecto [Allecto was one of the Furies] frightens me to death. Tear my heart, you horned serpents, or I shall end my pain with a sword." Period; *finis!*

If I'm Mozart and I say this is the moment, this is the moment that Electra has the stage and owns the audience and I'm handed these words, I utter that one word most necessary to the composer, "Rewrite!" But there is no rewrite because Mozart's a stud. Mozart says, "Look, she has much to feel and I've got to give her time to feel it." Let's read these words again, and then let's listen to what Mozart does with these useless, flat, unimaginative words in giving Electra one of the most galvanizing moments in the whole history of opera. Again, "I feel the torments of Orestes and Ajax in my breast. The image of Allecto frightens me to death." Frightens—one of the cues that Mozart is going to run with. He's going to run with fear and terror. Second verse: "Tear my heart, you horned serpents, or I shall end my pain with a sword." First, she says, tear my heart, mutilate me, hurt me, make me suffer, make me feel pain. I mean there's some real masochism here. And if you don't, I will end my pain with a sword. So, if you don't hurt me, I'll kill myself. You know the more we think about these words, the more we can see there's a great potential for hysterics here, and that's what Mozart gives us.

I'm going to point out a couple of things. We will listen. Then I'll point out these elements again, because I want us to hear what he does with these words. We're going to hear in the accompaniment *brrrrump, brrrump, brrrump*—these whipping, flagellating musical ideas, and she's virtually whipping herself, flaying her own flesh. This music fluctuates between violent self-abuse and deep pain.

Now if you had to write an aria like that where would you put these words in the soprano's *tessitura*, or her range? And there's a very useful word to use, my friends, if nothing else for crossword puzzles. *Tessitura* refers to the height of the singer's range. Well, where in the singer's *tessitura* will we put this? As high as possible. She has to screech. She has to scream. She cannot sound attractive and controlled. She has to sound out of control. So, Mozart will not only stick her high up, but she's going to be jumping all over the place, anything to sound out of control. We're going to have all kinds of obsessive repetitions. She's not just going to say, "Tear my heart, you horned serpents, you horned serpents, you horned serpents." She's going to say, "Tear my heart, tear, tear, tear my heart, my heart, my heart, my heart." Yes, she is going to get obsessive, and that sense of obsession will be translated into her madness.

At the very end, Mozart has a wonderful moment where we hear this absolutely mad laughter. I mean it sounds like something out of a bad horror movie, but of course, since horror movies are still a good 170 years away at the time Mozart writes this, we have to realize Mozart is coming up with this idea himself. This hysterical, strange and blood-curdling laughter that we hear at the end—let's just be really aware of it when it happens.

Let's jump in. Let's listen to this aria and let's ask ourselves, who's the dramatist? Varesco or Mozart?

"Of Orestes and Ajax" from *Idomeneo*. (musical example)

I can assure you, when you see *Idomeneo* and Electra sings this aria and she runs off the stage completely crazed at the end, everyone goes ape. It tells us two things. First of all, it tells us that the bad guys are always more interesting than the good guys. They are much more complex and they are frankly more fun. We don't necessarily want to date them, but we certainly want to watch their actions. And second of all, it tells us that Mozart is a magician. We knew that; but this reinforces what we know, that these words by themselves are flat, but with the application of music a whole three-dimensional person and character becomes visible.

We've been talking, and we will continue to talk as we move into the second lecture, about why opera has endured for 400 years. The first reason was the power of music to transmit information that words cannot. It is the music that makes her insane. It's those crazy leaps from low to high. It's the emphasis on her high vocal range. It's the obsessive repetition of words, that hysterical laughter at the end. It is the music that creates the character, and this is the first reason for the enduring popularity of opera.

I asked before, who is the dramatist here? Who creates this character? Now, my friends, in a stage play, it is indeed the actors that interpret the words, but in an opera, the composer has already interpreted the words by setting them to music in a specific way. It's up to the singer now to realize what the composer has created. Yes indeed, we could say that the singer is interpreting the composer, but not really. The singer should just be singing what's on the page and doing it as well they could. The words have already been interpreted; they've been interpreted by the composer. It is the composer who is the dramatist.

When we return for our second lecture, we will voyage into the second reason behind the enduring popularity of opera, and that has to do with the lasting dramatic effectiveness of the complementary nature of words and music. Until then, I thank you.

Introduction and Words and Music, II
Lecture 2—Transcript

Welcome back to "How to Listen to and Understand Opera." This is Lecture 2, and we are working our way through this introductory set of lectures. Right now, we're talking about the reasons behind the lasting expressive power and popularity of opera itself. The first reason, what we talked about back in Lecture 1, had to do with the expressive power of the purely musical experience—that is, those things that music can tell us that words cannot. We proceed.

Reason number two for the lasting dramatic effectiveness and popularity of opera has to do with the complementary nature of words and music: the self-reflective nature of words and the emotionally reflective nature of music. I quote from Eric Plaut's marvelous book, *Grand Opera*. "Words and music are our two most powerful languages for emotional communication. Speech expresses a form of symbolic thinking, and speech is unique in that it alone allows self-reflective thinking. Only through speech do we become able to think about thinking."

"The capacity for self-reflecting thinking comes, like most things in life, at some cost. Although it makes thoughts more precise and capable of generalizations and abstraction, its development results in the loss of potential for other capacities. Lost with the development of speech is some of the all-embracing quality of emotional response. The infant does not separate emotion from perception or sensation. The infant reacts in a total way." Indeed, those of us who have had or have infants know that to be true.

"With self-reflective speech, some of that quality of immediacy is lost. Music speaks to us in a language that is not self-reflective. Music retains more of the capacity for immediate, total emotional response that we lose with speech. Music does not have the capacity for logical reasoning and problem solving of self-reflecting speech." And neither, if I might add gratuitously, do musicians, generally, if you'll excuse me. "Rather, music can describe aspects of life and feeling that speech cannot."

For example, we're going to listen to and talk about a song. This is not from an opera. It's a song by Gustav Mahler, the marvelous, Bohemian-born and Austrian- and New York-careered composer and conductor. I would tell you a little about Mahler. I had to sneak him in somehow. This is kind of a surreptitious way to do it. He is one of my favorite composers, and he was simply the most famous opera conductor in his time. At the turn of the century, Mahler was the great conductor of operas and was considered an okay composer. But his great fame and fortune were made as a conductor. The great question everyone asked was, "Well, if he's such a great opera conductor"—which he was—"why doesn't he write operas?" And indeed, Mahler wrote symphonies; early in his life he wrote many songs, first for piano and voice and then for orchestra and voice; later in life, he wrote some more orchestral songs, capped by the marvelous "Das Lied von der Erde;" but essentially, he was a composer of instrumental symphonies. So, Mahler didn't write the opera he might have written for reasons we can't get into now; this is not a Mahler course. Suffice it to say for now he's a brilliant conductor of operas, a brilliant interpreter of vocal music, a brilliant writer of vocal music, and that's why I'm using him now; because we've got to understand the complementary power of words and music and Mahler's as good a vehicle as any.

This is a song from a group of songs called "The Songs of a Wayfarer," and it's a piece that dates from 1884 and the orchestral version that we will hear, from 1896. Mahler himself wrote the poems. He fancied himself, as all adolescents do, a very oversensitive person, capable of brilliant poetry. He learned later in life to stop setting his own poems. Nevertheless, early in life he did set them, and this poem has a certain rustic charm to it. Let me read it to you and then let's talk about the emotional and expressive content of the poem. Then, of course, we'll talk about Mahler's options. How will he set this to music? What will be the cues in the poem that will allow him to get an optimum musical setting that will intensify, distill and crystallize the meaning of the words?

The name of the poem is "Ging Heute Morgen Übers Feld—"As I Walked through the Field This Morning."

As I walked through the field this morning, the dew still hung upon the grass; the merry finch called out to me, "Hey, hey you there! Good day to you! Isn't this a splendid world? Splendid world? Tweet! Tweet! Fine and bright! O, how I love the world!"

And the bluebell in the field told of good cheer with its bell, ting-a-ling, as it rang its morning greeting: "Isn't this a splendid world, a splendid world? Ding, ding! Beautiful thing! O how I love the world! Hurrah!"

And all the world began to glow in the sunshine; in the sunshine all things took on color and sound! Flower and bird, things great and small. Good day, good day! Isn't this a splendid world? Hey, you there! Lovely world!

Will my happiness now flower, too? No, no! I know that it can never bloom for me!

The first three stanzas of this poem are completely happy and quite descriptive. Only the fourth stanza is self-reflective, and it's, of course, reflective of loneliness and unhappiness. As poetry, we only realize in the fourth stanza that the first three stanzas are an example of forced cheerfulness. Our disappointed young lover is wandering through nature and trying to feel good about himself and about the world. Or, I suppose this could be a young lady, although it was written for a male voice, trying to hide behind the beauties of nature, trying to hide from a broken heart. We might say that this gentleman is taking a trip in Egypt; he's in denial.

Anyway, look, we must ask ourselves two questions. What will Mahler's music tell us that the words do not and cannot? And secondly, how will Mahler's setting support the self-reflection of that final stanza, the fourth stanza? Will Mahler get real dramatic? Will there be agonized music used to illustrate the terrible realization that "Love will never bloom for me?"

Here's what Mahler does. First of all, this music is rustic and engaging, and it reflects a happy, out-of-doors nature that is described well in the first three stanzas of the poem. So, we should expect for this rustic, almost folk-like poetry a rustic and very sophisticated, if folk-like, melodic material to accompany it. By stanza three the music is going to begin to slow down, and Mahler tells us to start slowing down. Indeed, we will slow down noticeably. "Isn't this a splendid world!" becomes "Isn't this a splendid world?" with a question mark more than exclamation mark. Indeed, the emotional clock runs down over the entire course of this wonderful song. Stanza four slows the beautiful and rustic melody to a crawl. I would tell you that the sweetness of the music gives this stanza a bittersweet heartbreak; I mean a real sense of agony that histrionics and screaming never could. You know, it's true, and we all know this is true, sometimes it's better to make our point quietly, and elegantly, than with lots of screaming and howling.

Now, Electra needs to scream and howl. It is her nature as a member of the house of Atreus; but not for Mahler. Our gentleman simply winds down. I would tell you that as the poem, the song, reaches its climax; we have a complete emotional breakdown on the words, "Nimmer, nimmer;" never, never will love bloom for me. The song ends with a sustained instrumental sigh in the orchestra. This is a brilliant, deeply moving setting of these words.

Please, let's listen. Gustav Mahler, "Songs of a Wayfarer," Number 2, 1884, orchestrated in 1896. (musical example)

Isn't that something? Very effective, very brilliant, very simple, very direct. The best solutions are usually the obvious ones. He takes his cue from this fourth verse, this self-reflective verse, but everything in the song leads to that moment. It is a beautiful example of the self-reflective nature of words complemented by the emotionally-reflective nature of music.

Reason number three for the lasting dramatic effectiveness and popularity of opera has to do with the symbolic nature of opera and opera characters. Before I get into this, I just want to make a point. Because again, for the opera-haters—who I'm generally not speaking to, and I know I'm speaking to the choir in some cases here but we've got to make fans out of those who aren't quite sure—opera characters seem to be extreme human beings. I just don't mean the size of the diaphragms on the people who do the opera singing. I mean the nature of the characters themselves tends to be extreme, one way or the other.

Now, this is purposeful and it has to do with the nature of character archetypes and symbolism that permeate the entire history of opera. Yes, the symbolic nature of opera and opera characters is the Jungian vision of opera, if you will. It posits that operatic symbols and character archetypes, intensified and abstracted profoundly by the combination of words and music, draw on our collective unconscious—that deep reservoir of images derived from our ancestral experience. And so, certain characters are the way they are because they evoke both memory and reference to people we have known or perhaps even to ourselves. Opera characters are not your typical play characters. They are extremes. They are archetypes.

Robert Donington writes,

> We all contain within us and recognize elements of archetypes. Opera is the great purveyor of archetypal images. Confrontation with archetypal material is likely to be cathartic. Confrontation with archetypes is the chief business of opera. That's just the nature of the beast. Thus it is that an opera may come over to us as meaningful, even when the story is far from impressive. Something may stir in us, which is not literally recognition but is nevertheless akin to recognition. In every such case, I think we are getting the benefit of unsuspected associations beyond the visible exigencies of the plot and the audible suitability of the music for deepening our experience of that plot.

So, Donington is saying that opera characters carry within themselves, the nature of the characters, a whole series of memories and references that transcend the stories and even transcend the music.

For example, Bizet's *Carmen* of 1875. Let me set the scene in Act One. Carmen, of course, is that sexy little cigarette-factory worker, and she has been arrested for disorderly contact. Excuse me, disorderly conduct. You want to talk about a Freudian slip? Whoa! Yes, the disorderly contact actually comes in Act Two. But, all right, we'll get there in due time. She is being detained at this particular moment. Her hands are bound, incidentally, by a soldier named Don José, who has admired her from a distance. Don José, this poor schlepper, has not a chance. He's got this squeaky clean girlfriend named Micaela. He's a real mommy's boy; he's always saying, "How's Mom? How's Mom?" He's a corporal and someone who isn't going to rise a whole heck of a lot further in the service than he already is. He's clearly no match for Carmen. Even literally with her hands tied she dominates Don José. She verbally, and with her eyes, seduces him and convinces him to release her. These are the words that Georges Bizet was given by his librettists, Henri Meilhac and Ludovic Halévy, for this scene.

Carmen turns to Don José and sings:

> By the ramparts of Seville, at the place of Lillas Pastia, I'll go dance the seguidilla and take a glass of manzanilla. Yes, but by myself I'm bored, the only pleasure's one you can share, so I'll take along my man, and then we'll make a cozy pair. But my lover's…gone to hell! Last night he went out…on his ear! My poor heart's longing to forget, my heart is ever free as air! I count my beaux by dozens, but I'll have none of them. Here it is the end of the week, and who will love me? I'll love him! Who will take my soul? It's up for bids! You've come along at the right time, soldier boy. I can't wait a minute longer, for once I've got a brand-new lover…

And, of course, Don José is scandalized: "Be quiet! I told you not to speak!"

> I'm not speaking. I'm singing to myself! And thinking! There's no law against thinking! I'm thinking of a certain officer who loves me and whom I could maybe love myself.

And Don José says, "Carmen!"

And Carmen continues,

> My officer's not a captain. Why, he's not even a lieutenant, just a corporal; but that's good enough for a gypsy and I'm ready to make do with that!

Of course, Don José is in this cold sweat now. You know, his palms are dripping, his face is red, his hair is standing on end. "Carmen, I feel as if I'm drunk. If I give way, if I give in, your promise, you'll keep it? Ah, if I love you Carmen, Carmen, you'll love me?" Of course, Carmen says, "Oui." And he releases her and she runs off. Oh, Don José is a real wizard now, isn't he. One wonders if there's a little royal blood somewhere in Don José's family line.

Look, these lyrics border on the slutty, do they not? And Bizet, if he wanted to use music like "The Stripper," could make this a really sleazy exposé into the underside of Carmen's already jaded personality, but he does not. He takes his cue from the third line of the text, "I'll go dance the seguidilla." He sets this piece as a seguidilla—a bright, moderately fast Spanish dance in triple meter—that is, it's a three-step, like a waltz. In Bizet's setting, Carmen becomes a sly, sexy beguiling seductress. All of this with her hands tied. And she—well, is she teasing? Is she telling the truth? Don José doesn't know, but he doesn't have enough experience to know any better. All he knows is that his senses are completely overloaded. He releases her and his downfall begins. And all of this, my friends, is projected through the music.

Now let's just listen to the first portion of this aria up to the point where Don José comes in and says, "Be quiet," because I want you to hear how effectively Bizet creates this sense of teasing grace. This music dances. Even with her hands tied, Carmen has terrific humor, terrific power, and all of it comes through in the understatement of this vivacious dance. So, please; Bizet, *Carmen*, Number 10—that means this is the tenth number in the opera—"Seguedilla." (musical example)

I would tell you that poor Don José is lost. He has never had the attention of a woman like this. Of course, for her part Carmen has not a clue that she has just pulled the cork on a wellspring of sexuality that she is not going to be able to put the cork back into, and Don José's downfall will ultimately be hers. We will get to Carmen later in the course, but for now, we must talk about Carmen—the character of Carmen—as an archetype. Do we recognize Carmen? Do we know someone like Carmen? I hope we're not married to that particular person, but do we? Have we been tempted by someone or something like Carmen?

Carmen exists as three distinctly separate but mutually reinforcing archetypes. Archetype number 1: a character archetype. She comes from the *commedia dell'arte* character of Columbina. I should explain. I'll talk much more about *commedia dell'arte* later in the course, but for now, this is a fifteenth- and sixteenth-century phenomenon that starts in northern Italy. The commedia dell'arte are traveling troupes of singers and actors who put on shows, first across the Italian peninsula, but then these spontaneously semi-improvised shows become popular really all across Europe. So many of the character archetypes, so many of the plot devices we are familiar with, and everything from opera to television grew out of commedia dell'arte tradition.

In any case, there is a commedia dell'arte character named Columbina, and Columbina is the archetype for Carmen. She is a pretty young woman accustomed to getting her way through street smarts, femininity and guile. We're going to meet other Columbina archetypes in this course. For example, when we do Rossini's *The Barber of Seville*, we will meet Rosina. Rosina is a Columbina. If we were doing Mozart's *Cosi fan tutte*, which we're not, sadly, but if we were, we would meet a maid named Despina, again very sly, sexy and able to get her way through conniving and plotting. In the *Coffee Cantata*, which I have done in a previous Teaching Company course on Bach and the high baroque, we did a wonderful comic opera by Bach, called the *Coffee Cantata*, which features a character named Lieschen, who again is a young, attractive girl who has to use her wits in order to get her way.

First and foremost, Carmen is an archetype drawn from the commedia dell'arte. She is Columbina. Second of all, she is a biblical archetype. Carmen is the serpent, she is the apple, she is Eve, all rolled into one. She's a female. She represents temptation, and her sexuality is the apple itself. Don José, of course, becomes Adam, the dupe whose fall from grace becomes the essential storyline of the opera. Carmen is also a personal archetype, the third archetype. Carmen is that temptation—monetary temptation, sexual temptation, spiritual temptation—with which we've all come face to face at sometime or another; and if you haven't, too bad for you. We might know it's wrong, perhaps even self-destructive, but in the face of such temptation we are often powerless, sadly, to control ourselves. Don José's destruction at Carmen's hands becomes a metaphor, a surrogate for our own potential destructions.

Robert Donington continues,

> It is not in our nature to come up with images that mean nothing. The meanings may be more or less fragmentary or coherent, trivial or significant, but something will be welling up in even the most unpromising material, and far more interestingly when the material is shaped by a superior intellect and a keener vision; in a word, by a genius. Almost as immediately as dreams, and far more coherently, opera offers a royal road into our unconscious, drawing as it does on regions of the psyche where consciousness has little power to penetrate; this truly is the astonishing power of theater augmented with music.

Again, the symbolic, archetypal nature of music is the province of the composer. The uncanny ability of opera to delve into our unconscious, what T. S. Eliot, to repeat myself again, calls that "fringe of indefinite feeling, which we can only detect out of the corner of the eye"—this ability of opera to evoke this is due to music not to words.

All right. Let's bring all of this back around, do a little review and listen to one more marvelous aria. Again, an opera is a drama, which combines soliloquy, dialogue, scenery, action and continuous or nearly continuous music, the whole ever greater than the parts. Opera is human experience, and that means theater intensified, distilled, crystallized and communicated through music.

The great success of opera, varied and diverse though the genre may be, can be attributed to any number of mutually reinforcing elements. We've talked about these. Actually, we haven't talked about the first element and I should have brought it out right up front: the sheer beauty of vocal music and the excitement of theater. Music's beautiful, and theater's fun. Put them both together and it becomes compelling. Number two, more subtly, and more importantly as far as we're concerned, the incredible intensification of feeling and meaning when words and music are combined is the essence of opera. The non-verbal emotional nature of music can conjure moods and feelings beyond the capability of words alone. Number three, the ability of music married to words to evoke symbolic meaning and character archetypes.

All of these elements together have allowed opera to flourish, to develop, to continue to grow and evolve even as other arts, even as other entertainments, have fallen by the wayside. Again, opera is a very old tradition, given the age of traditions here in the West. It's a tradition that spans 400 years, and for something to last that long it has to be artistically flexible but it also has to appeal to something basic in all of us. Indeed, opera does. We should understand all of this, always in one main context, and that is that it is the composer that is the dramatist in an opera, not the writer of the libretto.

All right. The goals of this course, rather late arrived on, but better late than never, are fourfold: first, to provide an outline of the history of opera from 1600, with its invention, up to 1924. The latest opera we will listen to will be *Turandot* by Puccini, which we sampled back in Lecture 1. However, in our engaging the history of opera, we will go back to the world of ancient Greece to understand the precedents for opera set many thousands of years before its actual invention. The second goal of this course is to observe the development of "national schools" of opera with the understanding that we will spend the bulk of our time, as we should, with the Italian operatic tradition. The third goal of this course is to develop a methodology for listening to and understanding opera by reading a libretto first, then discussing a composer's interpretive options, and then observing the choices made by the composers in setting those words and thereby creating the characters and the dramatic situations. Fourthly, ultimately, this course is a celebration of the power of words and music. It should be fun. We should have a really good time.

One last glorious example of the power of music to distill and intensify the meaning of words, even while creating archetypes with which we can all identify. We turn to Rossini's *The Barber of Seville*, 1816, and the entrance aria. We heard an exit aria before; that's when Electra leaves the stage. Well, this is an entrance aria; this is when we first meet a character. Of course, this must also make a huge impression, because it's the entrance aria that tells us who a character is, what they're all about and what we can expect them to do in the near and even distant future.

This is the entrance aria for Figaro himself: "Largo al factotum della città," "make way for the jack-of-all-trades of the city." If there's anyone in the world that doesn't recognize this aria, it simply means that they have not come in contact with any European music. It is one of the most oft heard and greatest loved of all operatic arias. It is a classic comic number. Figaro is revealed immediately as a clever, fast-talking and streetwise and cocky character. He's a kind of male Carmen with all the sexual angst removed; a man of common birth, a man who's really happy with his career.

Let's listen to this aria in two parts. It's long and I want to go through the words because they're great fun. Anyway, we hear Figaro approaching from the distance. What do people do when they're walking and they're really happy? They sing, and so of course, he's singing as he approaches.

> La, la, la, la, la, la, la, la, la, la, la, la. Make way for the factotum of the city. La, la, la, la, la, la, la, la, la. Rushing to his shop for dawn is here. La, la, la, la, la, la. Oh, what a merry life, what gay pleasures for a barber di qualità—of quality. Yes, indeed.
>
> Ah, bravo Figaro. Bravo, bravissimo, bravo! La, la, la, la, la, la. Most fortunate of men, indeed you are! Ready for everything by day and by night, always in bustle, in constant motion. A better lot for a barber, a nobler life does not exist. La, la, la, la, la, la.
>
> Razors and combs, lancets and scissors, at my command everything's ready. Then there are the 'extras,' part of the trade of the ladies and the cavaliers…La, la, la, la, la, la. Ah, what a merry life, what gay pleasures, for a barber of quality."

Let's just sample this first half of the aria, please, and note the following two points: This bubbling, brilliant music reflects Figaro's *joie de vivre* and humor wonderfully. Second of all, the direct, almost pop song-like melodic material reflects Figaro's common birth.

(musical example)

Let's quickly move through the rest of the aria because we're all hopped up and movin' with it now and it's quite wonderful.

> All call for me, all want me. Ladies and children. Old men and maidens. I need a wig, I need a shave, leeches to bleed me. Here, take this note. All call for me, all want me, I need a wig, I need a shave. Here, take this note. Ho, Figaro, Figaro, Figaro, Figaro!

Indeed, the demands of Figaro's public pile one upon the other, becoming ever more insistent.

He continues,

> Heavens! What a commotion! Heavens! What a crowd! Uno alla volta. One at a time One at a time, for pity's sake. Yes, I only have two hands. How can I service you?

He becomes almost like a diva. Please! Trying to calm his captive audience. Quiet down. I'll get to you.

And then he continues, imitating all the people calling him.

> Ho, Figaro! I am here! Figaro here, Figaro there. Ho, Figaro I am here. Figaro here. Figaro there. Figaro up, Figaro down. Quicker and quicker, I go like greased lightning. Make way for the factotum of the city.

And then, the final phrase, picking up speed faster and faster and faster. As Figaro continues to service his public, the music gets louder and increasingly exciting.

> Ah, bravo, Figaro, bravo, bravissimo, on you good fortune will always smile. La, la, la, la, la, la. I am the factotum of the city.

The conclusion of this brilliant aria.

(musical example)

What an awesome entry aria. Do we like this guy? We're crazy about this guy, and everything he does from now on we will follow with rapt attention.

Figaro is also an archetype. He's a character archetype, the fast-talking, conniving servant. When we first see characters like this, I'm sure they predate Roman drama and comedy, but we first see them in Roman comedy. If you know the musical comedy, *A Funny Thing Happened on the Way to the Forum*, which updates some of these old, Roman comedic techniques, we know the character Pseudolus is Figaro. Indeed, the Roman servant, fast-talking and conniving, was updated by the commedia dell'arte to create a character called Arlequino or Harlequin, the quick-tongued clown. Damon Runyan's version of Figaro, of course, is Nathan Detroit. TV Figaro's? Well, the archetype continues. I think the best example would be Sergeant Bilko, but we could come up with lots of others; an underclass person who by street smarts, guile and humor gets what they want.

He's also a personal archetype. All of us, we admire Figaro's chutzpah, his intelligence, his joy, and we'd like sometimes to be able to work the world the way Figaro can work his. Now, Beaumarchais created the character, Figaro, and Cesare Sterbini wrote the libretto for Rossini; nevertheless, this Figaro is Rossini's creation. It's the music that makes him.

One last quote, and we move on to our next lecture. This was written by Edward Cone, a teacher of mine: "In any opera we may find that the musical and verbal messages seem to reinforce or to contradict each other. But, whether the one or the other, we must always rely on the music as our guide toward an understanding of the composer's concept of the text. It is this conception, not the text itself, that must be authoritative in defining the ultimate meaning of the work."

Indeed, in this exploration I have called "Words and Music," the essential point is that the composer is the dramatist. With this in mind, let us take our lecture break. When we return, a brief history of vocal expression in music from the world of ancient Greece to 1600. Thank you.

A Brief History of Vocal Expression in Music
Lectures 3 and 4

We are midway through our introductory set of ... four lectures, and for Lectures 3 and 4 we encounter the last part ... "A Brief History of Vocal Expression in Western"—meaning European-based—"Music." Really, the real title, my friends, should be "An All-Too-Brief History of Vocal Expression in Western Music," as we pave our way inevitably towards the invention of opera.

The phrase "music as a mirror" means that stylistic change in music and the arts reflects the greater realities of the society in which the composer, artist, and writer live and work. Musical style in the West (European sphere) has constantly adapted to ever-changing societal and cultural realities.

There are four tenets to the idea of music as a mirror. The first tenet is that Western music has exhibited ongoing stylistic change since the High Middle Ages. The second is that composers since the High Middle Ages have sought to express something of themselves or their world in their music. The third is that what is considered expressive changes from era to era, and the fourth is that the rate of change has increased exponentially as we move toward the present day.

We begin by considering the role of music in the ancient Greek world. The association of music with drama dates back to ancient times. The composers, poets, philosophers, and historians who invented opera believed they were recreating the environment and techniques of ancient Greek drama.

The ancient Greeks believed music to be a microcosm of all creation. Music was present everywhere in ancient Greece. It was played throughout sporting events. Probably most, if not all, ancient Greek drama was sung with accompaniment. Only about forty fragments of ancient (pre-Christian) music have survived.

As a musical example of music in ancient Greek drama, we consider the Stasimon Chorus from the drama Orestes, possibly composed by Euripides himself (408 B.C.E.). (A stasimon was the lip between the stage and the audience, where the chorus sat. This area today is called the "orchestra.") There are two essential elements in this style of music: A single voice is accompanied by a double reed instrument, and the setting is syllabic in that there is a single pitch for each syllable. This ensures clear articulation. The music is subservient to clarity of speech.

The Greek view of music was humanistic. Ancient Greeks believed that music represented the true heart of humankind and the order of the cosmos. They also believed that music could change the face of nature and alter the souls of people and animals. This view of music would last for about 1000 years.

In the developments in performance, words, and music that would culminate in opera, another key period was that of the Middle Ages (600–1400). During this period, an important nexus of musical—and cultural—development was the Church. Indeed, the Middle Ages were dominated by the church; thus the era is often called the Theocratic Age or the Age of Theocracy. By 600 C.E. or so, Roman municipal authority had collapsed, leaving the Rome-based Christian church as one of the few bastions against encroaching barbarity. The Rome-based Christian church was founded by Emperor Constantine in the 4th century. The survival of the Church provided a framework for the reemergence of European civilization around the years 900–1000.

During the first part of the Middle Ages—the Dark Ages (600–1000)—the great bulk of the music created was for use in worship. The predominant style was monophonic vocal music, as, for example, Gregorian chant. It has only one, unaccompanied melody. Instrumental music was discouraged, even outlawed by the church. Its earthy nature was not considered conducive to worship. A musical example is the Mass for Christmas Day, Introit, "Puer natus est nobis."

The High Middle Ages (1000–1400) saw the rebirth of Europe. Populations and food production grew, cities developed, universities were founded, and Romanesque and Gothic architecture developed. Vernacular literature also developed. The power of secular rulers grew, and trade and alliances formed ever-larger political units.

Ancient Greeks believed that music represented the true heart of humankind and the order of the cosmos. They also believed that music could change the face of nature and alter the souls of people and animals.

The High Middle Ages also saw the creation of several musical innovations. Polyphony was a major development in the 12th through 14th centuries. Composers became named and known, in contrast to the anonymous, itinerant composers of previous eras, and a new class of professional performers began to grow. Musicians began to develop a system of musical notation. In tandem with these developments, a new, secular audience began to grow, and they started adopting a new ritual of respectful listening. In general, increasingly complex modes of musical expression mirrored an increasingly complex world.

A new type of organum was developed at the cathedral of Notre Dame in Paris, France. Organum is an early type of polyphony. The new type of organum is illustrated by Leonin's "Alleluia pascha nostrum" and "Gaudeat devotio fidelium" (circa 1190). The poet/composer Leonin raised the art of polyphony to a new level. He combined different styles in one piece of music: the old form of plainchant is combined with a new florid organum in which a sustained plainchant in the lower voice is accompanied by faster-moving embellishments in the upper voice. He also added a very new type of dance-like rhythm. We will listen to an example of this in lecture.

Secular music grew by leaps and bounds as royal courts and the aristocratic classes grew. A school of troubadour composers of popular music sprung up. An example of this type of music is Bernart de Ventadorn's "Can vei la lauzeta mover" (circa 1170).

The 14th century saw an end to the absolute authority of the Church as a result of a series of events. First, the Babylonian Captivity occurred. This was a period between 1305 and 1378 when the entire papal court settled in Avignon, France. The Babylonian Captivity led to the Great Schism between 1378 and 1417, when there were two, or even three, claimants to the papacy at any one time. People grew tired of this chaos. Over time, the behavior of some high clergy became increasingly corrupt and scandalous. Additionally, the Black Death of 1348–50 caused widespread devastation and soul-searching, and the Hundred Years' War wreaked enormous havoc. Rulers became increasingly powerful. In general, the world was in transition from one dominated by the Church with its immutable rules to a new world of increasing secularism, humanistic pursuit, and doubt.

As a result of all of these changes and events, secular music became high art. Much of it exhibits a structural complexity not equaled again until the 1950s. As an example, we will consider Guillaume de Machaut's "Rose, liz" (circa 1350), a spiky, complex, and beautiful piece by one of the great poet/composers of the 14th century. The essence of this music is the control of emotion and polyphonic structure.

Another important historical period in the development of music, language, and performance was the Renaissance (1400–1600). This period saw the rediscovery of ancient Greek and Roman culture. Artists, architects, poets, dramatists, philosophers, and composers turned increasingly to pre-Christian models for their inspiration and guidance.

Renaissance composers wanted their music to have the same impact on their listeners as that which the Greeks attributed to their music. By the mid-Renaissance an entirely new view of vocal articulation and system of harmony had come into place to accommodate the new, more humanistic, expressive aims of composers. This was homophony in which one melody predominates with all other musical material heard as accompaniment.

Josquin des Prez (circa 1440–1521), the preeminent composer of the mid-Renaissance, was a master of sacred and secular music. There are several musical examples of this. First, "El Grillo" (circa 1480) exemplifies Josquin's use of homophony and word painting. Unlike the music of Machaut one hundred years before, this music serves the words. Also, "Je me complains" (circa 1480) is a polyphonic piece in which five voices weave in and out of each other. The clarity of the words is not the issue here. Two or three words are being sung simultaneously. The essence of this music lies in its expressive power. It is focused on a depiction of romantic malaise.

In the late Renaissance, the most important genre of secular music was the madrigal, a work for four to six singers, based on high art poetry, that freely mixes homophony and polyphony and focuses on word painting. Madrigals were sung at aristocratic gatherings at European courts, especially in Italy.

Thomas Weelkes' "As Vesta was from Latmos Hill descending" (1601) is a lighthearted madrigal of the late Renaissance in which word painting is taken to extremes. Note that "maiden Queen" and Oriana refer to the "Virgin Queen" Elizabeth I. Diana was the Roman goddess of virginity and Vesta was a virgin goddess. ■

A Brief History of Vocal Expression in Music, I
Lecture 3—Transcript

Welcome back to "How to Listen to and Understand Opera." We are midway through our introductory set of our opening four lectures, and for Lectures 3 and 4 we encounter the last part of that introductory set: "A Brief History of Vocal Expression in Western"—meaning European-based—"Music." Really, the real title, my friends, should be "An All-Too-Brief History of Vocal Expression in Western Music," as we pave our way inevitably towards the invention of opera.

Now, as I've already talked about briefly and will soon talk about in infinitely greater detail, the nature and content of opera has changed profoundly since the first court operas were produced around 400 years ago. While certain aspects of opera have changed inevitably—I mean, after all, nothing stays the same all the time—the vast changes in style and content over the last four centuries in opera are a reflection of something greater than just inevitable change. They are a reflection of a greater reality, and that reality is as follows; operatic style, musical style, artistic expression changes not randomly and whimsically, but changes inevitably as the world changes around the composer. I call this concept of change, of inevitable stylistic change, "music as a mirror." The reason why we call it "music as a mirror" is the way that stylistic change in music and the arts mirrors the greater realities of the society in which the composer, the artist, the writer lives and works. So, we've got to understand change, evolution, stylistic alteration not as random and seemingly indiscriminate, but as a function of a greater cultural reality—a cultural reality shared by composers, playwrights, writers and artists alike.

Please then, what I call the four basic assumptions, or the four tenets, of music as a mirror. Tenet or assumption number one: Western, meaning European, music has exhibited ongoing stylistic change. By the way, I keep saying "style." When we talk about musical style, all we're referring to is the way the music sounds. That's it. The feeling, the sensibility evoked by the sound of the music. Again, to assumption, tenet, number one: Western, that is European, music has exhibited ongoing stylistic change since the High Middle Ages, talking about the year 1000 or so.

Tenet number two: Since the High Middle Ages, composers have sought to express something of themselves, something of their world in their music. The result being that as the world around the composer changes, so does the style or the sound of that music.

Tenet number three of music as a mirror: What is considered expressive changes from era to era. Now, this might not be self-evident to us, because when we think of something being expressive, here in the late twentieth century, we think of emotion as being expressive. I mean, if we need to express ourselves, we're talking about something in the realm of our feelings. And indeed, we live in this cult of middle-class feeling—that is, whatever we feel is legitimate and worth being expressed. But I would tell you that this cult of individual feeling is a fairly recent phenomenon that we could trace back to poets like Byron and Keats, at the beginning of the nineteenth century. Really, before that, other things in music were considered essential to expression.

For example, for a great swatch of time between about 600 and 1400, worship of God and religion were the essence of musical expression. During the fourteenth century, as we will talk about in a few minutes, intellect and control were considered of essential expression. So, we have highly intellectualized, highly controlled music from the 1350s and the 1360s. At other times in musical history, emotional restraint and good taste were considered paramount in any musical or, indeed, any artistic expression—the age of Mozart and Haydn. I'm talking about the classical era. The 1760s, '70s, '80s and '90s were such an era of control and restraint. Emotions and feelings unrestrained? Well, that's an expressive ideal of the nineteenth and the twentieth centuries. So, please let's understand, that as time changes, so will what we consider essential and expressive to the arts.

And fourthly, the last assumption or tenet of music as a mirror: The rate of change in musical style, like everything else in our wild and wacky world, will increase exponentially as we move forward towards the present day.

I have a huge, important point to make before we move on any further, regarding change in music specifically and the arts in general. My friends, music and art are not linear. They don't build cumulatively on the work of predecessors as, let's say, science does. Scientifically, medically, technologically, even socially, are we better off today than we were 200 years ago? I think even the most abject Luddite would agree that we are indeed better off today than we were 200 years ago. But, are we better off artistically? Is Shakespeare better than Sophocles? Is Tom Stoppard better than Shakespeare? No. They're just different, and their differences are a reflection of a changing world around the composer, the artist, the poet, the writer. Is Richard Strauss better than Verdi? Is Verdi better than Mozart? Is Mozart better than Monteverdi? No, of course not. They're all different, and their differences reflect their times; although I might gratuitously add that nobody is better than Mozart.

So, a brief history of vocal expression in Western music. We will do this for two reasons: First, so we can trace the evolution of expression as it seen as we approach opera, and we will see antecedents for opera even as far back as the ancient Greek world; and number two, I need to prove to you this concept of music as a mirror. We've got to understand that musical style changes as a function of larger cultural change. The composer is not some idiot living in an ivory tower. The composer, the artist, the painter, the writer is one of us—is someone who lives in our community and reflects the same ideals and morals that surround all of us. The reason why this is important is we're going to have to understand changes in operatic style as a function of music as a mirror, as well as the music we're about to explore here in Lectures 3 and 4.

So, we go way back in our beginnings to the music of the ancient Greek world. Again, one more time. Opera is a drama, which combines soliloquy, dialogue, scenery, action and continuous or nearly continuous music—the whole ever greater than the parts. If you prefer, a synergy of complementary elements.

Although the earliest works we now call operas date back about 400 years, the association of music with drama goes back to ancient times. I'm going to say that again because it's really important. Although works we now call opera date back about 400 years, the association of music with drama goes back to the ancient world. The composers, poets, philosophers and historians who invented opera in the late sixteenth century firmly believed—almost religiously believed—that they were recreating, reinventing ancient Greek drama.

We must, in this and the following lecture, travel back to the musical world of ancient Greece and then move forward to the invention of opera. In doing so, we will examine the ongoing search for constantly relevant modes of musical expression, those modes of expression that do lead us ultimately to opera.

All right; the ancient world. I quote the eminent music historian Donald Grout:

> The word "music" had a much wider meaning to the Greeks than it has to us here today. It was an adjectival form of "muse", in classical mythology any one of the nine sister goddesses who presided over certain arts and sciences. The verbal relation suggests that among the Greeks, music was thought of as something common or basic to activities that were concerned with the pursuit of truth and beauty.
>
> In the teachings of Pythagoras and his followers, music and arithmetic were not separate arts. Numbers were thought to be the key to the whole spiritual and physical universe. So, the system of musical sounds and rhythms, being ordered by the numbers of the overtone series, exemplified the harmony of the cosmos and corresponded to it.
>
> The doctrine of ethos, of the moral quality and effects of music, fitted well into the Pythagorean view of music as a microcosm, a system of pitch and rhythm ruled by the same mathematical laws that operate in the whole of the visible and invisible creation. Music in this view, was not only a passive image of an orderly system of the universe, it was also a force that could affect the universe; hence, the attribution of miracles to the legendary musicians of mythology.

My friends, we will meet the most legendary of these musicians, Orpheus. Throughout the entire history of opera, Orpheus, as we will talk about him, is the personification of the operatic ideal—a singer with a golden voice, who can change the face of nature and the souls of people with music.

Back to Mr. Grout:

> The Greek idea of music as essentially one with the spoken word, has appeared in diverse forms throughout the history of music: in the invention of opera around 1600, for example, or in Wagner's theories about music drama in the nineteenth century.

We will talk, of course, about the invention of opera, but also about Wagner's ideas based on his view of ancient Greek theater and music in due time.

The upshot of all this is that music would seem to have been ubiquitous in the ancient Greek world. Music was used to accompany sporting events. I mean, can we imagine that here today? We have a band above one of the dugouts at a baseball game, not just playing fight songs to the crowd, but actually accompanying the players while they played. Or at a track meet? That would be a most interesting thing to letter in, varsity trumpet. It's just something we don't do any more. Indeed, in the Panhellenic games, singing and instrumental performance were sporting events. There were competitions in singing, in *kithara*—that is, this big lyre—playing, and so forth. There is also a great likelihood that much, if not most, if not all, Greek drama was actually chanted or sung.

Now, sadly, only 40 fragments of ancient music, that is pre-Christian music, have come down to us today. Of that incredible world, the ancient world, only 40 fragments of music. They've been destroyed by time, because, let's face it, if you write down music you're not generally going to be etching it in stone. It's going to go onto paper. It's going to go onto some very dissolvable medium. I would also tell you that, sadly, the early Christian church ravaged what they considered the repertoire of paganism. Much of what was destroyed was destroyed in the early days of Christianity as a way of removing pagan influences from a new world.

One of these surviving fragments of ancient music comes from a play named *Orestes*, by the famed dramatist Euripides. And we know who Orestes is; Orestes is, of course, the brother of Electra who killed... Well, I'll get into that in just a minute; first, the fragment. This fragment from Euripides' *Orestes* is on a papyrus, and the papyrus dates back to about the third century

B.C.E. My friends, "B.C.E." is a politically correct way to say "B.C." Instead of saying "before Christ," we say "before the Christian era." And now, of course, everyone can be included in this. The biggest problem is with A.D., *Anno Domini*, "year of our Lord." Better to say "C.E.," "Common Era" or "Christian Era."

In any case, of the fragment we have of Euripides' *Orestes*, or this bit of music, comes down to us on a papyrus that's dated to the third century B.C.E. The tragedy itself was written about 408 B.C.E., and it's possible that the music that has survived and come down to us on this later papyrus was even composed by Euripides himself, who was renowned for his musical settings. The fragment that has survived the ravages of time is a *stasimon*. It's an ode sung by the chorus as it stood in its place at the orchestra. The orchestra is that semi-circular lip beneath the stage, between the stage and the audience. Of course, in the early operas when instrumentalists started being put in the orchestra—that lip between the stage and the audience—the ensemble came to be known by the place where they were sitting, and that means the "orchestra." Anyway, this fragment that comes to us is a chorus, and that chorus would have been sung from that lip. The fragment is that; just a fragment, so any performance of course, will have to be a recreation. We will hear a recreated performance in a moment.

In this *stasimon* chorus, the women of Argos beg the gods to have mercy on poor Orestes, who, six days before the play began (as we all know from the discussion regarding Electra from Lecture 1), killed his mom, Clytemnestra, and her main squeeze, Aegisthus. Orestes and Electra together have plotted the killing in revenge for the murder of their own father, Agamemnon. The chorus begs that Orestes be released from the madness that has overwhelmed him since the killing. They sing this.

> You wild goddesses who dart across the skies seeking vengeance for murder, we beg you to free Agamemnon's son from his raging fury…. We grieve for this boy. Happiness is brief among mortals. Sorrow and anguish sweep down on it like a swift gust of wind on a sail-ship, and it sinks under the tossing seas.

So, the women are trying to say to the gods: "Remember this is a boy, remember he is a mortal; remember he was avenging his father in murdering his mother."

Let's listen, please, and I want you to be aware of the following two elements while we listen. It's a brief excerpt. This is being sung by a single voice accompanied by a double-reed instrument, an oboe-like instrument the Greeks called an "aulos," A-U-L-O-S. Secondly, and more importantly, note that this is what we call a "syllabic setting." What that means is that there is a different pitch for each syllable. When you syllabically set words, you guarantee maximum articulation—maximum clarity of the words. It also means that the rhythms of the music are completely dependent upon the words themselves. Everything is meant for clear articulation. Here is a case where the words are transcendent. The music accompanies the words, but clarity of word is the transcendent element in this excerpt.

Euripides' Stasimon Chorus from *Orestes*. (musical example)

All right. I don't think this is going to make anyone's Top 40 list of favorite tunes heard today. But please understand, in its context, this is most memorable and most tuneful in its context, a context 2500 years removed from today. The point is this; the ancient Greeks believed that music represented the true heart of humankind and the order of the cosmos. They believed that music could change the face of nature and alter the souls of people and animals. Now, this is a marvelous view of music; it's a deeply expressive view of music. It's an essentially humanistic view of music. And this humanistic view of music will be lost for about 1000 years, for reasons we will get into right now, because we must move forward to what we call the "Middle Ages."

By the year 600 C.E.—that is, 600 of the Common, or Christian, Era—Roman municipal authority, which had been the societal and cultural glue that had held most of Western Europe together for the last 700 years, had been almost completely destroyed. One Roman institution, however, survived. It stood as a lonely bastion against encroaching barbarity, brutality and ignorance. That, of course, was the Roman-based Christian church. The Roman Christian Church had been founded by the Emperor Constantine way back in the fourth century. This church had developed, by and large, its own hierarchy, its own structure, its own internal governance largely separate from that of the Roman state. So, the Church's survival into the Middle Ages was a function of its lack of dependence upon Roman municipal authority. I would also tell you that the Church's survival into the Middle Ages, for which we must be very grateful, and the subsequent Christianization of Western and Northern Europe, provided the necessary framework for the reemergence of a European civilization around the years 900 or 1000, or so.

I feel sometimes filled with guilt and remorse, the way we toss around these hundred, two, three, four hundred-year chunks as if they were but a day or a second. We've got to remember that culturally, societally, everything evolves slowly, geologically. And certainly if we were living back in 900, we wouldn't want to be told, especially if we were onion-eating peasants, that, "Congratulations, Europe's being reborn even while you live your life expectancy of 25 years, toothless and broken-boned that you are." Yes, we make these grand statements about huge chunks of history without taking into account the incredible details that make history what it is. I share my guilt with you as a way of purging it from myself. I continue.

We generally call the huge period of time between the years 600 and 1400—yes, talk about a big chunk of time—we call this huge period of time the "Middle Ages." Since the social, philosophical, artistic, even political institutions of the Middle Ages were, by and large, dominated by religion, issues of Christianity, we also call this 800-year chunk of time the "Theocratic Age" or the "Age of the Theocracy."

During the first part of this Theocratic Age, the so-called "Dark Ages," 600 to 1000, the great bulk of the music created was music to be used in Christian worship. This is the music of the Catholic Church. It is music of limited purpose; it was music created purposely to aid in worship. The Greek ideal of humanist expression, all that is lost or disregarded at this point. All pagan ritual, all pagan art was discarded in order to focus on the new liturgy, the new belief, the new spiritual cleanliness that was early Christianity.

Instrumental accompaniment was generally forbidden. This is a course on vocal music and opera, but please remember that instrumental music does not become a form of music unto itself until fairly late, until the 1600s. Before the 1600s, if you heard instrumental music, you would be hearing dance music. When instruments play dance music, what part of our body responds? I mean, what part of us starts to groove? Do we think about God? Do we ruminate upon our small place in the cosmos? No. No. The bottom half of our body moves—the part of our bodies that reproduces. And indeed, dance has often been called stylized reproductive ritual. Yes. Instruments can only make us think about those parts of our body most useless to praise and worship of God. So, instruments are discouraged if not outright outlawed in the early Church. Rather, plainchant—that is, unadorned singing sometimes called "Gregorian chant"—becomes the music of the Church. We have a huge and varied repertoire of this plainchant created to serve the liturgical needs of the Church.

Let's listen to such a plainchant. The repertoire is huge. I mean, you can't have a clue unless you've studied how much plainchant there is, how varied it is, depending on the region in which it was created. It was created over a period of four, five, six hundred years; and most of it, or much of it at least as of about 900 or so, was written down. This is a gigantic repertoire, perhaps the single largest chunk of music that exists in our Western culture.

It's easy to find, and it's hard to choose because so much of it is so beautiful and so representative. I chose for us to listen to now, the opening or the introit for the "Mass for Christmas Day," a number called "A Child is Born to Us." Here are the words that we will hear set to music: "A child is born to us, and a Son is given to us; whose government is upon His shoulder; and His Name shall be called the Angel of great counsel."

Now listen and note the following, please. This is music of great and enduring lyric beauty, and it is. But, it is also music utterly devoid of personal expression or ego. I mean, when we listen to this plainchant, do we say, "That must have been written by Father Billy of Bayonne? I mean, I recognize his style right away. Or, was that Padre Brad of Brugge, or maybe Reverend Bud of Berne?"

No. We can't identify the composer. This is generic-sounding music, which sounds like so much other music we cannot possibly say who the creator was. It is music intended as prayer, music intended as ritual—a mirror of its church, not of the individual ego that created it. Let's listen, and then we'll discuss it some more.

(musical example)

Very beautiful. I would ask us all to think now, what is being expressed in this music? What is this music about? Well, first and foremost, it's about peace, it's about love of God; it's a sublime, communally-sung religious song that celebrates a transcendent divinity. This music does not celebrate any particular individual's feelings, worldview or ego.

That's an important point, one we have to take with us as we enter the High Middle Ages, the era that sees Europe reborn between about 1000 and 1400. (Again, another huge chunk of time; again, I feel the hot coals of intellectual responsibility raked across my feet, but nevertheless we will address that huge chunk of time as the High Middle Ages.) This is the era that sees Europe essentially reborn. Political alliances grow, countries come into existence, the merchant class grows and develops, trade routes are reestablished, and so forth. Food production is increased hugely and, correspondingly, populations grow due to windmills, water mills, crop rotation and horse- as opposed to ox-drawn plows.

Population growth increases tremendously and cities develop: London, Paris, Venice, Brugge all grow. Please remember, a city is that greatest of all cooperative human ventures. Specialization can take place within a city, and if we can specialize, we can develop to much greater levels those things in which we are specializing, as opposed to everyone having to be a kind of generalist. We can never develop anything particularly if we all have to do everything all the time. Agrarian worlds tend not to be as sophisticated or specialized as one that has an urban center.

Universities are founded: Paris and Cambridge. Romanesque and then Gothic architecture develop. Huge, stunning, complex spaces are enclosed and controlled by the hand of the architect. Vernacular literature develops; that is, non-Latin and non-Greek literature develop. And the power of secular rulers is on the rise. That one is really important. The power of non-religious rulers and leaders is on the rise.

The musical innovations of the High Middle Ages are many and they are profound. First and foremost, polyphony—that is, multi-melodied compositions. Now think back on that plainchant, that introit from the "Mass for Christmas Day," for a second. We heard one melody and one melody only. We heard no accompaniment, we heard no instruments; we didn't hear any of the voices adding separate pitches. At any given time there was only one melody, despite the fact that it might have been sung by three, five or 10 different people. One melody.

We call such music *monophonic*, *mono* meaning one, *phone* meaning sound. A monophonic texture is one in which there is only one present melody. We can all create monophony wherever we are. Just start singing, now. I don't know, whatever comes to mind, "Inna Gadda Da Vida," whatever hits your head. That is a monophonic texture, unaccompanied, no other melodic lines interweaving within yours.

One of the most extraordinary musical inventions of the High Middle Ages is *polyphony*, *poly phony*, multiple melodies present at the same given moment. These multiple-melodied compositions at first employed plainchants, and we're going to hear an example of such a composition in a minute. That is, you'd have a plainchant—a Gregorian chant—in one voice, and then it would be decorated and embellished simultaneously in another, creating the effect of two simultaneous and different melodies.

It is during the High Middle Ages that the concept of composer and performer develops, that is, that these are separate people. One person writes the music and one person performs the music. And we should probably add a third element, because if you've got a composer and a performer, you hopefully have an audience—that is, someone whose only job it is to passively listen to the music. I would point out that an increasingly complex world demands increasingly complex modes of expression. So, we shouldn't be surprised by these evolutions.

The music of the High Middle Ages that I will play for you—and again a 400-year chunk offers us an extraordinary amount of repertoire, which I must limit to two pieces—the music I will play for us is very representative of its time and comes, in both cases, from Paris. The art of polyphony from the twelfth century (that is, from the 1100s) until the late fourteenth century (the late 1300s) developed primarily in Northern France, with Paris at the center, and radiated outwards to Europe from there.

The first composer that we feel comfortable calling a composer—that is, someone whose music is signed and someone who we know created this work and that work—is a gentleman named Leonin, who was born about the year 1135 and died, for sure, in 1201. He's one of the great Church-poet composers of his age and he worked out of the new Notre Dame Cathedral in Paris. Following in the footsteps of previous composers, he raises the art of polyphony to a new level.

The following musical example combines something new, something old and something very new. In the music of Leonin's time, the late 1100s and early 1200s, it was not atypical to combine all kinds of different styles within a single piece of music. We're going to listen to a piece of music called "Alleluia pascha nostrum" ("Hallelujah our Passover"), and then "Gaudeat devotio fidelium" ("Let the devotion of the faithful be raised in rejoicing"). We will hear these pieces performed as a singularity, as a continuity.

Here's what we're going to hear, three parts: something old, something new, something very new. Part One is new. It is what Leonin is a master of, florid organum. Organum is that sort of musical composition that puts a plainchant in a lower voice, usually sustained and very long notes, and then in an upper voice, a very fast embellishment of that plainchant. So we hear the long-held notes in the bass, and then the faster notes up top. Actually, I shouldn't call it the bass. I should call it by its proper term. The low voice with the sustained notes was called the "tenor" voice, and that comes from the Italian, or I should say the Latin, *tenere*, which means to hold or sustain. They were the sustaining voice, and that's where the word "tenor" comes from.

This florid organum, this upper voice, very flowery, is typical of what we call the Notre Dame School of the twelfth century, and Leonin is its greatest exponent. So, that's something new, this very flowery embellishment of a long-held plainchant.

The second part is something old. For a moment, we're going to hear a bit of plainchant without any polyphony, without any accompaniment whatsoever, followed by another little bit of organum. I'll point that out when we hear it; I'll say "Part Two." That's the old stuff.

Part Three is very new, cutting edge, modernistic, avant-garde, out there! What we're going to hear is a section of religious music, which has a dance-like feel to it. It's what we call the "descant" style, and that means the lower voices are going to move with the same dancing rhythms as the upper voice. It's going to be very physical music, very powerful music and very new-sounding music. These are the words that they are going to be singing.

"Let the devotion of the faithful be raised"—this is Part Three—"in rejoicing; the Word of the Father is made flesh, and a new child is given to us, and He has bestowed Himself upon us. The Salvation of the people has opened the gateway of life, for He in devotion has borne the punishment of death."

So, again, Part One, florid organum. All they're going to be singing is "Hallelujah our Passover." Part Two, a brief bit of old style plainchant followed by a little more organum, and then Part Three, this long poem in rhythms that are frankly more dance-like than they are prayer-like or contemplative. While listening, please ask yourself this following question: Is this music like plainchant—generic, egoless music of ritual—or does this music have the spark of originality and ego in it?

(musical example)

So, is this anonymous, generic music of ritual? Well, heck no. I mean, it moves, it grooves. It's got all kinds of contrasts, changing sections in there, and someone's got to make all these decisions. Someone's got to decide what notes we're going to hear at the same time, when one section will end and the next one begin, the degree of contrast, the sense of flow. We've got to have a composer, someone making a tremendous number of melodic, harmonic, rhythmic and structural decisions. And having made them, that composer has to have the means by which to notate them, write them down and give them to expert performers capable of performing that music. We've got a whole hierarchy here. Indeed, we have the evolution of a notational system capable of notating that last example, which is very engaged and, in its own way, very complicated music.

What is this music expressive of? Well, it's still religious, but compared to the plainchant, it's much more melodically diverse, rhythmically interesting, intellectual and personalized in its impact. It reflects a much broader, more complex world and a broader worldview. The composer's name is Leonin, Master Leonin to us, Lionheart to history.

I'm going to take a quick departure here because I have to bring something up. I'm crazy about the music of the High Middle Ages, and I'm going to play you some more examples before we end our investigation of the High Middle Ages. But, some would tell us that this differentiation between composer, performer and audience was heresy, that it destroyed Western music forever. And you know what? They could make a very good argument. They would say that, because of the High Middle Ages, because of the intrusion of ego into the soul of the performer and composer, music ceased to be the communal and shared activity that would bring us all together and simply started to be an activity that created a new ritual; you sit still and be quiet while I sing to you what they created for me to perform for you. This whole hierarchy takes away the communal music making, and it's true.

Here in the twentieth century, of course, we have advanced this ritual to a point almost past which we should not go. For example, let's talk about opera. You stand outside an opera house and people are dressed the same way. We have a listening ritual, do we not? We dress up in our coat, and our tie, and our suits because, if we're not properly dressed at the opera house, we're not showing respect. We go down there and we sit and we do our thing.

Listen, and this is a purely personal view of the world, I come from an informal generation and I wear my informality on my sleeve. I've always felt that ties were the whalebone corsets of the neck, something throttling and reducing the oxygen flow to my brain; that a jacket is kind of like a smelting oven for the body, something to raise my body temperature past the point of any degree of comfort. I don't generally like to dress up when I do anything. Someone might tell me, "That's showing disrespect for the singers and for the opera." But, of course, the singers couldn't care less what I was wearing. Frankly, we would do a whole lot of good in this country by telling everyone that would come to the opera, "Dress down, if you want to. If you want to!" Some people bemoan the lack of formality in our world today, but I say, "Be comfortable first." The singers don't know what we're wearing. They can't see us at all. The lights are in their eyes.

If we want to show respect for the singers, here's what we do. We sit quietly during a performance. We honor them properly by applauding and hooting at the proper moments. And, when the opera ends, we don't rush out to our cars with the fear that we're going to get in line at the garage and get stuck for an extra 10 minutes. No. We stay in our seats and we applaud the good work of the performers and the composer, whether the composer is alive or dead. My friends, there is nothing worse than jumping out of your seat during that initial round of applause and running to the car in the fear that it's going to be two or three more minutes and the applause will take too much time. No. If we want to show respect, it has nothing to do with our mode of dress. It has to do with our mode of behavior and response to what we've heard.

What is expressive in this music of the High Middle Ages? It is religious, but it also exhibits individual vision. It exhibits a complex series of musical events put together by the whim of the composer. When we reconvene for Lecture 4, we will continue to talk about the High Middle Ages, and we will continue exploring this ongoing development of expressive content as we move inevitably into the Renaissance and then the invention of opera. Thank you very much.

A Brief History of Vocal Expression in Music, II
Lecture 4—Transcript

Welcome back to "How to Listen to and Understand Opera." This is Lecture 4, and we continue our all-too-brief history of vocal expression in Western music as we pave our way forward to the invention of opera. We left off during the High Middle Ages, and that is where we will pick up again here in Lecture 4. We just listened to a piece by Leonin, one of the first composers who actually wrote his name on works and took credit as composer for that music that he produced. It's music that reflects an increasingly complex time in increasingly complex musical means. It's music that, in its own way, is quite expressive and very different from the more generic plainchants that had preceded the High Middle Ages during the Dark Ages.

The High Middle Ages, that era from about 1000 to 1400, also saw an explosion of secular—that means non-religious—music, as royal courts and aristocratic classes grew tremendously. Pop music, my friends, has always existed. But until the High Middle Ages, popular music was (1) an oral, not a notated tradition, and (2) the creators of popular music up to the High Middle Ages were anonymous, itinerant, low-life musicians—there's a self-canceling phrase, if you will—who traveled the countryside, earning a few copper coins for their trouble.

By the time we get to the High Middle Ages, these pop composers are also becoming known. Their music is becoming notated, and we know who they were. For example, one of the most famous musicians of the twelfth century was Bernart de Ventadorn, who lived a very brief life from about 1150 to 1180. He is one of the best-known troubadours of the twelfth century. One of his best-preserved songs is a song named "Can vei la lauzeta mover"—"when I see the lark beating its wings."

Let's listen and talk about this piece as an illustration of the beginnings of a popular musical culture during an age that increasingly celebrates things non-religious. By the way, the words of this song are in the language *Provençal*. Provençal is that language, now unused, of medieval Southern France. The song is a lover's complaint. I would point out that the lover's complaints comprise the main body of the entire repertoire of these courtly love songs, of which this is one. Lover's complaints also comprise the main body of torch songs, of tearjerkers, and probably 98 percent of all Country and Western are lover's complaints. What's that wonderful and terrible joke I once heard about C & W music? That if you play a Country and Western song backwards, it says, "My girl is back, the truck is running and the dog is alive." Lover's complaint stuff.

Anyway, the words to Ventadorn's "Can vei la lauzeta mover:"

> When I see the lark beating its wings joyfully against the sun's rays, which then swoons and swoops down because of joy in its heart, Oh! I feel such jealousy for all those who have the joy of love, that I am astonished that my heart does not immediately melt with desire!
>
> Alas! I thought I knew so much of love, and I know so little; for I cannot help loving a lady from whom I shall never obtain any favor. She has taken away my heart, and myself and herself and the whole world; and when she left me, I had nothing left but desire and a yearning heart.

Let's listen, please, and I would point out the following two things that I want you to listen for. In this performance, this song will be unaccompanied, as a troubadour might sing it in any company at any place. Secondly, while listening, ask yourself, "What is this song expressive of?"

Bernart de Ventadorn's "Can vei la lauzeta mover." (musical example)

It's very beautiful and for those who can hit a rewind button, I would suggest you rewind and re-listen to this again right away. Without harmonic accompaniment, the melody is harder to follow than if there had been an accompaniment. But it's an exquisitely beautiful melody, carefully wrought, and most descriptive, I think, of the mood that Ventadorn is trying to create.

I asked, "What was this expressive of?" Well, it attempts to express—with admittedly simple, but I think exquisite means—individual heartbreak, the pain of a single person's feeling at having been left behind by love. There's nothing generic in this song any more than there was anything generic in the Mahler song from "The Wayfarer" that we heard way back earlier in the course, which was about the same thing, about a broken heart in the face of love. Nature is celebrated for all its joy and beauty, but that's a joy and beauty that I don't have in my own soul. These two songs are very much alike, different traditions, different times, but the same impulse. There's nothing generic about this piece. It deals with common human feelings, if a bit prettified and idealized.

Now we move into the fourteenth century, or what the Italians call the *trecento*. Some people call this the Middle Ages, and some people call the fourteenth century just the fourteenth century, because it stands alone in the history of Western Europe for many reasons, which I will now go through.

Most importantly, the fourteenth century sees the end of the absolute authority of the Roman Christian Church. This end to its power and authority—not a complete end to its power, the Roman Church is still a most powerful institution—but the end to its absolute authority came about for a number of different reasons. I would quickly go through them right now. Between 1305 and 1378, we see something that is now called "The Babylonian Captivity." Due to huge municipal unrest in Rome, the entire papal court—and please remember that the Pope was not just a religious leader back in these days; the Pope was a monarch, controlling huge swatches of land and a great amount of financial resource. The Pope was not just a spiritual leader, but the Pope was also an earthly leader of tremendous power and influence—due to the problems in Rome, the entire papal court ups and leaves to Avignon in Southern France. This is a problem because Rome is supposedly the great European city of Catholicism, and by 1378, those still in Italy are tired of the Pope ruling from France.

So, from 1378 to 1417, we have what's called "The Great Schism;" two, and even sometimes three rival claimants to the papacy simultaneously. Now, do you see what this does to the whole Catholic hierarchy? The concept of the papacy is that the Pope is God's representative on earth and, of course, Catholicism is a single-god religion. I mean, there's only one great God, and the Pope is the God's voice on earth. What happens when you have two Popes? Three Popes? Well, which is the real one? Which one really represents God? They're all going to say, "It's me, it's me." This is a huge blow to the faith that's necessary to sustain belief in this particular religious system. Increasingly, the corrupt and scandalous life of the high clergy is drawing sharp criticism from both the middle and the lower classes. Add to all of these problems with faith, the Black Death between 1348 and 1350. How can the Church possibly explain this calamity, this catastrophe, of unimagined proportions?

We also have the Hundred Years' War going on between 1330 and 1453. It should be the Hundred and Twenty-Three Years' War, but that's hard on the tongue, so let's just stick with the "Hundred." Urban discontent and peasant unrest spread across Europe. Add to this increasingly powerful secular monarchs, who fill the vacuum created by the Church's administrative and spiritual problems. This is a time of great change, of great danger, of great turmoil where the old world slowly but inexorably moves to become the modern world.

What's the impact of all this on music? Well, there's an explosion of secular musical composition, and not just love songs like the Ventadorn we just heard. No, but complex and often hauntingly beautiful compositions. In these religiously troubled times, secular musical art becomes high musical art for the first time, at least the first time since the world of ancient Greece. Indeed, much of the music composed during the mid- to late-fourteenth century exhibits a complexity, I mean a structural complexity, in terms of melodic and harmonic schemes and formulas that will not be equaled again until the 1950s. This music well mirrors a complex and difficult world, a world in transition from being dominated by the absolute authority of the Church and its immutable doctrines to a new world of increasing secularity, humanistic pursuit and, for better or for worse, doubt.

The great composer of the mid-fourteenth century is a gentleman named Guillaume de Machaut, who was born about 1300 and died, for sure, in 1377. His elegant, spiky, incredibly complex music is utterly representative of this complicated and difficult time. We're going to listen to a piece by Machaut, and Machaut is the second of those Parisian-based composers I told you we would listen to. We listened to Leonin from the twelfth century and now we listen to Machaut, also based at Notre Dame, from the fourteenth century.

In this secular work, Machaut is both composer and poet. By the way, he was considered as great a poet as he was considered a composer. Here are the words to "Rose, liz" (circa 1350):

> Rose, lily, spring greenery, flower, balm, and the sweetest fragrance, beautiful lady, you surpass them all in sweetness. And all the gifts of nature you possess, for which I adore you. Rose, lily, spring greenery, flower, balm, and the sweetest fragrance.
>
> And, since beyond all creatures your virtue excels, I can honestly say: rose, lily, spring greenery, flower, balm, and very sweet fragrance, beautiful lady, you surpass them all in sweetness."

It's a very attractive poem, actually, even in translation. It's very attractive and very romantic, and I would tell you that this is music of extraordinary and haunting beauty, but also daunting complexity. Now, clearly I'm not going to explain the melodic and rhythmic schemes; there's no time. You will hear a certain spikiness to the music and this has to do with the formulas; but you'll also hear a composer at the top of his game, who can create great lyricism and great beauty, even given these formulas that he's wont to use.

Let me play this for you, and I would ask you to ask yourselves that key question: "What is expressive in this music?"

Guillaume de Machaut, "Rose, liz." (musical example)

What is expressive in this extraordinary music? Many things. It's lyrically very beautiful; and I trust any number of you, especially those of you who have sung in choruses, have some sense of how hard this must be to perform in a small, unaccompanied vocal ensemble like that. These are extraordinarily virtuosic singers. It's extremely virtuosic music, very foreign sounding to our ears because the harmonic system we are accustomed to has not evolved yet. I'm going to talk about that in about five minutes

Perhaps what this is most expressive of, might I suggest, is control; control of emotions charmingly stated and control of the complex musical means and the interweaving polyphonic lines and schemes that are intrinsic to this musical style. Perhaps the composers of the mid-fourteenth century were attempting to assert on their art the one thing that no one seemed to be able to assert on their environment, and that was a sense of rational control in a world, at that time perhaps, rootless and out of control.

The secularism of the fourteenth century, the loss of faith represented in the fourteenth century, the loss of authority, of absolute authority of the Roman Church in the fourteenth century leads inevitably to the Renaissance in the fifteenth century. The musical Renaissance, as we understand it, goes from about 1400 to 1600. The experience of rediscovering ancient Greek and Roman culture overwhelmed Europe in the fifteenth and sixteenth centuries. It could not help affecting the way people thought about music. To be sure, it wasn't possible for Renaissance men and women to hear actual ancient Greek music. None of it had been translated and interpreted yet. But a rethinking of music's purpose in light of what could be read in the writings of ancient philosophers, poets, essayists and music theories was not only possible, but some believed, urgently required. Those who read ancient literature asked themselves why their modern music did not move people to the various passions the way ancient music was said to have done for the ancients themselves. For example, Bernardino Cirillo wrote this: "Music among the ancients was the most splendid of all the fine arts. With it they created powerful effects that nowadays we cannot produce. Thus, the musicians of today should endeavor in their profession to do what the sculptors, painters and architects of our time have done who have recovered the art of the ancients." During the Renaissance, then, artists, architects, poets, dramatists, philosophers and composers turned to pre-Christian models for inspiration and guidance. Preeminent among those models are the models supplied by the ancient Greek world.

Now, of course, the impact on music is going to be just tremendous, just huge and just profound. Composers of both religious and secular music, and they are usually the same person, want to capture for their music the same power of expression the Greeks ascribed to their music. The question is, of course, how; how do we do that? Well, there are two general solutions that

Renaissance composers increasingly turned to, to make their music more expressive and to try to achieve this Greek ideal of moving the souls of people and changing the face of nature.

Solution number one had to do with articulation of the words. Renaissance composers believed firmly that since the message of any piece of music was in the words, clear articulation of words was of preeminent importance. Now, much as I love the Machaut "Rose, liz," frankly, clear articulation of the words is of secondary importance. The rhythmic and the melodic schemes are of more importance. So, if you land on a syllable that is supposed to be accented in language but in the music it's in an inconvenient place to accent, Machaut will not accent it; because the musical scheme comes first. Vocal articulation and clarity comes second. We're talking about the flip now, that the composers of the Renaissance, first and foremost, want their words to be heard clearly. If the meaning of the music lies in the words, the meaning of the words must be clear.

Solution number two: word-painting. The images and feelings described by these words must somehow be illustrated by the music. So whatever the music is doing, it must portray and illustrate what the words are saying. And what that means, we'll get into in just a moment.

Now listen; importantly, by the mid-Renaissance, by around 1500, an entirely new harmonic system was evolving, based on new examinations of the work of Pythagoras and other ancient Greek theorists. I'm just going to illustrate a couple of points as quickly as I can and then we'll move on. This evolution of what we call "functional harmony" has a huge impact on the future of music. I'm going to take a melody—and this is a melody that we will hear in a vocal piece in just another minute or so—and I'm just going to take the very beginning of this vocal piece, and first I'm going to play this melody monophonically: unaccompanied, one melody, one voice.

(monophonic musical example)

All right, not terribly engaging, but that is what we would sing if we were singing monophony, one melody and one melody only. Now I'm going to play it polyphonically in one of the most common sorts of polyphony, what we call "imitative polyphony," where one voice imitates another.

(polyphonic musical example)

Now, what happens during the Renaissance with this new investigation into Pythagoras and the overtone series, is the concept of chord evolves—that is, the sounding of three or more simultaneously different pitches. How do we coordinate these chords; how do we create laws by which these simultaneities can shift back and forth?

I will now harmonize that silly little line, using Renaissance-style harmonies.

(harmonized musical example)

Now, this sounds much more modern to our ears. This is also a texture; and here's the important point. If this was monophony (monophony example) and this was polyphony (polyphony example), then this we call *homophony*, because there's one main melody and all else is accompaniment (homophony example). We can juice those harmonies up, and believe me, the history of music from 1500 to 1900 is, to a great degree, about juicing up the chords. For example, (example of use of chords). Now if George Gershwin, or Duke Ellington, or Claude Debussy was playing this, they might do something like this (musical example). These harmonies get bigger and thicker with more and more added notes all the time. The point is: We have the first composed homophony, basically chordal music, in the Renaissance.

I'm going to jump ahead of myself and just make sure we all know why this is so important. Opera is a homophonic phenomenon: one voice; everything else perceived as accompanimental to support that voice. Until we have homophony, until we have the means to quietly and convincingly accompany one main melody, we cannot expect the operatic ideal of one person singing about how they feel to evolve.

So, the advent of homophony is the last of the three textures: First monophony, then polyphony and then homophony. It is a product of the reinvestigation of Greek theory that we see during the Renaissance. The upshot of all of this is as follows. The music we're about to hear sounds quite comfortable, quite modern to our ears as opposed to the spiky, more foreign-sounding music of Machaut, written 100 years before what we're about to hear. What we're about to hear was written by Josquin des Prez, born about 1450, died 1521. Josquin is the preeminent composer of the mid-Renaissance and one of my absolute favorites, I don't mind saying that, forever on the media. He's a master of both sacred and secular music.

We're going to listen to two of Josquin's shorter, vocal works as examples of mid-Renaissance vocal articulation, mid-Renaissance word-painting and mid-Renaissance harmonic practice. First we're going to listen to a cute little ditty called "El Grillo," "The Cricket," written around 1480 as best we can tell. It's written in Italian and it is an essentially homophonic work, depending on these block-like chords. It was the beginning of "El Grillo" that I was using just now in my textural demonstration. What will be word-painted, of course, is the jumpy nature of the music. Please, let's read the text first.

> The cricket is a good singer who holds a long note. Go ahead, drink and sing, cricket. But he is not like the other birds, who sing a little and then fly away, the cricket always stands firm. When it is hottest, he sings alone for love.

The way this piece will be painted, the way Josquin will make sure that we know this is about a cricket, is with the jumpy, almost hyperkinetic rhythms that we will hear, very clearly creating a kind of "insectile" texture. I would also point out that the articulation is crystal clear. He serves the words. We can follow every word with utter clarity. The harmony sounds modern. The piece is altogether humorous and engaging, a hugely far cry from the very foreign, if attractive-sounding music we heard from Machaut 100 years before.

Josquin, "El Grillo." (musical example)

As I said before, this is very modern-sounding music. Clearly it wasn't written yesterday, but clearly it uses a language with which we are all familiar and comfortable. And I didn't even point out this lovely bit of word-painting. How can Josquin—and by the way, I keep calling him *Josquin* because that's as he was known. If you to search for him in the CD bins of your local store, he will not be under *des Prez*, he will be under *Josquin* unless the person who is filing the music has not a clue of what they should call him; and then who knows where it will be.

In any case, Josquin has in the text here, "who holds a long note." Now what composer could possibly resist writing a long note when they're singing, "looooongo verso?" So, he doesn't resist. That's an example of word-painting, and that's the kind of phenomena we see first in the Renaissance. What is this music expressive of? Well, it's expressive of a wonderfully clever and humorous poem. The jumpy spirit of the cricket comes through loud and clear.

Let's listen to another brief work by Josquin, which illustrates another part of his art and another aspect of mid-Renaissance music. This is a piece called "Je me complains," "I complain." Well, there is something we all could use here and there. This, rather than Italian poetry, is French poetry; and please understand that composers needed to go back and forth easily between Italian and French poetry. Josquin himself was from the north of France, perhaps from Belgium, but probably he was from the north of France. He split his career between the rich French courts and the even richer courts on the Italian peninsula during the Renaissance, of course gathering tremendous wealth through trade.

This is a *chanson* as opposed to the *frotolla,* or the homophonic Italian work, we heard before. What makes this work really different is it is polyphonic. We have five voices, and they're all interweaving within each other all the time. Each part, in this five-voice polyphony we are about to hear—if you look at each part, you would see the declamation, the clarity of the words is absolute. Of course, when you stick those five parts together and they start swimming together like strands of spaghetti, the words might not be so clear any more because everyone is singing their own words at any given time.

If we were to sing "Row, Row, Row Your Boat" as a group, we would have no problem, if we were all singing the same melody at the same time, hearing the words. But, of course, when we sing it as a round and start overlapping, then it's harder to perceive individual words because at any given moment we're hearing three different words. So it is with polyphony. Even if the articulation of our individual lines is crystal clear, in a polyphonic texture when you combine all of these individual lines, clarity suffers. This will be a different kind of piece, and it will evoke a different expressive content.

The text:

> I complain about my friend, who usually comes to see me in the early morning, but now it's mid-morning, and now it's afternoon, and I don't have news of him. (Evening prayers) Vespers will soon be approaching. The knitting, the lovely knitting girl.

All right. She's sitting there, waiting for her boy to come, and he has not come. And she knits and she knits and she sorrows, quietly, but she sorrows. This is her complaint. Let me play this for you; and I would ask you, once again, what is this music expressive of, what is it reflective of?

(musical example)

So, what is this music reflective, expressive of? I would point out that the rhythms are not those jumpy, kinetic rhythms that we heard in "El Grillo;" rather this is a kind of languid and flowing music, basically dark in what we call the "minor mode." It's a kind of generalized mood, I think, one of romantic malaise. It's not a pointed mood; we don't have one person telling us how badly she feels, but there's a mood, a sensibility, an environment, if you will, that Josquin creates that's very lovely and very convincing. At the soul of these words is that malaise, that unhappiness.

Now we move to the late Renaissance, to the madrigal. The madrigal was the most important genre of Italian secular music in the late Renaissance. In part, I would tell you, that it is the rejection of the madrigal that led directly to the invention of opera. Madrigals were works for vocal ensemble of typically four to six different singers. They freely mixed polyphony and homophony. So, if we mixed together "El Grillo" and "Je me complains"— that is, a little homophony, a little polyphony, we would get what might happen in a single madrigal.

Madrigals were based—and this is what sets them apart from much of the vocal music around them—on serious, elevated poetry by serious poets. Increasingly, there is a feeling, even in this secular music of the Renaissance, that a higher level of poetry could bring about a higher level of music expression. So, madrigals are set to the poems of Petrarch, Ariosto, Tasso, and their like. Madrigals, like the two pieces we just heard, are expressive via word-painting, illustrating the literal meaning of the words. But I would tell you that madrigals take this word-painting to a sometimes excessive end. Madrigals would be performed in all sorts of social and courtly gatherings, and I would also tell you that the output of madrigals in Italy was enormous. These were popular all across Europe, not just in Italy. But in Italy alone, some 2000 collections, collections, of madrigals were published between 1530 and 1600.

The madrigal I'm going to use as an example is one of my favorites. It's by Thomas Weelkes, who is an Englishman, and this is "As Vesta was from Latmos Hill descending," from 1601. The reason why I love this madrigal is because it is in English; it is easier for us to follow the amusing word-painting that Weelkes indulges in. It is a light, brilliant and airy madrigal of great humor. I would tell you that Weelkes wrote this madrigal for an anthology called *The Triumphs of Oriana*. Twenty-three different English composers contributed madrigals to this collection, and while each of these madrigals had a different poem, they all had the same last two lines: "Then sang the shepherds and nymphs of Diana: long live fair Oriana!" All 23 of these madrigals ended with those same two lines. Oriana was the mythological name for Queen Elizabeth, then near the very end of her reign; and the nymphs and shepherds of Diana, the goddess of virginity, were her subjects. Now, in this particular poem, another goddess, Vesta, is walking down her hill in Rome accompanied by Diana's little androgynous darlings, the Vestal Virgins, who nevertheless desert Vesta, leave her in the dust as soon as they get light of Oriana, Queen Elizabeth, a real virgin, walking up the hill.

Here's what we get, and you'll excuse me for illustrating with my voice those things we'll hear Weelkes do in the poem.

> As Vesta was from Latmos Hill, from Latmos Hill, from Latmos Hill (high note on hill) "desceeeending, desceeeending, she spied a maiden queen the same time asceeeending, asceeeending, attended on by all the shepherds' swain; to whom Diana's darling came running down amain, running down, running down, running down amain, running down amain.

Over and over and over.

> First two by two (sung by two singers), then three by three (sung by three singers), then together (sung by everyone), leaving their Goddess all alone (sung by one singer), hasted thither; and mingling with the shepherds of her train, with mirthful tunes her presence did entertain. Then sang the shepherds and nymphs of Diana: long live fair Oriana!"

And as the men at the bottom of this group sing "loooong," they just hold the word "long". It's very cute. It's very brilliant. It's a perfect example of a late Renaissance madrigal where the word-painting is taken to extreme degrees.

(Musical example)

What is this music expressive of? To the nth degree, it's expressive about the meaning of the words, and that's it! Do we gain any insight, my friends, into the joy and euphoria that Oriana must feel having been drawn to all of these strange little creatures? (Plays melody in background) "You like me, you love me. You adorable things, you. And I love you, too." Do we feel the pain of Vesta, having been abandoned by these ingrates? In Ricky Waters' famous words, "For who? For what?" A mortal queen. Does she swear vengeance? (Plays harmonic melody in background) "You dirty rotten nymphs and shepherds, I'm going to get you and your little Vesta, too." No. There's no vendetta. There's no insight into personal feelings. I mean she doesn't even give them a guilt trip. It's not about individual feelings, this madrigal or any madrigal.

In its clever word-painting, does this madrigal embody that elusive Renaissance ideal, the Greek ideal, that music could and should change the face of nature and the souls of people by celebrating the sanctity and power of individual emotions? No. This madrigal does not celebrate individual emotions. Madrigals can't do that because there's too many people singing at the same time. So, the artistic search for the Greek ideal continues. Our next step—the invention of opera. Thank you.

The Invention of Opera and Monteverdi's *Orfeo*
Lectures 5–8

> The intermedio was important—in fact, vital—as a forerunner of opera for two essential reasons: first, because it kept alive in the minds of Italian poets and musicians the idea of close collaboration between drama and music; and second, because in these works, in these intermezzi, the external form of opera is already clear: a drama with interludes of music, dancing, splendid scenery, and spectacular stage effects.

We begin this lecture by reviewing the material we have discussed up to this point. First, the Greek ideal of music posited that music is a force that can move nature and change the hearts and souls of people. Second, the Renaissance saw a growing awareness of the Greek ideal of music. And third, the madrigal is a late-Renaissance experimental genre in which "expression" is based on word painting. Carlo Gesualdo's madrigal "Io parto e non piu dissi" (circa 1595) is expressive of a lovers' quarrel. It is full of unbelievable harmonic complexity. Major amounts of unresolved dissonance (known as chromaticism) correspond to the dissonance felt by the lovers. We will listen to a musical example.

We now move on to a consideration of the intermezzo/intermedio. This performance component developed alongside the madrigal. It was presented between the acts of spoken plays. Many intermezzi/intermedi became more interesting than the plays in which they were inserted, and they were an important forerunner of opera.

Another important development in the progression towards opera was the pastorale. This style of dramatic poetry dominated Italian theater in the late 16th and early 17th centuries. Pastorales feature sylvan settings and mild love adventures, usually ending happily.

From an intellectual and theoretical standpoint, another important event in the story of opera was the collaboration of the Florentine Camerata. The Florentine Camerata was a *ridotto*, or a private academy or intellectual club, that met in the home of Giovanni Bardi di Vernio from 1573 to 1592. Of special interest to this group was the nature of musical and dramatic expression. Among the members of the Florentine Camerata was Vincenzo Galilei, who wrote a scathing attack on the artificiality of expression in madrigals. Based largely on the ideas of scholar Girolamo Mei, the group decreed that true musical expression could only be achieved by a single singer employing an actor's dramatic and oratorical skills.

The Florentine Camerata developed a new theory of music. Their theory was based on the Greek expressive ideal and involved several rules for music and musical performance:

- The text must be sung by one singer, accompanied as simply as possible so that the words are clearly understood.

- The words must be sung the way they are spoken (natural declamation). No dance rhythms can be imposed upon the words.

- The music must depict the feelings and emotions of the character singing.

The first works that we today call operas were created by members of the Florentine Camerata. *Daphne* was created by the poet Ottavio Rinuccini and the composer Jacopo Peri in 1598. The music is lost today. *Euridice* was created by Rinuccini and Peri in 1600, and in the same year a second version was produced by Rinuccini and Giulio Caccini.

Euridice was first performed on October 6, 1600 in Florence, Italy. A fully staged production with alternating choruses, rhyming pop-type songs, and early recitative (*stile rappresentativo*), Peri's *Euridice* is a play set to music, not a play conceived musically. The character of Orfeo (Orpheus), with his ability to change souls and the very face of nature with his music, personifies both opera and the Greek view of music.

The first great composer of opera was Claudio Monteverdi (1567–1643). He did not invent opera but was inspired to create a new operatic ideal. Born in Cremona, Italy, he rose to the pinnacle of the musical profession in the 17th century as choirmaster at St. Mark's cathedral in Venice. Of his nineteen stage works only six have survived intact, including his first opera *Orfeo*, which represents the first completely successful attempt to apply the full resources of musical and dramatic art to the new genre of opera.

Orfeo (1607) is an extraordinary synthesis of the musical genres and compositional techniques available in the time when it was produced. The toccata (overture) demonstrates the large instrumental ensemble (around forty players) Monteverdi calls for in *Orfeo*. The character of Orpheus lies at the heart of the drama as the personification of dramatic musical art. He symbolizes the power of music. Yet while he can control external forces with his music, he cannot control his own emotions.

In Act 1 of *Orfeo*, there is happiness and joy in arcadia. Eurydice has finally agreed to marry Orpheus. They celebrate with friends. Monteverdi's style of recitative (half sung, half spoken music) is known as arioso, closer to actual song than Peri's. As a musical example, consider "In questo lieto." Another musical example is ballet/chorus, "Lasciate i monti." This chorus is full of sexual symbolism. The excitement builds up to the entrance of the star couple. Orpheus, appropriately, sings a richer arioso, "Rosa del ciel," than the other characters.

The first great composer of opera was Claudio Monteverdi (1567–1643). He did not invent opera but was inspired to create a new operatic ideal.

Act 1, like most first operatic first acts, is dramatically static. It represents an incredible synthesis of various musical forms: the toccata (opening music, or overture), ritornello (orchestral refrain), recitative (in Monteverdi's inimitable style), symbolic chorus ("Vieni, Imeneo"), ballet, popular song ("Lasciate i monti"), religious-type music ("Ma se il nostro"), and final, celebratory music.

In the second act of *Orfeo*, grief comes to paradise. Orpheus sings his last bit of joy in "Vi ricorda," but then the celebrations are cut short with the news of Eurydice's death. The messenger's story is a brilliant, masterful composition. She begins slowly, almost monotonically, and builds up to a powerful climax as she tells her tragic tale. Then, exhausted, she concludes on a bleak note. This is exemplified by "Ahi, caso acerbo." Orpheus's response, "Tu se' morta," is a profoundly moving and brilliantly written moment. It is followed by a madrigal-style chorus replete with word painting: "Ahi, caso acerbo." Monteverdi employs a stunning stroke. He brings back the ritornello heard at the beginning of the opera. Now it takes on a whole new dimension as it reflects both the tragic events of the act as well as Orpheus's determination to rescue Eurydice from death, armed with a single weapon—the power of music itself.

Act 3 involves the journey to Hades in search of Eurydice. The opening sinfonia is dominated by brass instruments, which were associated with the underworld. Charon, the boatman who takes souls to the underworld, is a deep bass, accompanied by a regal (reed organ). He sings "O tu, ch'innanzi morte." Orpheus's plea, "Possente spirito" is—as it should be—the crown jewel of the opera. While he does not succeed in softening Charon's heart and gaining entry to Hades, his music does have a beneficial effect on the formidable boatman. It puts him to sleep! A firm comment on the nature of opera audiences everywhere! For a musical example, we will listen to Orpheus's "Ei dorme."

In Act 4, Pluto presents a challenge and Orpheus experiences a downfall. Pluto, king of the underworld, agrees to allow Eurydice to follow Orpheus back up to the world of mortals as long as he does not look back at her. Orpheus disobeys and Eurydice is forced back to Hades. Her "Ahi, vista troppo" is memorable for its extraordinarily dissonant harmonies. Act 5 is marked by Orpheus's despair and Apollo's divine intervention.

In conclusion, we note that in *Orfeo* Monteverdi succeeds on every level. His opera synthesizes all the different genres. It is a brilliant example of the power of recitative to embody and magnify the power of words. It also represents the marriage of drama and music. The whole is greater than the parts. Additionally, in *Orfeo* the Greek ideal of the power of music to "calm every troubled heart and ... kindle the most icy souls", as described in the prologue, has been redefined and reinvented. ∎

Turandot

(1924)

Giacomo Puccini

Libretto by Giuseppe Adami and Renato Simoni

Calaf

Nessun dorma!
Nessun dorma!
Tu pure, o Principessa,
nella tua fredda stanza
guardi le stelle che tremano
d'amore e di speranza!
Ma il mio mistero è chiuso in me,
il nome mio nessun saprà!
No, no, sulla tua bocca
lo dirò,
quando la luce splenderà!
Ed il mio bacio scioglierà
il silenzio che ti fa mia!

Le donne

(interno; lontano)
Il nome suo nessun saprà . . .
E noi dovrem, ahimè! Morir! Morir!

Calaf

Dilegua, o notte! Tramontate, stelle!
Tramontate, stelle! All'alba vincerò!
Vincerò! Vincerò!

Calaf

No one shall sleep!
No one shall sleep!
You too, o Princess,
in your cold room
are watching the stars which
tremble with love and hope!
But my secret lies hidden within me,
no one will know my name!
No, no, I will reveal it
only on your lips,
when daylight breaks forth
and my kiss will break the silence
which makes you mine!

Women

(off stage; distant)
Nobody will know his name . . .
And we will have to die, alas! Die!

Calaf

Depart, o night! Quickly set, stars!
Quickly set, stars! At dawn I will
win! I will win! I will win!

Idomeneo
(1780)
Wolfgang Amadeus Mozart
Libretto by G.B. Varesco

Elettra	Electra
𝐴	𝐴
D'Oreste, d'Ajace ho in seno	I feel the torments of Orestes and
i tormenti,	Ajax in my breast,
d'Aletto la face già morte mi dà.	The image of Alecto* frightens me to death.
𝐵	𝐵
Squarciatemi il core, ceraste,	Tear my heart, you horned
serpenti, o un ferro il dolore	serpents, or I shall end my pain
in me finirà.	with a sword.
𝐴'	𝐴'
[A varied reprise of verse 1]	[A varied reprise of verse 1]
𝐵'	𝐵'

(*Alecto: one of the three Furies)

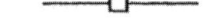

"Songs of a Wayfarer"
(1884)
Gustav Mahler
Poem by the composer

2. GING HEUT MORGEN ÜBERS FELD

Ging heut morgen übers Feld,	As I walked through the field this morning,
tau noch aud den Gräsern hing;	the dew still hung upon the grass;
sprach zu mir der lustge Fink:	the merry finch called out to me,
"Ei, du! Gelt? Guten Morgen!	"Hey, you there! Good day to you!
Ei gelt? Du!	
Wird's nicht eine schöne Welt?	Isn't this a splendid world?
Schöne Welt?	Splendid world?
Zink! Zink! Schön und flink!	Tweet! Tweet! Fine and bright!
Wie mir doch die welt gefällt!"	O how I love the world!"

Auch die Glockenblum am Feld
hat mir lustig, guter Ding
mit den Glöckchen klinge, kling,
ihren Morgengruß geschellt:
"Wird's nicht eine schöne Welt?
Schöne Welt?
Kling! Kling! Schönes Ding!
Wie mir doch die Welt gefällt!
Hei-a!"

Und da fing im Sonnenschein
Gleich die Welt zu funkeln an;
Alles, alles, Ton und Farbe gewann
im Sonnenschein!
Blum und Vogel, groß
und klein!
Guten Tag, guten Tag!
Ist's nicht eine schöne Welt?
Ei, du! Gelt? Schöne Welt!?

Nun fängt auch mein Glück wohl
an?! Nein! Nein! Das ist mein,
mir nimmer bluhen kann!

And the bluebell in the field
told of good cheer
with its bell, ting-a-ling,
as it rang its morning greeting:
"Isn't this a splendid world,
splendid world?
Ding, ding! Beautiful thing!
O how I love the world!
Hurrah!"

And all the world began to glow
in the sunshine; in the sunshine
all things took on color and sound!

Flower and bird, things great
and small!
Good day, good day!
Isn't this a splendid world?
Hey, you there! Lovely world!?

Will my happiness now flower
too? No, no! I know that it can
never bloom for me!

———□———

Carmen
(1875)
Georges Bizet
Libretto by Henri Meilhac and Ludovic Halévy

NO. 10 SÉGUEDILLA AND DUET

Carmen

Près des remparts de Séville,
chez mon ami Lillas Pastia
j'irai danser la séguedille
et boire du Manzanilla.
Oui, mais toute seule on s'ennuie,
et les vrais plaisirs sont à deux;
donc, pour me tenir compagnie,

Carmen

By the ramparts of Sevilla,
at the place of Lillas Pastia,
I'll go dance the seguidilla
and take a glass of manzanilla.
Yes, but by myself I'm bored,
the only pleasure's one you share;
so I'll take along my man,

j'emmènerai mon amoureux!
Mon amoureux . . . il est au diable,
je l'ai mis à la porte hier!
Mon pauvre coeur très consolable,
mon coeur est libre comme l'air!
J'ai des galants à la douzaine,
mais ils ne sont pas à mon gré.
Voici la fin de la semaine:
Qui veut m'aimer? Je l'aimerai!
Qui veut mon âme?
Elle est à prendre!
Vous arrivez au bon moment!
Je n'ai guère le temps d'attendre,
car avec mon nouvel
amant . . .

Don José

Tais-toi! Je t'avais dit de
ne pas me parler!

Carmen

Je ne te parle pas,
je chante pour moi-même!
Et je pense!
Il n'est pas défendu de penser!
Je pense à certain officier
qui m'aime
et qu'à mon tour, je pourrai
bien aimer!

Don José

Carmen!

Carmen

Mon officier n'est pas un capitaine:
pas même un lieutenant,
il n'est que brigadier; mais
c'est assez pour une Bohémienne et
je daigne m'en contenter!

and then we'll make a cosy pair!
But my lover's . . . gone to hell!
Last night he went out . . . on his ear!
My poor heart's longing to forget,
my heart is ever free as air!
I count my beaux by dozens,
but I'll have none of them.
Here it is the end of the week:
Who'll love me? I'll love him!
Who'll take my soul?
It's up for bids!
You've come at the right time!
I can't wait a minute longer,
for once I've got a brand-new
lover . . .

Don José

Be quiet! I told you
not to speak!

Carmen

I'm not speaking,
I'm singing to myself!
And thinking!
There's no law against thinking!
I'm thinking of a certain officer
who loves me
and whom I could maybe
love myself!

Don José

Carmen!

Carmen

My officer's not a captain:
not even a lieutenant,
he is only a corporal; but
that's good enough for a gypsy and
I'm ready to make do with that!

Don José

Carmen, je suis comme un homme
ivre, si je cède, si je me livre,
ta promesse, tu la tiendras,
Ah! si je t'aime, Carmen,
Carmen, tu m'aimeras!

Carmen

Oui.
*(Don José unties the rope holding
Carmen's hands.)*

Don José

Carmen, I feel as if I'm drunk,
if I give way, if I give in,
your promise, you'll keep it,
Ah! If I love you Carmen,
Carmen, you'll love me!

Carmen

Yes.
*(Don José unties the rope holding
Carmen's hands.)*

Il barbiere di Siviglia
The Barber of Seville (1816)
Gioacchino Rossini
Libretto by Cesare Sterbini

CAVATINA: "Largo al Factotum"

Figaro

𝐴
La ran la le ra la ran la la.
Largo al
factotum della città.
La ran la la, *etc.*
Presto a bottega
che l'alba è già
La ran la la, *etc.*
Ah, che bel vivere,
che bel piacere,
per un barbiere di qualità
𝐴'
Ah, bravo Figaro.
Bravo, bravissimo, bravo!
La ran la la, *etc.*
Fortunatissimo
per verità. Bravo!

Figaro

𝐴
La ran la le ra la ran la la.
Make way for the
factotum of the city.
La ran la la, *etc.*
Rushing to his shop
for dawn is here.
La ran la la, *etc.*
What a merry life,
what gay pleasures
for a barber of quality.
𝐴'
Ah, bravo Figaro.
Bravo, bravissimo, bravo!
La ran la la, *etc.*
Most fortunate of men,
indeed you are!

La ran la la, *etc.*

B
Pronto a far tutto
la notte, il giorno,
sempre d'intorno
in giro sta.
Miglior cuccagna
per un barbiere,
vita più nobile,
no, non si dà
La la ran la la ran la, *etc.*

B'
Rasori e pettini,
lancette e forbici.
Al mio comando
tutto qui sta.
V'è la risorsa
poi del mestiere,
colla donnetta,
col cavaliere . . .
La la ran la . . . la . . . la.
Ah, che bel vivere,
che bel piacere,
per un barbiere di qualità.

C
Tutti me chiedono,
tutti me vogliono,
donne ragazzi,
vecchi, fanciulle.
Qua la parrucca,
presto la barba,
qua la sanguigna,
presto il biglietto.
Tutti mi chiedono,
tutti mi vogliono.
Qua la parruca
presto la barba,
presto il biglietto.
Ehi, Figaro, Figaro, Figaro, *etc.*

La ran la la, *etc.*

B
Ready for everything
by night or by day,
always in bustle,
in constant motion.
A better lot
for a barber,
a nobler life
does not exist.
La la ran la la ran la, *etc.*

B'
Razors and combs,
lancets and scissors,
at my command
everything's ready.
Then there are "extras,"
part of my trade
business for ladies
and cavaliers . . .
La la ran la . . . la . . . la.
Ah what a merry life,
what gay pleasures,
for a barber of quality.

C
All call for me,
all want me.
Ladies and children.
Old men and maidens.
I need a wig,
I want a shave,
leeches to bleed me,
here, take this note.
All call for me,
all want me,
I need a wig,
I want a shave,
here, take this note.
Ho, Figaro, Figaro, Figaro, *etc.*

D
Ahimè! che furia!
Ahimè! che folla!
Uno alla volta,
per carità.
C'
Ehi, Figaro: son qua!
Figaro qua, Figaro là,
Figaro su, Figaro giù.
Pronto, prontissimo
son come il fulmine,
sono il
factotum della città.
C"
Ah, bravo, Figaro,
bravo, bravissimo,
a te la fortuna
non mancherà.
La la ran la, *etc.*
Sono il factotum della città.

D
Heavens! What a commotion!
Heavens! What a crowd!
One at a time,
For pity's sake.
C'
Ho, Figaro! I am here!
Figaro here, Figaro there,
Figaro up, Figaro down.
Quicker and quicker
I go like greased lightning.
Make way for the
factotum of the city.
C"
Ah, bravo, Figaro,
bravo, bravissimo,
on you good fortune
will always smile.
La la ran la, *etc.*
I am the factotum of the city.

Orestes

(ca. 408 BCE)

Euripides

STASIMON CHORUS

You wild goddesses who dart across the skies seeking vengeance for murder, we beg you to free Agamemnon's son from his raging fury. . . . We grieve for this boy. Happiness is brief among mortals. Sorrow and anguish sweep down on it like a swift gust of wind on a sail-ship, and it sinks under the tossing seas.

Mass for Christmas Day

INTROIT
"Puer natus est nobis"

Puer natus est nobis, et filius datus est nobis: cujus imperium super humerum ejus: et vocabitur nomen ejus, magni consili Angelus.	A child is born to us, and a Son is given to us; whose government is upon His shoulder; and His Name shall be called the Angel of great counsel.

---□---

"Alleluia pascha nostrum" and "Gaudeat devotio fidelium"
(ca. 1190)
Leonin

Alleluia pascha nostrum	Hallelujah our Passover
Gaudeat devotio fidelium; verbum patris incarnatur, nova proles nobis datur et nobis cum conversatur salus gentium. Vite pandit ostium, dum mortis supplicium, pie tolerat.	Let the devotion of the faithful be raised in rejoicing; the word of the father is made flesh, and a new child is given to us, and He has bestowed Himself upon us. The salvation of the people has opened the gateway of life, for he in devotion has borne the punishment of death.

---□---

"Can vei la lauzeta mover"
"When I see the lark beating" (ca. 1175)
Bernard de Ventadorn
Poem by the composer

Can vei la lauzeta mover
de joi sas alsas contral rai,
que s'oblid' e*s laissa chazer
per la doussor c'al cor il vai,
Ai! tan grans enveya m'en ve
de cui qu'eu veya jauzion,
meravilhas ai, car desse
lo cor de dezirer no*m fon.

Ai, las! tan cuidava saber
d'amor, e tan petit en sai,
car eu d'amar no*m posc tener
celeis don ja pro non aurai.
Tout m'a mo cor, e tout m'a me,
e se mezeis e tot lo mon;

e can se*m tolc, no*m laisset re
mas dezirer e cor volon.

When I see the lark beating its wings
joyfully against the sun's rays,
which then swoons and swoops
down because of the joy in its heart,
Oh! I feel such jealousy
for all those who have the joy of love,
that I am astonished
that my heart does not
immediately melt with desire!

Alas! I thought I knew so much
of love, and I know so little; for
I cannot help loving a lady from
whom I shall never obtain any favor.
She has taken away my heart and,
myself and herself and the whole
world;
and when she left me, I had nothing
left but desire and a yearning heart.

"Rose, liz"
"Rose, Lily" (ca. 1350)
Guillaume de Machaut
Poem by the composer

Rose, liz, printemps, verdure,
fleur, baume et tres douce
odour, belle,
passes en doucour,
et tous les biens de Nature,
avez dont je vous aour.
Rose, liz, printemps, verdure,
fleur, baume et tres douce
odour.

Et quant toute creature
seurmonte vostre valour,
bien puis dire et par honour:
rose, liz, printemps, verdure,
fleur, baume et tres douce
odour, belle,
passes en doucour.

Rose, lily, spring, greenery,
flower, balm, and the sweetest
fragrance, beautiful lady,
you surpass them all in sweetness.
And all the gifts of nature
you possess, for which I adore you.
Rose, lily, spring, greenery,
flower, balm, and the sweetest
fragrance.

And, since behond all creatures
your virtue excels,
I can honestly say:
rose, lily, spring, greenery,
flower, balm, and very sweet
fragrance, beautiful lady,
you surpass them all in sweetness.

"El Grillo"
"The Cricket" (ca. 1480)
Josquin des Prez

El grillo è buon cantore
che tiene longo verso.
Dale, beve grillo, canta.
Ma non fa come gli altri uccelli,
come li han canto un poco,
van' de fatto in alto loco,
sempre el grillo sta pur saldo.
Quando la maggior el caldo
alhor canto sol per amore.

The cricket is a good singer
who holds a long note.
Go ahead, drink and sing, cricket.
But he is not like the other birds,
who sing a little
and then fly away,
the cricket always stands firm.
When it is hottest,
he sings alone for love.

"Je me complains"
"I complain" (ca. 1480)
Josquin des Prez

Je me complains de mon amy,	I complain about my friend,
qui me vouloit tant venir veoir	who usually comes to see me
la fresche matinée,	in the early morning,
or est il prime,	but now it's mid-morning,
et c'est midi,	and now it's afternoon,
et si n'oy nouvelle de luy,	and if I don't have news of him,
s'aproche le vesprée.	Vespers will be approaching.
La tricoton, la belle tricotée.	The knitting, the lovely knitting girl.

"As Vesta was from Latmos Hill descending"
(1601)
Thomas Weelkes

As Vesta was from Latmos Hill descending
she spied a maiden Queen the same ascending,
attended on by all the shepherds' swain;
to whom Diana's darlings came running down amain
first two by two, then three by three together
leaving their Goddess all alone, hasted thither;
and mingling with the shepherds of her train,
with mirthful tunes her presence did entertain.
Then sang the shepherds and nymphs of Diana:
long live fair Oriana!

"Io parto"
"I am leaving" (ca. 1595, pub. 1611)
Carlo Gesualdo

"Io parto" e non più dissi che il
dolore privò di vita il core.

Allor proruppe in pianto e dissi
Clori con interroti omèi: "dunque
a i dolori io resto. Ah, non fia mai
ch'io non languisca in dolorosi lai."

Morto fui, vivo son che i spirti
spenti tonaro in vita a sì pietosi
accenti.

"I am leaving" and said no more,
for grief had robbed my heart of
life.
Then Clori began to weep, and
said, with interrupted cries of
"Alas: therefore, with my agony
I remain. Ah, may I never cease to
languish in such pain."
I was dead, and now am I alive, for
my dead spirits return to life at the
sound of such pathetic accents.

Euridice
(1600)
Jacopo Peri
Libretto by Ottavio Rinuccini

Dafne

Per quel vago boschetto,
ove, regando i fiori, lento
trascorre il fonte degl'allori,
prendea dolce diletto con le
compagne sue la bella sposa,
chi violetta o rosa
per far ghirland' al crine
togliea dal prato o dall'acute
spine, e qual posand' il fianco
su la fiorita sponda
dolce cantava al mormorar
dell' onda; ma la bella Euridice
movea danzando il piè sul
verde prato quand'ahi ria sorte
acerba, angue crudo e spietato
che celato giacea tra fiori e l'erba

Dafne

In the beautiful thicket,
where, watering the flowers, slowly
courses the spring of the laurel,
she took sweet delight with her
companions—the beautiful bride—
as some picked violets, others roses,
to make garlands for their hair,
in the meadow or among the sharp
thorns. Another, lying on her side
on the flowered bank,
sang sweetly to the murmur of the
waves. But the lovely Eurydice
dancingly moved her feet on the
green grass when—o bitter, angry
fate!—a snake, cruel and merciless,
that lay hidden among flowers and

punsele il piè con sì maligno dente,
ch'impalidì repente come raggio
di sol che nube adombri.
El dal profondo core,
con un sospir mortale,
sì spaventoso ohimè sospinse fuore,
che, quasi avesse l'ale,
giunse ogni Ninfa al doloroso
suono. Et ella in abbandono tutta
lasciossi all'or nell'altrui braccia.
Sparge il bel volto
e le dorate chiome un sudor viè
più fredd'assai che giaccio.
Indi s'udio 'l tuo nome tra le
labbra sonar fredd'e' tremanti
e volti gl'occhi al cielo, scolorito
il bel volto e' bei sembianti,
restò tanta bellezza immobil gielo.

Arcetro

Che narri, ohimè,
che sento? Misera Ninfa,
e più misero amante, spettacol
di miseria e di tormento!

Orfeo

Non piango e non sospiro,
o mia cara Euridice, ché sospirar,
ché lacrimar non posso.
Cadavero infelice, O mio core,
o mia speme, o pace, o vita!
Ohimè, chi me t'ha tolto,
chi mi t'ha tolto, ohimè!
dove sei gita?
Tosto vedrai ch'in vano
non chiamasti morendo il tuo
consorte. Non son,
non son lontano: io vengo,
o cara vita, o cara morte.

grass bit her foot with such an evil
tooth that she suddenly became
pale like a ray of sunshine that a
cloud darkens. And from the
depths of her heart, a mortal sigh,
so frightful, alas, flew forth,
almost as if it had wings;
every nymph rushed to the painful
sound. And she, fainting,
let herself fall in another's arms.
Then spread over her beautiful face
and her golden tresses
a sweat colder by far than ice.
And then was heard your name,
sounding between her lips, cold and
trembling, and her eyes turned to
heaven, her beautiful face and mien
discolored, this great beauty was
transformed to motionless ice.

Arcetro

What do you relate, alas,
what do I hear? Wretched nymph,
and more unhappy lover,
spectacle of sorrow and of torment!

Orfeo

I do not weep, nor do I sigh,
o my dear Eurydice,
for I am unable to sigh, to weep.
Unhappy corpse, o my heart,
o my hope, o peace, o life!
Alas, who has taken you from me?
Who has taken you away, alas?
Where have you gone?
Soon you will see that not in vain
did you, dying, call your
spouse. I am not
far away; I come,
o dear life, o dear death.

Orfeo
(1607)
Claudio Monteverdi
Libretto by Alessandro Striggio

PROLOGUE

Ritornello

La musica

Dal mio Parnasso amato
a voi ne vegno, incliti eroi,
sangue gentil de' regi, di cui narra
la fama eccelsi pregi, né giunge al
ver, perch'é tropp'alto il segno.

Music

From my beloved Parnassus I
come to you, illustrious heroes of
noble royal blood, whose glorious
virtues are proclaimed by fame
only incompletely, for they are
too many to number.

Ritornello

Io la Musica son, ch'ai dolci accenti
so far tranquillo ogni turbato core,

ed or di nobil ira ed or d'amore
posso infiammar le più gelate menti.

I am Music who, with sweet
sounds, knows how to calm every
troubled heart, and
now to noble anger, now to love,
can kindle the most icy souls.

Ritornello

Io, su cetera d'or, cantando soglio
mortal orecchio lusingar talora,
e in questa guisa a l'armonia sonora
de la lira del ciel più l'alma invoglio.

Singing to the golden lyre I am
accustomed sometimes to delight
mortal ears and I thus inspire the
soul at the sonorous harmony of
the lyre of Heaven.

Ritornello

Quinci a dirvi d'Orfeo desio mi
sprona, d'Orfeo che trasse al suo
cantar le fere e servo fe' l'inferno a
sue preghiere, gloria immortal
di Pindo a d'Elicona.

My desire now is to tell you of
Orpheus, of Orpheus who held
the wild beasts spellbound with his
song, who even subdued Hell with
his pleading, and won the immortal
fame of Pindos and Helicon.

Ritornello

Or mentre i canti alterno, or lieti or mesti, non si mova augellin gra queste piante, né s'oda in queste rive onda sonante, ed ogni auretta in suo cammin s'arresti.	Now during my songs, now gay, now sad, may the birds be silent on these trees, no waves be heard on these shores, and every breeze cease to blow.

Ritornello

---□---

ACT ONE

Pastore

A
In questo lieto e fortunato giorno
ch'ha posto fine a gli amorosi
affanni del nostro semideo,
cantiam, pastori, in sì soavi
accenti, che sian degni d'Orfeo
nostri concenti.
B
Oggi fatta è pietosa l'alma già sì
sdegnosa della bella Euridice.
Oggi fatto è felice Orfeo
nel sen di lei, per cui già tanto
per queste selve ha sospirato e
pianto.
A'
Dunque in sì lieto e fortunato
giorno, *etc.*

Shepherd

A
On this happy, auspicious day
which has put an end to the
lovesickness of our demi-god, let
us sing, shepherds, in such gentle
accents that our strains will be
worthy of Orpheus.
B
Today pity has stirred the soul, till
now so disdainful, of the lovely
Eurydice. Today Orpheus has
been made happy on her breast, for
whose sake he has already sighed
and wept so much in these woods.
A'
Therefore on such a happy,
auspicious day, *etc.*

---□---

Coro di ninfe e pastori

Vieni, Imeneo, deh, vieni,
e la tua face ardente
sia quasi un sol nascente ch'apporti
a questi amanti i di sereni e lunge
omai disgombre de gli affanni
e del duol gli orrori e l'ombre.

Chorus of Nymphs and Shepherds

Come, Hymen, o come,
and let thy blazing torch
be like a rising sun that brings days
of serenity to these lovers; and
drive far away the horrors and the
shadows of anguish and grief.

---□---

Balletto

Coro di ninfe e pastori | **Chorus of Nymphs and Shepherds**

Part 1
Lasciate i monti, lasciate i
fonti, ninfe vezzose a liete,
e in questi prati ai balli usati

vago il bel piè rendete.
Part 2
Qui miri il sole vostre carole
più vaghe assai di quelle
ond'a la luna la notte bruna
danzan in ciel le stelle.

Part 3

Part 1
Lasciate i monti, lasciate i
fonti, *etc.*
Part 2'
Po' di bei fiori per voi s'honori
di questi amanti il crine,
ch'or dei martiri dei lor desiri
godon beati al fine.
Part 3

Part 1
Leave the mountains, leave the
fountains, fair, happy nymphs,
and in these meadows, with
your usual dances,
bestir your beautiful feet.
Part 2
Here let the sun watch your
dances that are much lovelier than
those which the stars in the sky
perform around the moon in the
dark night.

Part 3
Ritornello
Part 1
Leave the mountains, leave the
fountains, *etc.*
Part 2'
Then with beautiful flowers adorn
the locks of these lovers,
who after the torments of longing
at last enjoy perfect bliss.
Part 3
Ritornello

Pastore primo

Ma tu, gentil cantor, s'a tuoi
lamenti già festi lagrimar
queste campagne, Perch'ora
al suon de la famosa cetra
no fai teco gioir le valli e i poggi?
Sia testimon del core qualche
lieta canzon che detti Amore.

Orfeo

Rosa del ciel, vita del mondo e

First Shepherd

But you, gentle singer, whose
laments once made this
countryside weep why do you not
now delight the valleys and hills
with the sound of the famous lyre?
May the testimony of your heart be
some happy song that speaks of love

Orpheus

Rose of the day, life of the earth

degna prole di lui che
l'universo affrena,
Sol, che'l tutto circondi e'l tutto
miri, da gli stellanti giri,
dimmi, vedesti mai
di me più lieto e fortunato
amante? Fu ben felice il giorno,
mio ben, che pria ti vidi,
e più felice l'ora
che per to sospirai,
poichè al mio sospirar to sospirasti;
felicissimo il punto
che la candida mano,
pegno di pura fede, a me porgesti.
Se tanti cori avessi
quanti occhi ha il ciel eterno e
quante chiome han questi colli
ameni il verde maggio, tutti
colmi sarieno e traboccanti di
quel piacer ch'oggi mi fa contento.

Euridice

Io non dirò qual sia nel tuo gioir,
Orfeo, la gioia mia, chè non ho
meco il core, ma teco stassi in
compagnia d'amore; chiedi lo
dunque a lui s'intender brami
quanto lieto gioisca e quanto
t'ami.

Coro de ninfe e pastori

Lasciate i monti, lasciate i
fonti, *etc.*

Vieni, Imeneo, deh, vieni,
e la tua face ardente
sia quasi un sol nascente
ch'apporti a questi amanti i
di sereni; *etc.*

and noble offspring of him who
guides the universe,
Sun, who surrounds and sees all
from your path among the stars,
tell me, did you ever see
a happier, more fortunate lover
than I? Blessed was the day,
my beloved, on which I first saw
you, and happier still the hour
when I sighed for you,
since you did return my sighs;
happy the moment when
you gave me your white hand
as a pledge of pure faithfulness.
Had I as many hearts as
the eternal heavens eyes and these
pleasant hills leaves in green May,
all would be full and overflowing
with the joy that has made me
happy today.

Eurydice

I'll not say how great is my bliss,
Orpheus, at your bliss: I do not
bear my heart within me, it
remains with you together with
my love; ask it if you would hear
how it rejoices and how much it
loves you.

Balletto

Chorus of Nymphs and Shepherds

Leave the mountains, leave the
fountains, *etc.*

Ritornello

Come, Hymen, o come,
and let thy blazing torch
be like a rising sun
that brings days of serenity to
these lovers, *etc.*

Pastore secondo

Ma se il nostro gioir dal ciel deriva,
com'è dal ciel ciò che quaggiù
s'incontra, giusto è ben che devoti
gli offriamo incensi e voti. Dunque
al tempio ciascun rivolga i passi a
pregar lui ne la cui destra è il
mondo, che lungamente il nostro
ben conservi.

Second Shepherd

But if our rejoicing comes from
Heaven, like everything around us
here, it is proper that we reverently
offer it incense and sacrifices. Let
each therefore turn his steps to the
temple to pray to him in whose right
hand the world rests, that he may
long preserve for us this happiness.

Ritornello

Pastore secondo e terzo

Alcun non sia che disperato in
preda si doni al duol, benchè talor
n'assaglia possente si che
nostra vita inforsa.

Second and Third Shepherds

Let nobody fall prey to despair,
surrender to grief, even though it
assails us so powerfully that it
endangers our life.

Ritornello

Ninfa, pastore primo e quarto

Chè, poi che nembo rio, gravido
il seno d'atra tempesta, inorrridito
ha il mondo, dispiega il sol più
chiaro i rai lucenti.

Nymph, First and Fourth Shepherds

For after the terrible clouds, laden
with dark storms, have frightened
the world, the sun shines all the
more brightly.

Ritornello

Pastore primo e secondo

E dopo l'aspro gel del verno ignudo
veste di fior la primavera i campi.

First and Second Shepherds

And after the bitter frost of bare
winter the spring clothes the fields
with flowers.

Coro di nife e pastori

Ecco Orfeo, cui pur dianzi furon
cibo i sospir, bevanda il pianto.
Oggi felice è tanto che nulla
è più che da bramar gli avanzi.

Chorus of Nymphs and Shepherds

Here is Orpheus, for whom sighs
were once food and weeping was
drink. Today he is so happy that
nothing more remains for him to
desire.

ACT TWO

Sinfonia

Orfeo

Ecco pur ch'a voi ritorno,
care selve e piagge amate,
da quel sol fatte beate
per cui sol mie notti han giorno.

Orpheus

Behold, I return to you,
dear woods and beloved hills,
made blessed by that sun
through which alone my nights
turn to day.

Ritornello

Pastore secondo

Mira ch'a sè n'alletta
l'ombra, Orfeo, di que' faggi,
or che infocati raggi
Febo dal ciel saetta.

Second Shepherd

See how the shade of these
beeches allures us, Orpheus,
now that Phoebus sends
fiery rays from the sky.

Ritornello

Pastore terzo

Su quell'erbose sponde
posiamci, e in vari modi
ciascun sua voce snodi
al mormorio de l'onde.

Third Shepherd

On these grassy banks let us rest
and in our various ways
let each join his voice
with the murmur of the waves.

Ritornello

Pastore secondo e terzo

In questo prato adorno
ogni selvaggio nume
sovente ha per costume
di far lieto suggiorno.

Second and Third Shepherds

On this adorned meadow
every god of the woods has
frequently been accustomed
to spend happy hours.

Ritornello

Qui Pan, dio dei pastori,
s'udì talor dolente
rimembrar dolcemente
suoi sventurati amori.

Here Pan, god of shepherds,
was sometimes heard sadly
and gently recalling
his unhappy loves.

Ritornello

Qui la Napee vezzose,
schiera sempre fiorita,
con le candide dita
fur viste a coglier rose.

Coro di ninfe e pastori

Dunque fa' degni, Orfeo,
del suon della tua lira
questi campi ove spira
aura d'odor sabeo.

Here the charming Napaeae,
a group always garlanded,
with their white fingers
were seen plucking roses.

Chorus of Nymphs and Shepherds

Then, Orpheus, make worthy
with the sound of your lyre
these fields, over which wafts the
aura of oriental perfumes.

---◻︎---

Ritornello

Orfeo

Vi ricorda, o boschi ombrosi,
de' miei lunghi aspri tormenti,
quando i sassi ai miei lamenti
rispondean fatti pietosi?

Orpheus

Do you remember, o shady
woods, my long, bitter torments,
when the stones responded
to my laments compassionately?

Ritornello

Dite, allor non vi sembrai
più d'ogni altro sconsolato?
Or fortuna ha stil cangiato
ed ha volto in festa i guai.

Say, did I not then appear to you
more disconsolate than any other?
Now fortune has smiled on me and
has turned my woes into a feast.

Ritornello

Vissi già mesto e dolente:
or gioisco e quegli affanni
che sofferti ho per tant'anni
fan più caro il ben presente.

I used to live sadly and woefully;
now I rejoice, and those sufferings
that I bore for so many years
make my present joy all the more
precious.

Ritornello

Sol per te, bella Euridice,
benedico il mio tormento:
dopo il suol si è più contento,
dopo il mal si è più felice.

Only for you, lovely Eurydice,
do I bless my former torments;
after grief one is more content,
after pain one is happier.

---◻︎---

Pastore secondo

Mira, deh mira, Orfeo,
che d'ogni intorno ride il bosco
e ride il prato; segue pur col
plettro aurato d'addolcir l'aria
in sì beato giorno.

La messaggera

Ahi, caso acerbo, ahi, fato
empio e crudele, ahi, stelle
ingiuriose, ahi, cielo avaro!

Pastore secondo

Qual suon dolente il
lieto dì perturba?

La messaggera

Lassa, dunque debb'io, mentre
Orfeo con sue note il ciel consola,
con le parole mia passargli il core?

Pastore primo

Questa è Silvia gentile, dolcissima
compagna de la bella Euridice;
oh, quanto è in vista dolorosa;
or che fia? Deh, sommi dei,
non torcete da noi benigno il
guardo.

La messaggera

Pastor, lasciate il canto,
ch'ogni nostra allegrezza in
doglia è volta.

Orfeo

Donde vieni?
Ove vai?
Ninfa, che porti?

Second Shepherd

Look, Orpheus, o look
how all around laughs the wood
and laughs the meadow; so continue
with thy golden plectrum to sweeten
the air on such a happy day.

The Messenger

Ah, bitter occurrence, ah, wicked
and cruel fate, ah,
unjust stars, ah miserly Heaven!

Second Shepherd

What sound of sorrow disturbs
this happy day?

The Messenger

I am wretched, for while Orpheus
soothes the heavens with his notes,
with my words I must pierce his
heart.

First Shepherd

This is the lovely Sylvia, sweetest
companion of the fair Eurydice;
o how full of grief is her
appearance; what has happened?
O mighty gods, do not turn away
from us your benign glances.

The Messenger

Shepherd, cease your singing,
for all our joy has turned to
grief.

Orpheus

From where do you come?
Where are you going?
Nymph, what bring you?

La messaggera

A te ne vengo, Orfeo,
messaggera infelice
di caso più infelice e
più funesto.
La tua bella Euridice . . .

Orfeo

Ohimè, che odo?

La messaggera

La tua diletta sposa è morta.

Orfeo

Ohimè!

La messaggera

In un fiorito prato
con l'altre sue compagne
giva cogliendo fiori
per farne una ghirlanda a le sue
chiome, quand'angue insidioso,
ch'era fra l'erbe ascoso,
le punse un piè con velenoso dente.
Ed ecco immantinente scolorirsi il
bel viso e ne' suoi lumi sparir que'
lampi ond'ella al sol fea scorno.
Allor noi tutte sbigottite e meste
le fummo intorno, richiamar
tentando gli spirti in lei smarriti
con l'onda fresca e con possenti
carmi; ma nulla valse, ahi lassa,
ch'ella i languidi lumi alquanto
aprendo e te chiamando, Orfeo,
dopo un grave sospiro
spirò fra queste braccia; ed io rimasi

The Messenger

To you I come, Orpheus,
unhappy messenger
of the most unhappy and
most tragic happening.
Your beautiful Eurydice . . .

Orpheus

Woe is me, what do I hear?

The Messenger

Your beloved wife is dead.

Orpheus

Woe is me!

The Messenger

In a flowery meadow
with her other companions
she was collecting flowers
to make a wreath for her hair,
when a treacherous serpent,
hidden in the grass, bit her foot
with its poisonous fangs.
And behold, all at once
her beautiful face turned pale,
and her eyes lost that brilliance for
which the sun envied them. And
now we, all horrified and woeful,
stood around her and tried to re-
awaken the spirit that had fled
with fresh water and powerful spells;
but all in vain, ah, wretched am I,
for she briefly opened again her
dying eyes and calling you, Orpheus,
after a deep sigh expired

piena il cor di pietade e di spavento.

Pastore secondo
Ahi, caso acerbo, ahi, fato empio
e crudele, ahi, stelle in ingiuriose,
ahi, cielo avaro.

Pastore terzo e secondo
A l'amara novella rassembra
l'infelice un muto sasso che per
troppo dolor non può dolersi.

Ahi, ben avrebbe un cor di tigre o
d'orsa chi non sentisse del tuo
mal pietade, privo d'ogni tuo ben,
misero amante.

Orfeo
Tu se' morta, mia vita, ed io
respiro? Tu se' da me partita per
mai più non tornare, ed io rimango?
No, che se i versi alcuna cosa
ponno, n'andrò sicuro a' più
profondi abissi, e, intenerito il cor
del re de l'ombre, meco trarrotti a
riveder le stelle; o, se ciò
negherammi empio destino,
rimarrò teco in compagnia di
morte.
Addio terra, addio cielo e sole,
addio.

in these arms; and I remained with
my heart full of anguish and fear.

Second Shepherd
Ah, bitter occurrence, ah wicked
and cruel fate, ah, unjust stars,
ah, miserly Heaven.

Third and Second Shepherds
At this bitter news the unhappy
one resembles a lifeless boulder, so
overcome by grief that he cannot
lament.
Ah, he would have the heart of a
tiger or a bear who did not feel
pity for your pain, deprived of all
thy happiness, wretched lover.

Orpheus
You are dead, my life, and I am
breathing? You have left me,
nevermore to return, and I remain?
No, no, if my verses have any
power at all, I will surely go down
to the deepest abysses, and, having
softened the heart of the King of
Shadows; lead you back with me
to see the stars; or, if impious fate
denies me this, I shall remain with
you in the company of death.
Farewell earth, farewell sky and
sun, farewell.

———□———

Coro di ninfe e pastori

Ahi, caso acerbo, ahi, fato
empio e crudele, ahi, stelle
ingiuriose, ahi, cielo avaro.
Non si fidi uom mortale
de ben caduco e frale,
che costo fugge, e spesso
a gran salita il precipizio è
presso.

Chorus of Nymphs and Shepherds

Ah, bitter occurrence, ah wicked
and cruel fate, ah,
unjust stars, ah miserly Heaven.
Do not trust, o mortal man,
the perishable and frail happiness
which soon vanishes, and often
in a great ascent the precipice is
near.

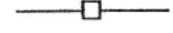

Coro di ninfe e pastori

Ahi, caso acerbo, ahi,
fato empio e crudele, ahi,
stelle ingiuriose, ahi, cielo avaro.

Chorus of Nymphs and Shepherds

Ah, bitter occurrence, ah
wicked and cruel fate, ah,
unjust stars, ah miserly Heaven.

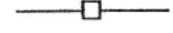

ACT THREE

La speranza

Ecco l'atra palude, ecco il
nocchiero che trae gli ignudi
spirti a l'altra riva, dove ha
Pluton
de l'ombre il vasto impero.
Oltre quel nero stagno, oltre quel
fiume, in quei campi di pianto e
di dolore, destin crudele ogni tuo
ben t'asconde.
Or d'uopo è d'un gran core e
d'un bel canto.
Io sin qui t'ho condotto, or più
non lice teco venir, chè amara
legge il vieta, legge iscritta col
ferro in duro sasso de l'ima reggia
in su l'orribil soglia, che in queste
note il fiero senso

Hope

Here is the dark swamp, here the
boatman who bears the naked
spirits to the other bank, where
Pluto
has his vast empire of the shadows.
Beyond this black bog, beyond this
river, in those fields of lamentation
and grief, cruel fate hides your
dearest possession.
Now you need a great heart and
a beautiful song.
I have conducted you as far as here,
no further am I permitted to
accompany you, since a stern law
forbids it, a law inscribed with iron
in hard stone of the gateway to the
deepest kingdom of terror, express-

esprime: Lasciate ogni speranza voi che entrate.

ing its fierce meaning in these words: Abandon all hope, ye who enter here.

Dunque, se stabilito hai pur nel core di porre il piè nella città dolente, da te men fuggo e torno a l'usato soggiorno.

Therefore, if your heart be truly steadfast and your feet able to enter the city of sorrow, I will flee from you and return to my usual abode.

Caronte

O tu, ch'innanzi morte a queste rive temerario ten' vieni, arresta i passi: solcar quest'onde ad uom mortal non dassi, nè può co' morti albrego aver chi vive.

Che vuoi forse, nemico al mio signore, Cerbero trar de le tartaree porte?
O rapir brami sua cara consorte, d'impudico desire acceso il core?

Bon freno al folle ardir,
ch'entr'al mio legno non
accorrò più mai corporea salma,
sì de gli antichi oltraggi ancor
ne l'alma serbo acerba memoria
e giusto sdegno.

Charon

O you, who dare before death to approach these shores, halt your steps: to cross these waters is allowed to no mortal, neither can he who lives dwell with the dead.

Will you, perhaps, hostile to my lord, drag Cerberus from Tartarus's gates?
Or do you, your heart aflame with shameless desire, want to steal his beloved wife?
Give up thy foolish intention, into my boat will I never admit a bodily being, for the ancient outrages again awaken in my soul bitter memories and just anger.

Sinfonia

Orfeo

Possente spirto e formidabil nume, senza cui far passaggio a l'altra riva alma da corpo sciolta in van presume.

Orpheus

Mighty spirit and awesome divinity, without whom the souls freed from their bodies hope in vain to cross over to the other bank.

Ritornello (2 violins)

Non viv'io, no, che poi di vita è priva mia cara sposa, il cor non è più meco, e senza cor com'esser può ch'io viva?	I am not alive, no, since of life is deprived my beloved wife, my heart is no longer with me, and without a heart how can it be that I live?

Ritornello (2 cornets)

A lei volto ho il cammin per l'aer cieco, a l'inferno non già, ch'ovunque stassi tanta bellezza il paradiso ha seco.	To her I have turned my steps through the dark air, not towards Hell, for whoever has so much beauty has Paradise.

Ritornello (2 harps)

Orfeo son io, che d'Euridice i passi segue per queste tenebrose arene, ove giammai per uom mortal non vassi. O de le luci mie luci serene, s'un vostro sguardo puo tornarmi in vita, ahi, chi niega il conforto a le mie pene? Sol tu, nobile dio, puoi darmi aita, né temer dei, chè sopra un'aurea cetra sol di corde soavi armo le dita contra cui rigida alma in van s'impetra.	I am Orpheus, who follows the steps of Eurydice through these gloomy plains, to which mortal man never has access. O serene lights of my eyes, if only one glance from you can restore me to life, ah, who can deny me comfort in my torment? Only you, noble god, can aid me, fear not, for it is only the sweet strings of a golden lyre I use as a weapon against which rigid souls implore in vain.

Caronte

Ben mi lusinga alquanto dilettandomi il core, sconsolato cantore, il tuo pianto e'l tuo canto. Ma lunge, ah, lunge sia da questo petto pietà, di mio valor non degno effetto.

Orfeo

Ahi, sventurato amante! Sperar

Charon

Much am I flattered by such delight to my heart, disconsolate singer, by thy lament and thy song. But far, ah, far from my breast be pity, which is beneath my dignity.

Orpheus

Ah, unhappy lover! Am I then not

dunque non lice ch'odan miei prieghi i cittadin d'Averno?	allowed to hope that the citizens of Hades will hear my pleas?
Onde, qual ombra errante d'insepolto cadavere e infelice, privo sarò del cielo e de l'inferno?	Must I therefore, like a wandering shadow of an unburied and unhappy corpse, be deprived of Heaven and of Hell?
Così vuol empia sorte che in quest'orror di morte da te, cor mio, lontano chiami tuo nome in vano e pregando e piangendo io mi consumi? Rendetemi il mio ben, tartarei numi!	Does impious fate thus will it that I, in this horror of death, far from you, my beloved, call your name in vain and waste away in imploring and weeping? Give me back my love, gods of Hell!

Sinfonia

Ei dorme, e la mia cetra, se pietà non impetra ne l'indurato core, almen il sonno fuggir al mio cantar gli occhi non ponno. Su, dunque, a che più tardo? Tempo è ben d'approdar su l'altra sponda, s'alcun non è ch'il nieghi. Vaglia l'ardir se foran vani i prieghi. E vago fior del tempo l'occasion, ch'esser dee colta a tempo.	He sleeps, and even if my lyre stirs no compassion in the heart of stone, at least his eyes cannot escape sleep at the sound of my singing. Up, then, why do I delay? The time is right to cross to the other bank if nobody is there to prevent me. Let boldness prevail where entreaties were vain. A short-lived flower of time is opportunity, which must be plucked at the right moment.
Mentre versan quest'occhi amari fiumi, rendetemi il mio ben, tartarei numi!	While these eyes shed floods of tears, give me back my love, gods of Hell!

ACT FOUR

Proserpina

Signor, quell'infelice
che per queste di morte ampie
campagne va chiamando Euridice,
ch'udito hai tu pur dianzi
cosi soavemente lamentarsi,
mossa ha tanta pietà dentro al
mio core ch'un'altra volta io
torno a porger prieghi perchè il
tuo nume al suo pregar si pieghi.

Proserpine

My lord, this unhappy man
who over the wide fields of death
calls for Eurydice,
whom you have just now heard
lamenting so sweetly,
has awakened so much pity within
my heart that I return again
to entreat you
to yield to his imploring.

Plutone

Benché severo ed immutabil fato
contrasti, amata sposa, i tuoi
desiri, pur nulla omai si nieghi
a tal belta congiunta a tanti
prieghi.
La sua cara Euridice contra l'ordin
fatale Orfeo ritrovi;
ma pria che tragga il piè da questi
abissi non mai volga ver lei gli
avidi lumi, ché di perdita eterna
gli fia certa cagion un solo
sguardo.

Io così stabilisco. Or nel mio
regno fate, o ministri, il mio voler
palese, sì che l'intenda Orfeo
e l'intenda Euridice, né di
cangiarlo altrui sperar più lice.

Coro di spiriti

Pietade, oggi, e amore
trionfan ne l'inferno.

Pluto

Although stern and immutable
fate opposes your wishes, beloved
wife, nothing indeed shall now
refuse such beauty joined with
such entreaties.
His beloved Eurydice
Orpheus shall find again, contrary
to the decrees of fate;
but before his feet have borne
him from these abysses,
he may not turn round to look
at her, for eternal loss
will result from a single
glance.

I ordain it so. Now in my
kingdom make, o ministers, my
will known, so that Orpheus hears
it and Eurydice hears it, and
nobody shall hope to change it.

Chorus of Spirits

Pity and love today
have triumphed in Hades.

Spirito primo

Ecco il gentil cantore che sua
sposa conduce al ciel superno.

Ritornello

Orfeo

Quale onor di te fia degno, mia
cetra omnipotente, s'hai nel
tartareo regno piegar potuto
ogni indurata mente?

Luogo avrai fra le più belle
immagini celesti, ond'al tuo
suon le stelle danzeranno in giri
or tardi or presti.

Io per te felice appiano
vedrò l'amato volto,
e nel candido seno de la
mia donna oggi sarò raccolto.

Ma mentre io canto, ohimè, chi
m'assicura ch'ella mi segua?
Ohimè, chi mi nasconde
de l'amate pupille il dolce lume?
Forse d'invidia punte
le deità d'Averno,
perch'io non sia quaggiù felice
appieno, mi tolgono il mirarvi,
luci beate e liete, che sol col
guardo altrui bear potete?

Ma che temi, mio core?
Ciò che vieta Pluton, comanda
Amore. A nume più possente
che vince uomini e dei,
ben ubbidir dovrei.

First Spirit

Here is the gentle singer, who
leads his wife to the skies above.

Ritornello

Orpheus

What honor is worthy of thee, my
omnipotent lyre, that you have,
in the infernal realm, been able to
overcome every hardened spirit?

Ritornello

You will find a place among the
most beautiful images of Heaven,
and to your sound the stars will
dance in circles, now slowly, now
quickly.

Ritornello

I, made perfectly happy through
you, will see the beloved brow
On the white breast
of my lady I shall rest today.

But while I am singing, alas, who
will assure me that she is
following? Who keeps the beloved
eyes hidden from me?
Perhaps pierced by envy
the gods of Avernus forbid me,
so that my happiness will not be
complete, to look at you, blessed
happy lights that can make others
blessed with one glance alone.

What do you fear, my heart?
What Pluto forbids, Cupid
commands. A more powerful
divinity, who conquers men and
gods, I must obey.

(There is a noise behind him.)
Ma che odo, ohimè lasso?
S'arman forse a' miei danni
contal furor le furie innamorate
per rapirmi il mio ben?
Ed io'l consento?
(He turns around.)
O dolcissimi lumi, io pur vi
veggio, io pur: ma quale eclissi,
ohimè, v'oscura?

Spirito terzo

Rott'hai la legge e se' di
grazia indegno.

Euridice

Ahi, vista troppo dolce e troppo
amara; così per troppo amor
dunque mi perdi? Ed io, misera,
perdo il poter più godere
e di luce e di vita e perdo
insieme te, d'ogni ben più caro,
o mio consorte.

Spirito primo

Torna a l'ombre di morte,
infelice Euridice,
né più sperar di riveder le stelle,
ch'omai fia sordo a' prieghi tuoi
l'inferno.

Orfeo

Dove ten' vai, mia vita?
Ecco, io ti seguo, ma chi me'
l niega, ohimè? Sogno o vaneggio?
Qual occulto poter di questi
orrori, da questi amati orrori
mal mio grado mi tragge e
mi conduce a l'odiosa luce?

(There is a noise behind him.)
But what do I hear, alas?
Do the Furies arm themselves to
hurt me, madly desiring with such
frenzy to rob me of my beloved?
And I allow it?
(He turns around.)
O sweetest lights, I can indeed
see you, I can, but what eclipse,
alas, obscures you?

Third Spirit

You have broken the law and are
unworthy of mercy.

Eurydice

Ah, sight too sweet and too bitter;
so by too much love you thus
lose me? And I, poor one, lose
the happiness of returning
to light and life, and lose at the
same time you, dearest of all
possessions, my husband.

First Spirit

Return to the shades of death,
unhappy Eurydice,
hope no more to see the stars
again, for henceforth to thy pleas
Hell will be deaf.

Orpheus

Where are you going, my life?
Behold, I follow you, but who,
alas, prevents me? Is it a dream?
What hidden power of these
horrors drags me from these
beloved horrors against my will,
and leads me to the hateful light?

Sinfonia

Coro di spiriti

E la virtute un raggio di celeste
bellezza, pregio de l'alma,
ond'ella sol s'apprezza.
Questa di tempo oltraggio
non teme, anzi maggiore ne l'uom
rendono gli anni il suo splendore.
Orfeo vinse l'inferno e vinto poi
fu da gli affetti suoi.
Degno d'eterna gloria
fia sol colui ch'avrà di sé vittoria.

Chorus of Spirits

Virtue is a ray of heavenly
beauty, prize of the soul,
where alone it is valued.
The devastation of time
it does not fear; in man the years
make its splendor brighter.
Orpheus overcame Hell and was
overcome by his passions. Eternal
fame is deserved only by him
who will have victory over himself.

Sinfonia

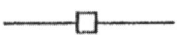

ACT FIVE

Orfeo

Questi i campi di Tracia, e quest'è
il loco dove passommi il core
per l'amara novella il mio dolore.
Poi che non ho più speme
de ricovrar pregando,
piangendo e sospirando
il perduto mio bene, che poss'io
più se non volgermi a voi,
selve soavi, un tempo conforto a'
miei martir, mentr'al ciel piacque
per farvi per pietà meco languire
al mio languire? Voi vi doleste,
o monti, e lagrimaste, voi, sassi, al
dipartir del nostro sole, ed io con
voi lagrimerò mai sempre e mai
sempre darommi, ah doglia,
ahi pianto!

Orpheus

These are the fields of Thrace, and
this is the spot where my heart was
pierced by sorrow at the bitter news.
Now that I have no longer any
hope of recovering by praying,
weeping or sighing,
my lost happiness, what else
remains for me but to turn to you,
gentle woods, once comfort to
my torments, as Heaven in pity
for me let you languish at my
languishing? You have mourned, o
mountains, and wept, o stones, at
the departure of our sun, and I will
weep with you forever, forever
make myself suffer and lament.

Eco

Hai pianto!

Echo

Lament!

Orfeo

Cortese Eco amorosa, che
sconsolata sei e consolar mi vuoi
ne' dolor miei,
benchè queste mie luci sien già per
lagrimar fatte due fonti,
in così grave mia fera sventura
non ho pianto però tanto che basti.

Orpheus

Kind, loving Echo, who are
disconsolate and wish to console me
in my grief, although these eyes of
mine through so much weeping are
made two fountains, in my serious
misfortune I have not yet
wept enough, not yet enough.

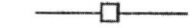

Apollo

Perchè a lo sdegno ed al dolor in
preda così ti doni, o figlio?
Non è, non è consiglio
di generoso petto servir al proprio
affetto; quinci biasmo e periglio
già sovrastar ti veggio, onde movo
dal ciel per darti aita. Or tu
m'ascolta e n'avrai lode e vita.

Apollo

Why to rage and to grief do you
give yourself as prey like this, o son?
It is not the counsel of a great heart
to be servant to one's own passions;
by shame and peril I already see you
threatened wherefore I hasten from
Heaven to help you. Now listen to
me, and you will have fame and life.

Orfeo

Padre cortese, al maggior uopo
arrivi, ch'a disperato fine con
estremo dolore m'avean condotto
già sdegno ed amore. Eccomi
dunque attento a tue ragioni,
celeste padre: or ciò che vuoi
m'imponi.

Orpheus

Kind father, you find me in greatest
distress, anger and love have led me
already, with extreme grief, to a
bitter end. Behold me then,
attentive to your reasoning,
heavenly father: command what
you will.

Apollo

Troppo, troppo gioisti di tua lieta
ventura; or troppo piangi tua sorte
acerba e dura. Ancor non sai
come nulla quaggiù diletta e dura?

Dunque se goder brami immortal
vita vientene meco al ciel,
ch'a sé t'invita.

Apollo

Too soon did you rejoice at your
happy lot; now you weep too
much at your hard and bitter fate.
Do you not yet know that no
delight is lasting here below?
Therefore if you desire to enjoy
immortal life, come with me to
Heaven, which beckons you.

Orfeo

Sì non vedrò più mai
de l'amata Euridice i
dolci rai?

Apollo

Nel sole e ne le stelle
vagheggarai le sue sembianze
belle.

Apollo e Orfeo

(ascendono al ciel cantando)
Saliam cantando al cielo,
dove ha virtù verace degno
premio di sé, diletto e pace.

Orpheus

So shall I never again see
the sweet eyes of my beloved
Eurydice?

Apollo

In the sun and the stars
you shall recognize her beautiful
likeness.

Apollo and Orpheus

(rise singing to Heaven)
Let us rise, singing, to Heaven,
where true virtue
has its own reward: joy and peace.

The Invention of Opera and Monteverdi's *Orfeo*, I
Lecture 5—Transcript

Welcome to "How to Listen to and Understand Opera," Lecture 5. Lectures 5 through 8 are conceived as a set and they are entitled as a group "The Invention of Opera and Monteverdi's Orfeo."

Before we get into the invention of opera and Monteverdi's *Orfeo*, it is absolutely necessary for us to do a brief but intense review of some of the most salient things discussed in Lecture 4. We go back to the Greek view, the Greek ideal, of music. Ancient Greek culture celebrated music as a force of nature that could change the souls of human beings and animals—a very powerful and ultimately humanistic view of music. During the Renaissance—and we're talking about the musical Renaissance now, that period in Europe that spans approximately the years 1400 to 1600—we see a growing awareness of this Greek view, this Greek ideal of music. Even if the Renaissance scholars and philosophers and artists and composers had not a clue of what Greek music actually sounded like, they did have the literature written by the Greeks that said, our music was capable of these tremendous expressive effects. This essentially humanistic, emotionally expressive view of music galvanized the thinkers and musicians of the Renaissance. We can imagine Renaissance composers thinking to themselves, "My goodness! I want my listeners to respond to my music the way the ancient Greeks said that their listeners responded to their music."

Perhaps the most important experimental genre of music of the Renaissance was the madrigal—a late sixteenth century genre, which based expression on what we call "word-painting" or "tone-painting;" that is, expression became the words being sung. And the job of the composer was to illustrate the meaning of the words with the proper musical gesture. In the last lecture, Lecture 4, we listened to a madrigal by an English composer, Thomas Weelkes, "As Vesta was from Latmos Hill Descending," and we heard all kinds of wonderful musical effects that illustrated the meaning of the words. When we hear the word "descending," the music descends and so forth. This is what word-painting and tone-painting are.

We're going to listen to another madrigal now, because one madrigal does not a study make. Frankly, an English madrigal is pleasant, nice and bubbly, but it's not really representative of the true Italian madrigal, and that's what we've got to deal with right now. We're going to listen to a madrigal, a true Italian madrigal, by Carlo Gesualdo, Prince of Venosa, called "Io parto e non piu dissi." This piece dates from about 1595. It wasn't published until 1611, but certainly it dates from the late sixteenth century.

Let me read you this text, and while I read you this text ask yourselves, please, what's this all about?

> "I am leaving" and I said no more, for grief had robbed my heart of life.
>
> Then Clori began to weep, and said, with interrupted cries of "Alas; omèi, Alas: therefore with my agony I remain. Ah, may I never cease to languish in such pain."
>
> I was dead, and now I am alive, for my dead spirits return to life at the sound of such pathetic accents.

My goodness! What could this be about? Well, first of all, it's much more typical of your basic madrigal, bosom-beating text. It's about a breakup. It's about two people parting their ways. "'I am leaving' and said no more, for grief had robbed my heart of life." Okay, that's me. "Then Clori," the other person, "began to weep, and said, with interrupted cries of 'Omèi.'" Look, this word "omèi"; we're going to hear so many omèis today it's going to be coming out of our ears, noses and anywhere else you want to imagine. Without the word "omèi" or "alas," it would seem that all late madrigals and early opera would be impossible. One encounters it rather almost too often.

"'Omèi: therefore, with my agony I remain,' says Clori. 'Ah, may I never cease to languish in such pain.'" Oh, she's pathetically unhappy. And then I respond again "I was dead, and now I am alive, for my dead spirits return to life at the sounds of such pathetic accents." Yes, she's so unhappy that, even though I thought I was dead I've got to be alive, because only a living person could feel so rotten hearing all of this pathetic carrying on.

There's our text for this madrigal, and here's the word-painting I want you to be aware of while we listen to it: first, and most importantly, the unbelievable degree of harmonic complexity. My friends, this music is going to sound like a barbershop quartet well into its fourth pitcher of martinis. The harmonies are going to be slipping and sliding all over the place. This complexity, this lack of resolution, this oily move from one key to the next seemingly inexplicable in motion, reflects the sense of emotional turmoil and irresolution that the story is all about.

The second thing I want you to be aware of, whenever they mention the word *dolori*, grief, sadness, sorrow. *Dolori* will always be expressed in long notes: *doooloooriii*, languorous and unhappy. Whenever we hear the word *vita*, life, it will always be in fast, upbeat notes: *vita, vita, vita, vita*. Whenever we hear the word *morte*, death, we will hear it expressed in the longest, lowest possible tones: *Moooooorrteeeee*. Is this starting to sound a little silly? It is a little silly, but it is a very engaging piece.

Spirti spenti, exhausted, dead spirits will be portrayed with descending wraithlike lines. Lastly, the very last word of this madrigal is this word *accenti*, and this is a *double entendre*. An *accento* was a flourish, an embellishment, a stepwise embellishment. If you said to a singer at this time, "I want you to add an *accento*," they would do one of these little embellishments. But, of course, *accenti* also means "accents," or statements in this case. So, when a singer utters the word *accenti*, meaning Clori's pathetic cries, he uses this wonderful little embellishment as an illustration; so it's a *double entendre*, both a musical statement and the word itself in its meaning.

Let's listen. Let's be aware again of this incredibly complex harmonic stuff that creates a sense of irresolution and dissatisfaction. And always, while listening to this ask yourselves, "What is being expressed in this music?"

Gesualdo, "Io parto." (musical example)

I trust we heard that extraordinary dissonance when Clori says, *dolorosi*. For the listener of this particular recording hearing it for the first time, one might think, "My goodness, they're singing wrong notes." Oh, no. They're singing precisely what Gesualdo wrote, major amounts of dissonance, unresolved dissonance that corresponds with the dissonance being felt by the characters at this particular moment.

Now I asked you before, I ask you again, what's being expressed in this music? First, and foremost, the text itself with these long notes on *morto* and these short notes on *vita* and so forth. And a certain generic melancholy and unfulfillment is, of course, created by the tremendous amount of "chromaticism"—that's what we call this harmonic irregularity and complexity—and a lack of harmonic resolution.

But here's the big point, and I'm making it for the second time in two lectures, while the incredible harmonic and polyphonic complexity of this madrigal—it's for five voices singing something different all the time; wow—this complexity can evoke a mood. Can this complexity evoke the sense of individual, pointed, singular and personal emotion? No, it cannot.

So, as I said in Lecture 4, the search for other expressive musical means that can, continues. Which brings us now to another late Renaissance genre of music called the "intermezzo" or the "intermedio." Parallel to the late sixteenth century development of the madrigal was the intermezzo or the intermedio. It's the same thing; we just have two terms. Opera historian Donald Grout tells us that "Intermezzi and intermedi were a class of sixteenth-century works in which the role of music was to offer diversion in connection with a regular spoken play." So what Grout is telling us is that these intermezzi, or intermedi, were musical diversions occurring in the course of a regular theatrical spoken play.

As is well known, one of the features of the Renaissance was the revival of secular drama. The movement began in Italy towards the end of the fifteenth century, that's the end of the 1400s, with performances of Latin plays in the original or in translation under courtly auspices at various centers of which Ferrara, Rome, Florence, Mantua and Venice were particularly prominent. I would add that those cities will soon become the early centers of Italian opera, given as they are to theatrical entertainment. Many new plays were written in Latin or in Italian, imitated from classical models. Practically all these plays made use of music to a greater or lesser extent, though in a subordinate, decorative fashion. There were occasional solos or duets, choruses (these especially in tragedies based on Greek originals), madrigals and even sometimes instrumental pieces. The general tendency was to separate the musical numbers from the play itself by placing the musical numbers in the prologue, that means at the very beginning, or at the ends of the acts, so that they appeared as a intermezzo or an intermedio—that is, something intermediate to the actual action of the play.

Often because of the quality of the music, which was high in these intermezzi, or simply because of the scale of their productions, the intermezzi became more interesting than the play that they were plugged into itself. John Addington Symonds wrote, or rather, he "sniffed" unhappily, in his book *Renaissance Italian Culture*, "For the majority of the audience, the music and the pageants formed the chief attraction. It is therefore no marvel if the drama, considered as a branch of high poetic art, was suffocated by the growth of its mere accessories." Music as a mere accessory. Well, Mr. Symonds, one could say that your drama was a mere accessory to our music. But I would never say such a thing.

The intermedio was important, in fact, vital as a forerunner of opera for two essential reasons—first, because it kept alive in the minds of Italian poets and musicians the idea of close collaboration between drama and music; and second, because in these works, in these intermezzi, the external form of opera is already clear: a drama with interludes of music, dancing, splendid scenery, and spectacular stage effects. As soon as the drama itself would be set to music—that is, as soon as we'd actually set the words to music—opera would be achieved.

What almost all of these intermezzi or intermedi had in common is that they were based in plays that were what we call "pastorales." Let me tell you a little bit about the content of these actual plays, these pastorales. The pastorale was a style of dramatic poetry that dominated Italian theater in the late sixteenth and early seventeenth centuries, that's the late 1500s and the early 1600s. In 1598, Antonio Ingegneri, who, I would tell you, was the foremost writer on theater of his time, wrote this, "If it were not for the pastorales, it might be said that the theater was extinct." Probably the sort of overstatement critics are given to, but the point is clear; and that is, it would seem that whatever theater you go to it's another pastorale. Another pastorale; why not some science fiction? Why not something else? Well, that's what's popular, so that's what's being staged.

A dramatic pastorale is a poem, lyric in substance but dramatic in form, intended for either reading or for stage presentation. It's got shepherds and shepherdesses and various sylvan deities as its main characters, and uses, as background, fields and forests and other rather Arcadian and attractive natural scenes. The dramatic action is typically restricted to mild love adventures and the kind of incidents that arise out of pastoral life. Almost invariably, my friends, these pastorales end happily.

We've listened to a pastorale. You didn't even realize it. "As Vesta was from Latmos Hill descending," admittedly very limited in its scope, is a pastorale. We've got these sylvan deities, these nymphs, these shepherds, these goddesses and so forth, all portrayed against this beautiful natural scene. Shakespeare's *A Midsummer Night's Dream* is a pastorale, and the first operas based as they are on the legends of Orpheus and Eurydice, are also pastorales.

A momentary diversion, please. Take this stuff about pastorale and put it not in deep memory but in middling memory, because I've got to introduce another chunk of information and then we'll get back to these pastorales. We've got to talk about the so-called Florentine Camerata. A camerata was a club or a coterie. We must talk about the ridotto, because actually what the Florentine Camerata was, was a ridotto, R-I-D-O-T-T-O, that means a private academy or intellectual club. Many such were established in Italy during the Renaissance. It would be a mistake to think of a ridotto as merely a boys' club, a poker night, a bowling team. It was much more than that, but they weren't quite what we would think of today as "think tanks." What they were, were groups of professionals or intellects, or self-styled intellects, who were fascinated by a certain topic. They would band together with others who were fascinated with like topics, and discuss, and write tracts, and carry on into the night about their favorite topics. Kind of like a faculty meeting, frankly. I would compare these ridotti to faculty meetings and groupings of well-educated but often hostile or at least self-interested people, arguing the merits of their point of view of their favorite discipline.

The so-called Florentine Camerata was a ridotto, and they met in the home of a rich Florentine patron named Giovanni Bardi di Vernio. Bardi lived from 1534 to 1612; the Camerata met in his house. If you go to Florence, there is a plaque on the palace, it's still there, that says, "This is where met the Florentine Camerata from 1573 to 1592." He hosted them for 19 years. What did the Camerata in Florence talk about? They talked about literature and science and art, indeed, but especially they talked about music and drama. These were the topics that most fascinated the members of this group—the nature and power of musical and dramatic expression.

Among the members of the Florentine Camerata that met in Bardi's house, was Vincenzo Galilei. Vincenzo Galilei was born in 1533 and died in 1591, so he was an exact contemporary of the host, Bardi. And by the way, he was also the father of the astronomer, Galileo Galilei. Vincenzo Galilei was a student of ancient Greek music and theater, or so he fancied himself, given as much as was known about ancient Greek music at this time. Galilei's ideas regarding ancient Greek music and theater were powerfully influenced by the work of a Florentine scholar named Girolamo Mei. Now stay with me. I'm giving you a lot of names but I'll tie them together in a second. Mei was older than all of these people. He was born in 1519 and he died in 1594. Mei's research, incidentally, inspired and titillated the entire Florentine Camerata, not just Galilei, but we'll find out why Galilei is the most important of the group in a moment. But, back to Mei. Mei had come to the conclusion through his research, mostly conducted in Rome, that the Greeks were able to obtain powerful effects with their music because it consisted of a single melody—a single melody, whether sung solo, accompanied, or sung by a chorus. This single melody could affect the listeners' feelings since it would exploit the natural expressiveness, the rise and falls and the register of the single human voice.

In 1581, Vincenzo Galilei wrote a tract, a treatise entitled "Dialogue Concerning Ancient and Modern Music," where he, and by extension the entire Florentine Camerata, declared open-hunting season on the Italian madrigal as they knew it. Of course, this tract was based on the writings and works of Girolamo Mei. Claude Paliska tells us what Galilei wrote all about:

> Following the doctrines of Mei, Galilei attacked the theory and practice of vocal counterpoint as exemplified by the Italian madrigal. His argument was, in brief, that only a single line of melody with appropriate pitches and rhythms could express a given line of poetry. Therefore, when several voices simultaneously sang different melodies and words, music could never deliver the emotional message of the text.

The emotional message of the text, my friends; not the meaning of the words, the emotions beneath the words. Paliska continues,

> When some voices were low and others high, some rising and others descending, some moving in slow notes and others in fast, the resulting chaos of contradictory impressions served only to show off the cleverness of the composer and the ability of the singers. Word-painting, imitations of sighing, and the like, Galilei dismissed as childish. The correct way to set words, Galilei said, was to use a solo melody, which would follow the natural speech inflections of a great orator or actor.

So, the Camerata develops a theory of new music, what they called the "three corollaries," based on the Greek ideal of expressivity as enumerated by Girolamo Mei. These are the three corollaries. Number One: The text must always be clearly understood. This goes far beyond the ideas of articulation we've talked about in previous lectures, because what the Camerata is saying is that the only way for the text to be understood is for it to be sung by one singer—one at a time, period—accompanied as simply as possible with no vocal polyphony.

Corollary number two: The words must be sung with correct and natural declamation. That means they should be sung the way they would be spoken, with the same accents, the same pacing, the same rise and fall. There should be no dance rhythms asserted upon these words, and we should avoid textual repetitions except for rhetorical reinforcement; except for rhetorical reinforcement; except for reinforcement, rhetorical.

And thirdly, the melody must not depict mere graphic details as we would in word- or tone-painting, but rather must interpret the feelings and emotions of the character seeing them.

Do we see the huge difference with this theory? The Camerata is positing that we must seek the emotions beneath the words, rather than illustrate simply the literal meaning of the words. Very influential tract, and it gets a lot of folks, especially in Florence, to thinking about what kind of music would result if we did all of these things.

Let's continue to trace the history of the Camerata a little further. Starting around 1592, the Camerata was sponsored and hosted by a new patron, this one named Jacopo Corsi. By now, the Camerata includes among its members some very important artists, and they're all artists of the next generation. I'll give you their birthdates, and we'll hear they're all born 25 or 30 years after the earlier Camerata members were. These are very important artists. Camerata members now include Giulio Caccini, who's a well-known composer and a singer—he was born in 1546 and died in 1618; Jacopo Peri, composer, singer, organist, director of the ducal court—that is, the music in the court of the de Medici—he was born in 1561, died in 1633; and Ottavio Rinuccini, a poet born in 1562 and died in 1621. My friends, with talent like this hanging out together, we now have a think tank. We now have the equivalent of a very high level, college faculty, research facility trading important ideas about art and the nature of expression. These three gentlemen, Caccini, Peri, and Rinuccini invent opera in the last years of the sixteenth century.

By the way before I go on and talk about the invention of opera, I just have to mention one last thing. Today, when we get together and we chat in think tanks and research groups, we chat about economics, we chat about the globalization of our world, we chat about technology. We chat about these essential issues, which seem to affect our world. In 1595, they chatted about art and communication and about expression, because these were as intrinsic and singular to their culture as economics, globalization, politics and technology are to our culture. Frankly, they had it better off. I would think it would be marvelous if we had whole research groups dedicated to the nature of human expression and communication through the arts. I would like to be party to that one. So, please, let's take this very seriously and let's understand that these people lie at the philosophical and intellectual cutting edge of their culture and that opera also lies at the philosophical and cutting edge of its culture. It's not merely an entertainment, at least not yet.

The first operas. The first opera was a piece called *Daphne*. Ottavio Rinuccini wrote the libretto and Jacopo Peri wrote the music. They teamed up in 1598 to create this piece, but sadly the music has been lost, so we don't know what *Daphne* sounded like.

Then, Rinuccini wrote a libretto about the Orpheus and Eurydice story, and it was set two times in the same year. Twice in the year 1600 with a few changes here and there, Rinuccini's *Euridice* was set. It was set by Giulio Caccini in 1600 and produced in 1602; and Rinuccini's *Euridice* was also set by Jacopo Peri, also in 1600. But Peri's version of this story was first performed, also in 1600, and then was published immediately in 1601, February 1601. So, for our purposes, and rightly, the first opera or the oldest surviving opera must be Jacopo Peri's *Euridice*, libretto by Ottavio Rinuccini.

Let's jump in. Peri's *Euridice* was first performed on October 6, 1600 at the Pitti Palace in Florence as part of the wedding festivities of Henry V of France and Marie de Medici. It is a fully-sung theatrical work alternating three elements, two old and one very new. The old elements first. We hear choruses; indeed, the chorus is used in the Greek way to comment on the action and to narrate what's going on. We also hear rhymed, that is pop-style songs, used as interludes to the action at scene ends and at scene beginnings. This should sound to all of you just like an intermezzo, because this is what happens in an intermezzo—we hear songs and choruses at the beginnings and ends of scenes as commentaries. Those are the two old elements.

But now, the new element, element three. The body of the text of the play was also sung in what was called the *stile rappresentativo*, the representative style. This is early recitative, early recitation, and it lies at the heart and soul of this new Florentine music. Peri wrote about this *stile rappresentativo*. I quote Peri: "I believed that the ancient Greeks and Romans who, according to the opinion of many, sang their tragedies throughout, used a kind of music more advanced than ordinary speech but less than the melody of singing;

thus, taking a middle position between the two." Peri's *stile rappresentativo* is not quite song, and it's not recitative in the later sense, as we will hear in Mozart, for example. Its basis is on an absolutely faithful adherence to the natural rhythms, inflections and accents of the spoken word, of the text. So it's going to sound kind of chant-like with a rise and fall of pitch, but the rhythms are absolutely the rhythms of spoken language.

Quickly, the story of Orpheus and Eurydice and then we'll move on and sample a bit of the Peri. Please remember Orpheus is a demi-god; that is, he's the son of Apollo, a god, but of a mortal woman. Why we don't call him a "semi-god," I don't know, maybe we should. Anyway, Orpheus is half and half. He's also a cocky, golden-tongued singer and lyre player, whose songs can change the face of nature and even change the hearts of the gods. My friends, the significance of Orpheus, then, in the history of opera is clear. Orpheus is the personification of the Greek view of music, and therefore, he becomes the personification of the power of opera, the power of words and music. The Orpheus legend has been set to music more than any other single story in the history of opera. We have Peri's Orpheus, we have Puccini's, we have Monteverdi's, we have Gluck's, we have Stravinsky's, we have others I haven't mentioned. We even have a bossa nova, samba Orpheus. Go out and rent the movie "Black Orpheus." It's a wonderful version of the story that takes place in Rio during Carnival. And the music, most of which is by Antonio Carlos Jobim, combines both Brazilian samba and bossa nova.

Back to our story. Eurydice is the beautiful but haughty nymph that Orpheus is in love with, and he finally, through constant singing and cajoling, convinces her to marry him. During the preparation for the wedding, Eurydice is out plucking flowers for a garland for her hair when, of course, Murphy's Law being what it is, she puts her foot down right next to a venomous snake who bites her and, of course, pow! She drops dead. But, just before she dies, what does she say? She calls for Orpheus.

There's a very famous scene in almost every Orpheus story, where the messenger, some young nymph, has to come and tell Orpheus what's happened. It's a moment of signal drama when the world changes, when our golden-tongued singer is struck dumb. And, of course, he is informed by the messenger whose name is Sylvia, sometimes Daphne, sometimes…

whatever. He's informed, and then he speaks the famous words: "I will go down to Hades and with my lyre as my only weapon, I will bring her back to the sunshine of the overworld." Indeed, he charms his way into the court of Pluto, convinces Pluto that he should bring his woman back to the top. But Pluto lays down the famous condition: "You may bring her back to the overworld. We will set this precedent just for you, providing you don't turn around to see if she's really behind you." Orpheus cannot control himself. He does turn around. She was there; she falls back forever into Hades. Disconsolate Orpheus comes to the upper world. He forswears women forever, which, of course, incenses a mob of Furies, who then proceed to tear him apart, throwing his head into a river, which floats downstream. Those darn Furies. We've met them in a previous lecture, didn't we? They hounded Orestes into madness. My friends, safety hint: don't mess with the Furies.

Back to Peri's *Euridice*. Let's listen to the messenger's song and Orfeo's, that's the Italian for Orpheus, Orfeo's response, because we want to hear what this new *stile rappresentativo*, this early recitative, sounds like. The messenger's name in this version is Daphne. Please, I would read. "In the beautiful thicket"—she's telling the story to Orpheus and the shepherds.

> In the beautiful thicket, where, watering the flowers, slowly courses the spring of the laurel, she took sweet delight with her companions—the beautiful bride—as some picked violets, others roses, to make garlands for their hair, in the meadow or among the thorns. Another, lying on her side on the flowered bank, sang sweetly to the murmur of the waves.

It's a very idyllic, sylvan scene.

> But the lovely Eurydice dancingly moved her feet on the green grass when—o angry, bitter fate!—a snake, cruel and merciless, that lay hidden among flowers and grass bit her foot with such an evil tooth that she suddenly became pale and like a ray of sunshine that a could darkens. And from the depths of her heart, a mortal sigh, so frightful, alas, ohimè, flew forth almost as if it had wings; every nymph rushed to the painful sound. And she, fainting, let herself fall into another's arms. Then spread over her beautiful face and her

> golden tresses a sweat colder by far than ice. And then was heard your name, sounding between her lips, cold and trembling, and her eyes turned to heaven, her beautiful face and mien discolored, this great beauty was transformed to motionless ice.

Orpheus cannot speak. He's struck dumb, so one of the shepherds speaks for him. "What do you relate, ohimè, what do I hear? Wretched nymph and most unhappy lover, spectacle of sorrow and of torment!"

And finally, Orpheus finds his voice, slowly at first.

> I do not weep, nor do I sigh, o my dear Eurydice, for I am unable to sigh, to weep. Unhappy corpse, o my heart, o my hope, o peace, o life! Ohimè, who has taken you from me? Who has taken you away, ohimè? Where have you gone? Soon, soon you will see that not in vain did you, dying, call your spouse. I am not far away; I come, o dear life, o dear death.

Three points before we listen to this section of music. First, if you can hear it, I want you to notice that there's a natural progression to Daphne's speech. At first, it's emotionally neutral as she sets the scene. But as she tells the story of the snakebite, more and more harmonies come, more and more dissonance is heard to correspond with her feelings and the story. Second point: I want you to note the growing sense of conviction we hear in Orpheus's voice as he communicates his intent to go and get his Eurydice. And thirdly, I want you to note the declamation. Clear, oratorical declamation lies at the heart of this *stile rappresentativo*; the words are crystal clear. Let us listen.

Peri's *Euridice* of 1600. (musical example)

I know what some of you are thinking right now: you're thinking, that's it? Because it sounds a little flat to our ears. We're used to histrionics, we're used to singing, we're used to up and down. Yes, that's it. That's the first experiment with this new *stile rappresentativo*, the new recitative, but it's a fabulous and important beginning for reasons I'll mention in just a moment.

One last note about *Euridice* before we move on. Peri's orchestra, if we can call it that, for *Euridice* employed but four instruments, hidden behind the screen so that they wouldn't distract the audience. This ensemble of four instruments consists of a harpsichord, two large lutes, and a *lira grande*, a big, early, bowed, stringed instrument. The smallness of this ensemble tells us something that we already suspect. *Euridice* is, *Euridice* was, a drama with music, not a musical drama. It's very important we make that distinction. It's a play set to music, rather than a play conceived musically. But, minimal though the music may have been, Peri's *Euridice* was and is an epochal and important work. There can be no doubt that these first composers of dramatic recitative at Florence, towards the end of the sixteenth century, believed that they were renewing a musical practice of the ancient Greeks, and that in doing so, they were accomplishing something of revolutionary importance. Indeed, they were.

Which brings us to Claudio Monteverdi, 1567 to 1643. My friends, opera was invented by original and talented men, people like Rinuccini and Caccini and Peri. They were intent on recreating the ancient Greek expressive ideal. The continuation of opera, however, the flowering of opera, came at the hands of a great genius, and that was Claudio Monteverdi. When we return for Lecture 6, we will talk about Monteverdi and this signal and most important early opera, *Orfeo*, of 1607. Thank you.

The Invention of Opera and Monteverdi's *Orfeo*, II
Lecture 6—Transcript

Welcome back to "How to Listen to and Understand Opera." This is Lecture 6; the second of a four-lecture set entitled "The Invention of Opera and Monteverdi's *Orfeo*." We have been brought to the edge, my friends. We have witnessed the invention of opera. Right now, it's still basically a dramatic production with the addition of music, but now opera transcends its early beginnings very quickly. I mean it takes just seven years from the time of the first opera to the time of the first operatic masterwork; and that's what Monteverdi's *Orfeo* is, the first operatic masterwork created by the first great genius writing in the operatic medium.

I would take this moment to introduce one of the many gratuitous statements I make during this course, and this is something I've said before and will undoubtedly say again. I've got a special soft spot in my heart for Monteverdi, aside from the fact that he's a brilliant composer who can write in any style, and we'll talk about that in a moment, but especially it's his name—"Monteverdi," "mountain green." It's Greenberg in Italian. And that's why it's important when people spell my name that they spell the end "-berg," which means mountain, as opposed to "-burg," which means town. Exactly. I'm "green mountain" and Monteverdi is "mountain green," darn it. At some spiritual level we've got to be *paisani*, we've got to be perhaps even *cugini*, cousins. I would love to think so. Anyway, onward please.

Monteverdi was born in Cremona, that marvelous Northern Italian city of madrigals and violins. He's trained by Marc'Antonio Ingegneri, the head of music at the Cremona Cathedral. In 1590, Monteverdi enters the service of Vincenzo Gonzaga, the Duke of Mantua; and 12 years later, in 1602 he becomes master of the Ducal Chapel. In 1613, and indeed until the time of his death 30 years later in 1643, Monteverdi becomes choirmaster at St. Mark's Cathedral in Venice. This is as good a gig as exists in Italy, and Italy is as good a place to live as exists in the seventeenth century. The only other job of such equal status as choirmaster at St. Mark's would be the choirmaster at the Sistine Chapel in Rome, the private chapel, of course, of the Pope.

Now, Monteverdi was equally adept at writing in any style. He produced books and books and books of Renaissance-style madrigals. He could write in what we call the "polychoral" style of St. Mark's Cathedral. That is, St. Mark's has these huge choir lofts, and composers took to writing for multiple, simultaneous choirs, and Monteverdi wrote brilliant pieces like his "Vespers" that employed this technique. He was equally adept at the new operatic style, the new art. Monteverdi wrote 19 stage works, and only six of these stage works have survived intact. If anyone is listening and would love to make a life's contribution to the arts and Western civilization, please find the other 13. I'd love to think that they were around somewhere, buried in a cistern in some place or another. I mean here we have one of the great opera composers and only six of his works have survived intact. Among the ones that have survived intact, are his first opera, *Orfeo,* of 1607 and his last opera, *The Coronation of Poppea*, of 1642.

It is in Monteverdi's hands that opera passes out of the experimental stage. His operas become models for the next four generations of composers. Donald Grout tells us, "The music of *Orfeo* was greeted by contemporaries as another example of the Florentine style." And indeed, the general plan of the opera—that is, it's a pastorale and it uses lots of recitative—would seem to justify this view. Nevertheless, the differences between Monteverdi and what came before him are fundamental. Monteverdi was a musician of genius, soundly trained in technique, concerned very much with musical and dramatic truth and very little with antiquarian theories. He combined the madrigal style of the late sixteenth century with the orchestral and scenic apparatus of the old intermezzi and a new conception of the possibilities of recitative and solo singing. *Orfeo* represents the first attempt to apply the full resources of the art of music to opera unhampered by any limitations. In the words of Robert Donington, "We do not praise Monteverdi for originality but for inspiration." That's an important point, because as we talk about *Orfeo*, we will remind ourselves that what makes it so brilliant is that it synthesizes all that exists about Monteverdi into a single piece. Inspiration. He didn't invent opera, but he was inspired to create a new operatic ideal.

Orfeo, 1607, libretto by Alessandro Striggio. We will examine this opera from two different points of view; first, as a self-contained drama with music, simply as an opera. But as I just said, we will also examine it as an incredible synthesis of musical genres and compositional techniques; indeed, a synthesis of genres and techniques that were extant and available in 1607. It is in many ways an early *gesamtkunstwerk*, a term coined by Wagner many centuries later to mean the "all-inclusive artwork." Well, Monteverdi's *Orfeo* is an all-inclusive artwork, inclusive of everything that was available to a composer in 1607. He combines, he synthesizes, first, this awesome unique talent for dramatic recitative. There is no such thing as an aria yet; we'll talk about that in later lectures. He combines with this amazing recitative a full range of instrumentation and instrumental lighting techniques. He combines with that, madrigal choruses; and he combines with that, rhymed, pop-style songs and dances.

Let's begin at the beginning with what he calls the *toccata*, or what we would more modernly call the "overture." That *Orfeo* was meant to be performed in a very large hall, as opposed to the small room the Peri would be performed in, becomes abundantly clear at the very first notes of this overture. Monteverdi's instrumental ensemble is, by the standards of his time, gargantuan. We hear 40 or more players employing a dazzling variety of different instruments. I would list them for you now, and I say 40 or more because this ensemble can be, and has been, augmented to be even larger.

We have a score that calls for two harpsichords; two double-bass viols, which means big basses; 10 *viole da braccio*, these would be arm-rested viols—they are the ancestors of the modern violin; one double harp; two *violini piccoli alla Francese*, these are these pint-sized French dance fiddles that he asks for; two large lutes, which are called *chittarone*. Remember that, because I'm going to invoke the *chittarone*. The *chittarone,* when they are plucked, sound, from Monteverdi, like the lyres of the ancient world. So, when Orfeo is singing and playing his lyre, we will be hearing one or both of the *chittarone*; two organs with wooden pipes; three bass viols, the equivalent of a modern cello; four trombones; a portable organ; two cornets; a medium, alto recorder; one high trumpet; three muted trumpets; a harp; a guitar; three soprano recorders; and optional percussion. And there are those extra instruments that could be added. My goodness, where are they going to put all these people? Well, that's the problem of the stage director. Monteverdi calls for a band of huge size.

The toccata is a brilliant and expanded version of the sort of fanfare which customarily began theatrical entertainments. It's scored for full orchestra in three parts. In Part One, we hear the fanfare and everyone plays it. Part Two repeats the fanfare but now played a little more quietly by just strings and winds. Then, Part Three, everyone comes back and plays the whole fanfare again. Let's listen to the toccata and let's ask ourselves what sort of production this music will be preparing us for.

Monteverdi, *Orfeo*, toccata. (musical example)

Now by any measure that really swings, and it also gets our attention big time. That's a lot of music; it fills a lot of space; and we're going to expect a drama as big, as swollen, as dramatic as that overture gives us, and we will indeed get it. At the heart of the drama, at the heart of the opera, lies Orpheus the character, and at the heart of Orpheus the character lies his ultimate inability to control himself. The chorus of spirits that concludes Act Four, this is after Orpheus has failed and lost Eurydice, sings this: "Orpheus overcame Hell and was overcome by his passions. Eternal fame is deserved only by him who will have victory over himself."

Let's talk about Orpheus the character, please. I quote from Joseph Kerman's wonderful book *Opera as Drama*,

> Myths contain in them the lasting problems of humankind. The myth of Orpheus, furthermore, deals with a person specifically as artist, and one is drawn inevitably to see in the Orpheus myth the peculiar problems of the opera composer. Initially, Orpheus is the supreme lyric artist. But for Orpheus the lyric singer, the crisis of life becomes the crisis of his lyric art. Art must now move into action onto the tragic stage of real life.

What Kerman is talking about, of course, is that Orpheus can go around singing all he likes—that's art. But when he decided to go to Hades and use his singing to bring back Eurydice, art must not intrude into the action of real life.

It is a sublime attempt. Can its symbolic boldness have escaped the musicians of 1600 seeking a new power in new forms of drama? Orpheus's new triumph is to fashion the lament that heralds Hell out of his own great sorrowing emotion. This, too, the early opera composers must have identified with, wrestling as they were with new emotional means, harrowing, dangerous to manage. But the fundamental conflict of the myth transcends that time and this medium and extends to every artist. It is the problem of emotion and its control. Orpheus, as an artist, achieves everything. He changes Hell with his art of song, but as a man, he cannot shape his emotions to Pluto's shrewd challenge. Face to face with the situation, he looks back and fails. Real life and art are not necessarily one.

That Monteverdi and Alessandro Striggio were aware of this allegorical relationship between Orpheus the man and the problems of the librettist and composer, is revealed immediately in the prologue, which follows the toccata we just heard. Let's move on to the prologue.

The prologue begins with a *ritornello*. A *ritornello* is a musical refrain. The word *ritornello* comes from the Italian *ritornare*, which means to return to. So, a *ritornello* is a refrain, a melody that comes back and back and back again. This gorgeous and melancholy instrumental refrain will return time and time again across the span of the opera, so it's very important we get it in our ears now so that we hear it and recognize it when it returns at later times.

Just the *ritornello* theme that initiates the prologue. (musical example)

This striking and memorable *ritornello* appears at the end of Act Two, right after Orpheus is determined to go to Hades. It appears at the beginning of Act Five, after Orpheus has failed in his mission. And, it becomes a sort of leitmotif symbolizing the melancholy of the story, the power of music as it is expressed right here in lines five and six of the prologue. "I am Music, who, with sweet sounds, knows how to calm every troubled heart." This is the music that represents all of these elements, so it's an important chunk of music and we'll hear it again in just a moment.

But please, let me read through the prologue and we will hear it in its entirety. Yes, this is the voice of La Musica, introducing us to the story and the characters. We have five verses. The first verse is, I suppose, the expected obsequious one that says "thank you" to all the royal people who have come and commissioned this work.

"From my beloved Parnassus I come to you, illustrious heroes of noble royal blood"—yes, she's speaking right to the Gonzagas—"whose glorious virtues are proclaimed by fame only incompletely, for they are too many to number." My goodness. All right, this obsequious, tushy-smooching out of the way, La Musica can now get on to rather more important topics. And now, in verse two, she stops being accompanied by a harpsichord and starts being accompanied by one of those *chittarone*, which sounds just like a lyre. So now, we hear, in many ways, the voice of Orpheus.

> I am Music who, with sweet sounds, knows how to calm every troubled heart, and now to noble anger, now to love, can kindle the most icy souls.

The *ritornello* returns again, verse three:

> Singing to the golden lyre I am accustomed sometimes to delight mortal ears and I thus inspire the soul at the sonorous harmony of the lyre of Heaven.

Ritornello, verse four:

> My desire now is to tell you of Orpheus, of Orpheus who held the wild beasts spellbound with his song—

When she sings that, I want you to notice this gorgeous violin elaboration. It is the voice of Orpheus in the background.

> Who even subdued Hell with his pleading, and won the immortal fame of Pindos and Helicon.

Again, the *ritornello*.

> Now during my song (verse five) now gay, now sad, may the birds be silent on these trees, no waves be heard on these shores, and every breeze should cease to blow.

What she's saying here in verse five, she's saying, "Keep it down out there. No noise; just shut up and listen." That's a great verse, to end the introductory music with a stern warning, "Let everything be quiet while I tell you this story." Then we hear the *ritornello* two more times.

The last thing I would point out, because I am intellectually bound to do so, is that this entire prologue is a *passacaglia*; that is, the melody of each of these five verses is different but the baseline, the underpinning, is the same over and over and over again. Do I expect you to notice that? No. Would a fellow composer notice that? Yes, instantaneously. I need to point out these things because we need to know what a great technician Monteverdi is, aside from being a great dramatist. This work succeeds at every level, my friends—technical, aesthetic, dramatic.

All right. Let's jump in. Let's listen to this marvelous prologue, which begins again with the *ritornello*, which will come and punctuate each of the five verses.

(musical example)

All right. We're ready for Act One. Act One is about happiness and joy in Eden or Arcadia or Sylvania, call it whatever you want, just don't call it North Jersey. The opening recitative is sung to us by a shepherd, and it reflects the joyful and dancing spirit of this opening act; and it also gives us a chance to talk about the nature of Monteverdi's recitative, which is so different from Peri's or Caccini's. First, I would read what the shepherd sings to us:

> On this happy, auspicious day which has put an end to the lovesickness of our demi-god, let us sing, shepherds, in such gentle accents that our strains will be worthy of Orpheus.
>
> Today, pity has stirred the soul, till now so disdainful, of the lovely Eurydice. Today Orpheus has been made happy on her

breast, for whose sake he has already sighed and wept so much in these woods.

So, what is the shepherd saying? Well, Eurydice has finally said, "Yes. All right! Okay! I'll marry you. Now leave me alone." Yes, we can imagine that Orpheus has wept and sighed and sung and has finally convinced her; and everyone, including Eurydice herself, is filled with joy. Our shepherd continues to repeat his first lines again: "On this happy auspicious day…" and so forth and so on.

I want us to listen to this opening recitative, these first moments of Act One, and I want us, most importantly, to compare the sense of depth, melodic spirit, and musicality of this recitative to what we heard in Peri's *Euridice*, which I think we admitted was—if Peri's *Euridice* was food, it would be a saltine cracker with nice, brook water. All right, what food then might this recitative by Monteverdi be?

(musical example)

Now that's nice. It moves; it has melodic contour; there's a sense of directionality; there's a real sense of musical substance here that goes way beyond anything we heard in the Peri. If this was food—all right, it might not be chateaubriand with an old and fine Bordeaux—we'll get to that in due time. But certainly there's enough substance here to feed us and feed us happily. This is a whole different story than the kind of recitative we heard in the early operas. It's almost song, but not quite. And this is Monteverdi's recitative, really much closer to song—a harmonic underpinning that pushes the music forward, a sense of melody and contour that gives this life. One might call this *arioso*, and often Monteverdi's recitative is called *arioso*—almost song-like, *arioso*. Not to be confused with Aristotle Onassis.

Joseph Kerman writes of Monteverdi's particular form of recitative: "Recitative was Monteverdi's greatest achievement. It forms the basis for *Orfeo* and completely dominates and determines his masterpiece of 35 years later, *The Coronation of Poppea*." Recitative is one of the fundamental constant elements of operatic dramaturgy. But actually, it already began to decay into convention with Monteverdi's pupils, and in spite of impressive renewals in later centuries, it has never again been used with Monteverdi's confidence, imagination, and conviction. As a result, it's hard for us today to think of recitative as anything but second-best, as a necessary link between arias. I would point out that, in 1600, there was, as of yet, no concept of abstract instrumental musical expression—musical expression that was not tied to words—the sort of expression we hear in, let's say, a Bach organ work or a Beethoven symphony. In the musical tradition that Monteverdi grew up with, musical expressivity, as we know, had been tied to word-painting, as in the madrigals that we've listened to.

Joseph Kerman continues:

> Now, there was a new, specifically neo-classic ideal. Music should imitate the accents of passionate speech as represented by the grand, exaggerated rhetoric of a great actor. Music should follow the cadence, and thus the moving implications, of the individual word. The result was recitative, tumbling emotion, a continuing heart cry, undistanced, the naked human voice behind the measured voice of the poet. Its magnificence and immediacy stem from its impulsive nature, from its lack of formal control. Monteverdi met this ideal of recitative with a perfect genius for declamation. Words formed themselves musically for him, and to whip the recitative line into passion, he harrowed every available musical means. For tension, declamation guided him to sudden halts and spurting cascades of rhythm and to precipitous, intense rises and falls in his melodic lines. This art of recitative is what Monteverdi brought to the story of Orpheus, an artist who could move Hell by his grief, a lover who could not dominate his passions.

Let us continue. We hear a chorus of nymphs and shepherds, which will allow us now into a brief insight into the nature of symbolism in Alessandro Striggio's libretto. Following that just heard recitative, we hear a chorus of nymphs and shepherds sing a joyful, congregational prayer in honor of Orpheus and Eurydice.

Here's what they sing:

> Come, Hymen, o come, and let thy blazing torch be like a rising sun that brings days of serenity to these lovers; and drive far away the horrors and the shadows of anguish and grief.

That's kind of like a toast to their impending marriage. Let's just listen to this brief chorus, and then let's talk about the symbolism inherent in these words.

(musical example)

This seemingly inconspicuous little chorus is filled with the sort of symbolism that absolutely permeates this entire opera. Mythological Orphic doctrine states that the sun equals divine truth, goodness, and masculinity. Again, the sun equals divine truth, goodness, and masculinity—machismo. With this concept of masculine machismo in our ears, let me read the opening lines again and let's see how innocent these words are.

"Come, Hymen, and let thy blazing torch be like a rising sun that brings days of serenity to these lovers." This is not just sun worship but clearly phallic and reproductive symbolism as well. And we thought that it was going to be safe to let the kids watch this? No. Warning label music: Hide 'em.

Let's continue. Now, of course, the references to the sun, which are many here in the first act, and the brightness of the upper world stand in sharp contrast with the shadowy darkness of the underworld, where the great drama of Orpheus and Eurydice will eventually be played out. Robert Donington points out, "Opera started at a period, the late Renaissance, when deliberate symbolism was at the very height of fashion, not to mention sophistication. All the protagonists of classical mythology survived or returned to carry the projections of just those aspects of our own personalities, which we are least able or least willing to recognize directly within ourselves." This is, of course, that conversation we had in a previous lecture about archetypes and about the cathartic nature of opera. We see in the characters of opera ourselves, and as a result, we suffer or experience emotional catharsis through the operas.

We know for a fact that the librettists, such as Ottavio Rinuccini, who wrote Peri's *Euridice*, and Alessandro Striggio, who wrote Monteverdi's *Orfeo*, were powerfully influenced by another poet named Pierre de Ronsard. Ronsard instructed his fellow poets too, and now I quote Ronsard: "Dissemble and conceal fables thickly and disguise well the truth of things with a fabulous cloak, so as to make enter into the minds of ordinary people by agreeable and colorful fables the secrets, which they could not understand when the truth is too openly disclosed." So, this kind of purposeful symbolism, of hiding truths within fables and fabulous characters, is intrinsic to the opera and the art of this time.

Donington concludes:

> By Orphic doctrine the sun is God and the moon, for God is day and night. I think this doctrine must convey an intuitive understanding of the two constants of our human destiny. First, that the masculine luminosity of the sun is complemented by the feminine numinosity of the moon. And second, that we most certainly have our dark sides as well as our light side, and that for the soundest of psychological reasons, we have somehow to accept both these polar opposites as part of that curious package deal, which is the human being.

All of this from that little chorus? Yes, all of this from that little chorus.

Which brings us to the next episode in our opera, a dance and song of celebration of the upcoming marriage. A joyful and pastorale song and dance follows a prayerful chorus, which followed our prologue, which followed our *toccata*. Already we should be becoming aware of the extraordinary synthesis we are witnessing, different kinds of music all brought together and held together by the extraordinary dramatic line of the story. We started with the instrumental *toccata*. We immediately went to the prologue with its marvelous *ritornello*, then we went to the recitative, very personalized, very melodic; then we went to the chorus, very symbolic in its meaning. And now we go to a pop song and pop dance episode.

The music of this song and dance, the *Lasciate i monti*—that is, "leave the mountains"—is in three parts. In Part One, the voices, the dancers—and by the way this would be danced at most performances—successively enter in canon. A canon, like "Row, Row, Row Your Boat," is when each individual voice, or group of voices, comes in a period of time after the last one. The beauty of starting a dance this way is obvious. Each dancer comes on stage with their music, until finally everyone is on stage and in position.

So, let's listen to Part One of *Lasciate i monti*. "Leave the mountains, leave the fountains, fair, happy nymphs, and in these meadows, with your usual dances, bestir your beautiful feet." This is Part I of this song and dance, and I would also point out it's in what we call "four." That is, we would count four: one-two-three-four, one-two-three-four, one-two-three-four. Listen.

(musical example)

Part Two of *Lasciate i monti*. Everyone is now in position and they sing, "Here let the sun"—there's that sun again—"Let the sun watch your dances that are much lovelier than those which the stars in the sky perform around the moon in the dark night." Again, the celebratory tone continues. I would point out that Monteverdi switches the meter from four to three. We go from one-two-three-four, one-two-three-four, to one-two-three, one-two-three, one-two-three, one-two-three. It's a wonderful bit of metric movement. Part Two.

(musical example)

Part Three of *Lasciate i monti* is a rollicking instrumental *ritornello*, which continues this triple meter. Part Three.

(musical example)

We will hear this sequence of events three times. First, the dancers will enter in canon singing in four, then we will hear Part Two sung in three, then the instrumental *ritornello*, and then that sequence with a couple of small changes will be heard again. The progression continues. The sense of celebration and excitement grows with each new number. Let's listen to this entire song and dance, *Lasciate i monti*.

(musical example)

We should be excited. We should be tapping our toes and we should be prepared now for a very important event; and Monteverdi has led us right to the edge. What's that event? Well, it's time to hear from Orpheus and Eurydice. We are primed and ready. All our blood's moving. It's time for the star couple to come out and sing for us. And sing for they shall, but we will have to wait for the next lecture to hear from them. So, with this in mind, we will conclude Act One and will move on to Act Two, in our third lecture concerning Orpheus and Eurydice, Lecture 7 of our set. Until then, I thank you.

The Invention of Opera and Monteverdi's *Orfeo*, III
Lecture 7—Transcript

Welcome back to "How to Listen to and Understand Opera." This is Lecture 7, the third of a four-lecture series entitled "The Invention of Opera and Monteverdi's *Orfeo*." We continue in Act One, and we continue in a signal moment. Finally, we hear and meet Orpheus and Eurydice. Orpheus is introduced, typically, by one of his shepherds. I say "typically," because Orpheus never seems to be without his shepherds.

> But you, gentle singer, whose laments once made this countryside weep, why do you not now delight the valleys and hills with the sound of the famous lyre? May the testimony of your heart be some happy song that speaks of love.

What's the shepherd saying? He's saying, "How about a song, big fella?" Indeed, it's a song opportunity, an aria opportunity, even; though we don't really have arias yet, so should we say it's a recitative opportunity. Now please, before I read the content of this recitative, I would just remind you that when we listen to this, you should listen especially for the fact that Orpheus's recitative is of an even higher melodic level than the ones we've heard the shepherds do up to this point. Again, that aspect of *arioso*, of almost song-like recitative, is especially true when Orpheus sings. He will have the most melodic material, and that makes great sense. He's supposed to be the golden-tongued singer, after all. Let's notice these gradations of recitative in this piece. Again, Monteverdi's recitative is probably the best ever created.

Orpheus sings to his Eurydice who is at his side:

> Rose of the sky, life of the earth and noble offspring of him who guides the universe, Sun, who surrounds and sees all from your path among the stars, tell me, did you ever see a happier, more fortunate lover than I? Blessed was the day, my beloved, on which I first saw you, and happier still the hour when I sighed for you, since you did return my sighs; happy the moment when you gave me your white hand as a pledge of pure faithfulness. Had I as many hearts as the eternal heavens eyes and these pleasant hills leaves in green May,

all would be full and overflowing with the joy that has made me happy today.

Eurydice responds, and please notice they do not sing in duet as they might in a later opera; rather, they sing consecutively. This is still a play that's been set to music. They're not singing concurrently in the sort of operatic duet that we have become familiar with but which doesn't really exist yet. Eurydice replies:

> I'll not say how great is my bliss, Orpheus, at your bliss: I do not bear my heart within me, it remains with you together with my love; ask it if you would hear how it rejoices and how much it loves you.

So, they've spoken like good little cooing lovebirds and immediately the joyful ballet music we heard before, *Lasciate i monte*, returns in closing Orpheus's and Eurydice's confession of love. Immediately after we hear the reprise of the ballet music, we hear a reprise of the chorus: "Come, Hymen, o come, and let thy blazing torch be like a rising sun that brings days of serenity to these lovers." Monteverdi is recycling previously heard material, and it's a brilliant stroke, because what he does all at once is create a large-scale form within this first act. By bringing back both the celebratory dance music and the benediction of the chorus, we no longer have a series of discrete events, but rather a larger structure, which we can perceive. And all of this, of course, is his doing. This is the composer as dramatist.

From the introduction of the shepherd to Orpheus's very melodic love song to Eurydice's brief reply, the reprise, the ballet, and then the beginning of the reprise of the benedictory choral section:

(musical example)

And so forth. The act comes to its conclusion moments later with a noble song of thanksgiving, introduced in recitative by a single shepherd. I would just read you quickly this introduction.

> But if our rejoicing comes from Heaven, like everything else around us here, it is proper that we reverently offer it incense and

sacrifices. Let each therefore turn his steps to the temple to pray to him in whose right hand the world rests, that he may long preserve for us this happiness.

This brief recitative is followed by a really brilliant chunk of instrumental music, and I'm going to play it for you because it's so moving. It sounds for all the world like church music, and indeed at this point, we must give thanks. So, Monteverdi writes a heavy, powerful *ritornello*—it's the theme that will come back and back again here at the end of the act—which at once reinforces the rural nature of this act, but also imbues the finale with a powerful sense of religiosity.

I would also add, for people interested in such things, that this *ritornello* is a *ricercare* in five parts; that is, a piece of music built on a series of pitches that is heard lower and lower each time it's repeated in the bass. Now again, this is a structural thing, a constructive thing that you won't hear on the surface, but these are the things that intrigue composers; how is it put together? And it's put together very carefully with great technical acumen. Let's just be aware of that, even if we don't hear it.

Let's just listen to this wonderful and powerful church music introduced near the end of Act One.

(musical example)

After the hymn of thanksgiving, and after we've heard this church music a few times, the act concludes on another rollicking note of celebration.

Some conclusions to draw about Act One before we move on to the second act. It is dramatically static; that is, there is very little real action. But that shouldn't come as a surprise. Most operatic Act Ones we're going to hear across the course of this course will be static. The job of Act One is what we've heard in the Act One here: It's to introduce us to the characters, introduce us to the essential dramatic information, which is the love between Orpheus and Eurydice. And, in the case of this Act One, we are also introduced to this pastorale paradise of the outer world, filled with light and sun, which will stand in great, polar opposite to the darkness of the underworld, which we will deal with later.

The other point I want to make about Act One before we move on is what an incredible synthesis we have heard. I talked about this before but we've got to drive the point home. We began with that blaring, blazing toccata; and now of course, the blazing aspect of it, the sun-like aspect of that toccata becomes clear to us. Then we heard the ritornello-dominated prologue. Then we heard the shepherd's first recitative, and we got a taste of what recitative is going to be like when Monteverdi gets his hands on it. And need I to remind us, this is Monteverdi's first opera. It's not that Monteverdi has been writing operas over and over and has perfected his craft. His craft is completely intact in the first opera; that is, this is something he does not have to work towards. He is already doing it better than anyone had done it, certainly, and better than most will do it for the next 400 years.

After this opening recitative we hear the symbolic chorus, that benedictory chorus. Then we have the ballet pop song, *Lasciate i monti*, then we have the love song between Orpheus and Eurydice, religious contemplation, and finally, the unrestrained joy of the conclusion. That's a lot of stuff, and it all holds together because of Monteverdi's organization of refrain material that comes back and the incredible dramatic line that he creates. It just keeps getting better, my friends, so let's continue.

Act Two, sadness and grief invade paradise. Now, we wouldn't know that at first, because at the beginning of Act Two we have music that is as brilliant and as joyful as anything we've heard in Act One. So initially, the spirit of Act One continues. Orpheus says, "Behold, I return to you, dear woods and beloved hills, made blessed by that sun through which alone my nights turn to day." Again, the brilliance of the sun is mirrored in brilliant and upbeat music. We go through a whole long number celebrating the sun and how good everyone feels until finally, after this number, a chorus of nymphs and shepherds sings: "Then, Orpheus, make worthy with the sound of your lyre these fields, over which wafts the aura of oriental perfumes." Again, the gathered throng is asking Orpheus to sing a number.

More and more Orpheus is reminding me of a kind of Arcadian Elvis-type character. I mean, let's face it. He's the unofficial king of Arcadia. He's got this whole entourage of homeboys, of shepherds that wanders around and asks him to sing all the time. And frankly, Orpheus is a rock-and-roller; and the next tune we're going to hear is as close to rock-and-roll as you're going to get before 1954. Let's move and groove, my friends. This is Orpheus at the highest he will be. It is a—I was about to say "aria;" I have to hold myself back—it's a pop song that transcends pop songs called "*Vi ricorda*"—"Do you remember"—and it's Orpheus, I say, at his most joyful. He could win the heart of any one of us with this song; and he will. Sadly, it's his last joyful moment in this opera, and the high that he brings us to will make the fall that much more profound when it happens in just a few minutes. So, let's enjoy the sun while we can.

I would point out that this *Vi ricorda* begins with a brilliant *ritornello* set in the rhythms of a Renaissance dance. We have an alternation back and forth of a group of six, followed by a group of three: one-two-three-four-five-six, one-two-three-four-five-six, one-two-three; one-two-three-four-five-six, one-two-three-four-five-six, one-two-three; one-two-three-four-five-six, one-two-three. Back and forth, back and forth—a familiar sort of metric scheme for someone of his time. It just adds a lot of juice and rhythmic complexity to this dancing song. Here's what he sings. Actually, let's listen to the ritornello first.

(musical example, with professor counting in background: "One-two-three-four-five-six, one-two-three; one-two-three-four-five-six, one-two-three; one-two-three-four-five-six, one-two-three.")

There's the rhythm I was talking about, and it does dance. It does boogie. All right. Now he sings:

> Do you remember, o shady woods, my long, bitter torments, when the stones responded to my laments compassionately?
>
> Say, did I not then appear to you more disconsolate than any other? Now fortune has smiled on me and has turned my woes into a feast.

> I used to live sadly and woefully; now I rejoice, and those sufferings that I bore for so many years make my present joy all the more precious.
>
> Only for you, lovely Eurydice, do I bless my former torments; after grief one is more content, after pain one is happier.

We really don't want to see happen what we know is about to happen. I mean it's almost too good right now. Again, we talked about it before, Murphy's Law of love: the higher you get, the farther the fall. I don't know what the particular number of that one is, but it's got to be out there somewhere.

Let's listen to the entire *Vi ricorda*; the energized climax of the good part of this opera is reached. Let's be aware of that marvelous dancing *ritornello* as it appears between each of the stanzas of the song.

(musical example)

All right. We are at the moment when the messenger, and the message she brings, must come. Monteverdi creates an incredible contrast between the happy shepherds and the approach of the miserable messenger. A happy shepherd continues to sing in rhyme immediately after the *ricorda*, "Look, Orpheus, o look how all around laughs the wood and laughs the meadow; so continue with thy golden plectrum to sweeten the air on such a happy day." As our shepherd completes that bit of recitative, this is the music we hear the shepherd sing.

(musical example)

It's very pleasant and it's very nice. Now I want you to hear what happens to the bass, because it twists up horribly at the anticipated approach of the messenger, and we should all say, "Oh no, bumissimo…"

(musical example)

Now listen. (musical example)

This chord (musical example) becomes this chord (lower example). Yuck. This can't be good news, and it's not. In the distance we hear these words "Ah, bitter occurrence, ah, wicked and cruel fate, ah, unjust stars, ah miserly Heaven!" It is the messenger approaching from afar, and I would point out that the Italian is wonderful here. The words spill one into the next: "*Ahi, caso acerbo, ahi, fato empio e crudele, ahi, stelle ingiuriose, ahi, cielo avaro!*" That's good work on Striggio's part to create words that just, ooooh—it's almost like one entire cry of pain.

It is the messenger and she approaches. Please, from this last bit of good feeling, sung in rhyme, by the shepherd through that horrible upwards twisting in the bass and the shepherd's approach:

(musical example)

Bummer is right. Our Arcadian party dudes cannot believe what they're hearing. It's as if a black cloud has just swept across the sky and covered our once bright sun. The second shepherd says, "What sound of sorrow disturbs this happy day?" And then the messenger, "I am wretched, for while Orpheus soothes the heavens with his notes, with my words I must pierce his heart."

First shepherd: "This is the lovely Sylvia, sweetest companion of the fair Eurydice; o how full of grief is her appearance; what has happened? O mighty gods, do not turn away from us your benign glances." The messenger responds, "Shepherd, cease your singing, for all our joy has turned to grief."

Orpheus can't stand it. What's going on here? And he butts in: "From where do you come? Where are you going? Nymph, what bring you?" I would point out that at this moment Orpheus and the shepherds are no longer, for the first time in the opera, singing, talking in rhyme. This is not good. This is not good at all.

The news is the worst imaginable. The messenger continues, "To you I come, Orpheus, unhappy messenger of the most unhappy and most tragic happening. Your beautiful Eurydice..." And Orpheus butts in again, "Ohimè, Woe is me, what do I hear?" The messenger continues, "Your beloved wife *è morta,* is dead," on a low note. Orpheus basically buckles under his own weight and simply can say only, "Ohimè!, Woe is me!"

Let's listen to this extraordinary phrase because this is a true operatic interchange, with constant changes of key and instrumentation during this dialogue between the messenger and Orpheus. I would also point out that the harmonies seem almost irrational, in order to portray the terrible fantasy come to life of this dramatic moment. Of course, at its conclusion when Orfeo collapses and says "Ohimè," he's struck dumb. He's not going to be able to say anything else for a good period of time.

The report. (musical example)

After a long pause, Sylvia, the messenger, tells the terrible story. I would point out that, at first, it's a monotone. She's just suffering from her own grief. But as her anguish builds so does the music, and it's brilliantly done. I would also point out that when we hear this, note that she is accompanied by a small organ and a single *chittarone*—one of these big lutes. The plaintive, veiled tones of these instruments add well to the dark and somber mood.

> In a flowery meadow with her companions she was collecting flowers to make a wreath for her hair, when a treacherous serpent, hidden in the grass, bit her foot with its poisonous fangs. And behold, all at once her beautiful face turned pale, and her eyes lost that brilliance for which the sun envied them. And now we, all horrified and woeful, stood around her and tried to reawaken the spirit that had fled with fresh water and powerful spells; but all in vain, ah, wretched am I, for she briefly opened again her dying eyes and calling you, Orpheus, after a deep sigh expired in these arms; and I remained with my heart full of anguish and fear.

Across the span of the conclusion of this dramatically told story, we have a large, long descent, which drives the deathly message home that much more powerfully.

The golden-tongued Orpheus is still speechless. It's up to the homeboys to respond. The second shepherd uses the same words we heard when the messenger approached: "Ah, bitter occurrence, ah wicked and cruel fate, ah, unjust stars, ah, miserly Heaven." Then another shepherd says, "At this bitter news the unhappy one resembles a lifeless boulder, so overcome by grief that he cannot lament. Ah, he would have the heart of tiger or a bear who did not feel pity for his pain, deprived of all thy happiness, wretched lover."

Let's listen to the messenger's message—this terrible report, the response of the shepherds, and then let's be aware of how brilliantly Monteverdi sets up Orfeo's response, which we will talk about after we've heard this body of music.

(musical example)

Everything about the messenger's song is brilliant, and sets this so far apart from the one we heard by Peri as to be almost two different universes. The way she begins quietly and almost monotone, as the words start tumbling one on the other as the terrible event is remembered. The way she reaches a terribly moving high note when she remembers Eurydice calling "Orpheus," and then the almost whispered conclusion, exhausted from the trouble, from the time, from the energy telling this story. It's just a fabulous bit of writing by any standard at any time. As we discussed before listening to it, the shepherds well set up Orpheus's response, which happens next.

Now, Orpheus for his part slowly finds his voice, though at first, he hardly seems conscious at all. His tone gradually rises, his energy gradually rises as he decides to reclaim his Eurydice from death.

> You are dead, my life, and I am breathing? You have left me, never, never to return, and I remain? No, no, if my verses have any power at all, I will surely go down to the deepest abysses, and, having softened the heart of the King of Shadows; lead you back with me to see the stars.

An excellent climax is reached when Orpheus rises to the word "stars." He continues:

> Or, if impious fate denies me this, I shall remain with you in the company of death. Farewell earth, farewell sky and sun, farewell.

That last farewell, that last *addio,* is again very moving. He leaps downward a stunning distance from "sun" to that final *addio.* I would simply play the melody for you, so you can expect to a degree what will happen. He says "*e sole*"—"and sun" (piano musical example), and then leaps downwards (lower piano example) as if to say, "If I do not succeed, I will stay with Eurydice in Hades. I will not go back without her." Orpheus's growing sense of determination, this glorious desire to bring her back to sun and stars, is all portrayed in the music. It has nothing to do with the words. The composer is the dramatist.

Orpheus's response. (musical example)

It's a profoundly moving moment and a brilliantly written moment; and it's followed immediately by a madrigal chorus. This is the public response to Orfeo's grief and Eurydice's death. By the way, I would point out that this chorus begins with the same lines that initiated the messenger's approach and that initiated the shepherd's response to the messenger.

I read the chorus of nymphs and shepherds:

> Ah, bitter occurrence, ah wicked and cruel fate, ah, unjust stars, ah miserly Heaven. Do not trust, o mortal man, the perishable and frail happiness which soon vanishes, and often in a great ascent the precipice is near.

When we're highest, the fall is the furthest. Now I said this was a madrigal chorus and indeed it is. When they talk about heaven, *cielo,* we will hear an ascent in the voices. It's word-painting. When they say, "scatter," the word *fugge,* which means flight, the voices will seem to scatter apart very rapidly and very rhythmically. And of course, when they say "*precipizio,*" a precipice, they will leap downwards. So, we have Renaissance-style tone-painting here, illustrating the meaning of the words. It's a straight-on, old madrigal.

Let's listen to this public response to the catastrophe of Eurydice's death.

(musical example)

Following this madrigal chorus, the shepherds and nymphs singly and collectively continue to express their guilt—excuse me, their grief! The act concludes powerfully and very tragically with the reprise of the first two, and by now familiar, lines of that madrigal chorus. The act concludes with, "Ah, bitter occurrence, ah wicked and cruel fate, ah, unjust stars, ah miserly Heaven."

Following this reprise, once again, of those two lines—and this is just a fabulous and stunning stroke on Monteverdi's part—we hear a reprise of the *ritornello* theme from the prologue way back at the beginning of the opera. Now, what began the opera, an invocation of the power of music, thus ends the second act. Orpheus and his lyre will not be denied.

Let's listen to these final two lines, which again express the sense of unjustness at the death of Eurydice, and then that brilliant reprise of the *ritornello* from the prologue.

(musical example)

So ends Act Two, which had begun so brilliantly and ends so tragically. Again, the *ritornello* theme from the prologue now takes on a whole new dimension. It now reflects both the tragic events of the act, as well as Orpheus's determination to rescue Eurydice from death itself, armed with his singular weapon, the power of music. When we return, we will meet Orpheus again, but now in the underworld. Thank you.

The Invention of Opera and Monteverdi's *Orfeo*, IV
Lecture 8—Transcript

Welcome back to "How to Listen to and Understand Opera." This is Lecture 8, the fourth of four lectures from a group entitled "The Invention of Opera and Monteverdi's *Orfeo*." We are now to Act Three, and now we will witness Orpheus in the underworld.

Act Three begins with an instrumental introduction called a *sinfonia*. The dark and indeed, my friends, malevolent environment of the underworld is well depicted by a brass-dominated introduction, brass instruments being, in Monteverdi's day, those instruments associated with the underworld. Let's listen to this nasty bit of introductory music and get in the properly gloomy mood we need to have.

(musical example)

Welcome to Hades, big fella! Either that or you're at a brass-section rehearsal. Either way this is a potentially ugly place to be.

The goddess Hope, *la Speranza*, guides Orpheus as far as she can. She can guide him as far as Charon, the boatman, who crosses souls across the river Styx to the underworld. She says,

> Here is the dark swamp, here the boatman who bears the naked spirits to the other bank, where Pluto has his vast empire of the shadows. Beyond this black bog, beyond this river, in those fields of lamentation and grief, cruel fate hides your dearest possession. Now you need a great heart and a beautiful song. I have conducted you as far as here, no further am I permitted to accompany you, since a stern law forbids it, a law inscribed with iron in hard stone of the gateway to the deepest kingdom of terror, expressing its fierce meaning in these words: *Lasciate ogni speranza voi che entrate*, Abandon all hope, ye who enter here. Therefore, if your heart be truly steadfast and your feet able to enter the city of sorrow, I will flee from you and return to my usual abode.

Well thanks, doll. I mean, Hope has left him at the very moment when he needs Hope the most. Hope's departure leaves poor Orpheus close to panic, but he has very little time to quiver and quake because he is face to face with Charon himself, the boatman of the underworld.

Charon says to him—and please remember, he is a scabrous, brutally ugly giant of a man:

> O you, who dare before death to approach these shores, halt your steps: to cross these waters is allowed to no mortal, neither can he who lives dwell with the dead.
>
> Will you, perhaps, hostile to my lord, drag Cerberus from Tartarus's gates? Or do you, your heart aflame with shameless desire, want to steal his beloved wife? Give up thy foolish intention, into my boat will I never admit a bodily being, for the ancient outrages again awaken in my soul bitter memories and just anger.

Needless to say, Charon is a basso, a very low basso, singing at the very bottom of the male range. I would also point out that he is accompanied by a regal; this is an organ with reed pipes and it's going to make an ugly, buzzing sort of noise when we hear it. He is grotesque and bitter, filled as he is with memories of violation and deceit.

Let's listen to Charon's little song, shall we? (musical example)

Whoa! Beastly. Terrifying. I mean, this is like a Department of Motor Vehicles employee on steroids—a dangerous person. And this is where Orpheus must be strong, where he must summon everything he has. This is the moment that he's been waiting for, and Monteverdi gives us the best of his best, a piece called "*Possente spirto*." It is the crown jewel of this opera, "Mighty spirit" in translation. This is Orpheus's song, his entreaty, his serenade to Charon, the boatman of Hades. It is a preeminent and awesome example of Monteverdi's incredible dramatic and his lyric art. Can music move the soul of the soulless? That is the challenge.

Striggio, the librettist, uses a rhyme scheme called *terza rima*, which is the same rhyme scheme that we have in Dante's *Inferno*—a detail, but a most interesting one. Now in this magnificent plea, we hear in the first three stanzas, respectively, accompaniment from first, two violins, then from two cornets, and then from two harps. These instruments, which accompany stanza one, two, and three, represent the love of Orpheus and Eurydice; and as these instrumental lines curl and intertwine, they represent Orpheus' love for Eurydice and Eurydice's love for Orpheus. They offer a subtext, then, throughout this aria.

Let's read through and then listen to this superb and magnificent example of Monteverdi's art. In the first verse, Orpheus decides to rely on flattery. I mean, what better way to start an entreaty than to say, "Hey big guy, you're looking really good today," and that's essentially what he does. "Mighty spirit, possente spirto, and awesome divinity..." He's talking to Charon. I mean, no one's called him an awesome divinity in ages, I can assure you. "Mighty spirit and awesome divinity, without whom the souls freed from their bodies hope in vain to cross over to the other bank." So, he's going to try to butter him up first.

Then we hear as an interlude, a wonderful solo of two violins, again representing the intertwining love of Orpheus and Eurydice. Verse two: He decides now he's got to be as pathetic as he possibly can. I mean, he's got to try to get some pity out of this monstrous creature. "I am not alive, no, since of life is deprived my beloved wife, my heart is no longer with me, and without a heart how can it be that I live?" Indeed, this talk of death brings brass instruments to the fore, and now we hear two cornets intertwine and play a solo following these three lines, following this second verse.

The third verse: He decides to offer hope, a sense that there is a future for himself and for Eurydice: "To her, I have turned my steps through the dark air, not towards Hell, for whoever has so much beauty has Paradise." In invoking Paradise, what instruments would we expect to hear? Well, harps, of course. They are the instruments, since it would seem the beginning of time, we have associated with Heaven. After this third verse, we hear two harps intertwine beautifully, gracefully and quite romantically.

Then the last verse, the fourth verse, and this is the forceful one, my friends, this is the punch line. Orpheus knows he's got to go for the jugular now, if he's got any hope. So this is what he says.

"I am Orpheus,…" But I would point out that Monteverdi has provided a tremendously elaborated embellished line. So while he's saying "Oooorrrrrfeeeoooo," it sounds as if he is weeping, weeping in agony. It's a brilliant compositional calculation.

> I am Orpheus, who follows the steps of Eurydice through these gloomy plains, to which mortal man never has access. O serene lights of my eyes, if only one glance from you can restore me to life, ah, who can deny me comfort in my torment? Only you, noble god, can aid me, fear not, for it is only the sweet strings of a golden lyre I use as a weapon against which rigid souls implore in vain.

And he finishes.

Let us listen to *Possente spirto* in its entirety. It's a fairly long chunk of music, running close to nine minutes; but as I say, it's the crown jewel of this opera. It represents what Monteverdi can do better than anyone else living at his time, and that is project operatically and dramatically this incredibly rich, and yet complex, and yet memorable, vocal and dramatic line.

Possente spirto. (musical example)

So ends *Possente spirto*, forcefully and powerfully. And of course, for Orpheus to sound at his best and most convincing, Monteverdi has to be at his very best and his most convincing, and he is.

Charon's response? Not what Orpheus had been hoping for. In the same music as before, Charon refuses him outright. I think this should come as a surprise for most of us. Charon says, "Much am I flattered by such delight to my heart, disconsolate singer, by thy lament and thy song. But far, ah, far from my breast be pity, which is beneath my dignity." Basically, he tells him, "Look, you're singing up the wrong tree, pretty boy." So, Orpheus is going to take one more shot at it, one final plea. My friends, this is a tough gig. This is a tough crowd. I think Orpheus is beginning to feel like a comic from the Aryan Brotherhood playing a rabbinical convention; nevertheless, he decides to go for it one more time, and he says this:

> Ah, unhappy lover! Am I not then allowed to hope that the citizens of Hades will hear my pleas? Must I therefore, like a wandering shadow of an unburied and unhappy corpse, be deprived of Heaven and of Hell? Does impious fate thus will it that I, in this horror of death, far from you, my beloved, call your name in vain and waste away in imploring and weeping? Give me back my love, gods of Hell! Give me back my love, gods of Hell! Give me back my love, gods of Hell!

Three times he says that last line. All at once, he's forceful, pathetic, pleading, princely. Will it work?

Let's listen first. (musical example)

Again, he is forceful, he is pathetic, he is powerful, he is princely. Will it work? How does Charon react to this incredible, impassioned plea from Orpheus? Well, we'll never know, because Charon fell asleep while Orpheus was singing this last plea. Now is this great, or what? He's acting just like a good old opera audience is supposed to act during an aria, just kind of snoozes on off. Yes, we hear an instrumental introduction that represents Charon's snoring, then Orpheus sings: "He sleeps, and even if my lyre stirs no compassion in the heart of stone, at least his eyes cannot escape sleep at the sound of my singing." Yes, a very firm comment on the nature of all audiences everywhere.

> Up, then, why do I delay? The time is right to cross to the other bank if no one is here to prevent me. Let boldness prevail where entreaties were vain. A short-lived flower of time is opportunity, which must be plucked at the right moment.

So, he enters the boat and rows himself across the river. Meanwhile we can imagine Charon is going to be in the deep stuff when he wakes up, but that's his problem and that's at another time. Then Orpheus says again, "While these eyes shed floods of tears, give me back my love, gods of Hell!"

Act Three concludes with a madrigal chorus of spirits celebrating Orpheus's victory over Charon. It's not the victory we might have anticipated, but it's a victory nonetheless. He's gotten through the door. Act Four takes place in the court of the king and the queen of the underworld, Pluto and Proserpina. The act begins with Proserpina's plea on Orpheus's behalf. Yes. She's speaking to her husband and this is what she says.

"My lord, this unhappy man who over the wide fields of death calls for Eurydice"—I would point out something at the piano because it's very striking. When Proserpina begins this recitative, she's singing in minor, so it's a dark-colored sound (musical example). But when she says, "Eurydice," suddenly she goes to major, and it's a very shocking, almost a brutal change to the better (musical example). Virtually, in one moment, the evocation of the beautiful Eurydice allows an opening up of the musical sound, a much brighter and more brilliant sound to occur. In any case, back to Proserpina's plea—"whom you have just heard lamenting so sweetly, he has awakened so much pity within my heart that I return again to entreat you to yield to his imploring."

Now isn't this neato? Obviously, the intercom of Hades has been switched to "on," and all of that trouble in *Possente spirto* was not wasted after all. Proserpina has been listening all this time to Orpheus, and her heart—her female heart—has been melted by the love that he bears for his wife, and so she is interceding on Orpheus's behalf. Let's just listen to the beginning of her plea, that segment I just read.

(musical example)

She continues to implore on behalf of Orpheus with other lines. For example, she reminds her husband that "I followed you down here out of the light, because this was where your job was." And she tells him that "If I pleased you, if I have given you joy, then you must do this for me." She chooses those lines, which she knows are liable to evoke the most positive response.

Pluto responds with a condition. He says:

> Although stern and immutable fate opposes your wishes, beloved wife, nothing indeed shall now refuse such beauty joined with such entreaties. His beloved Eurydice Orpheus shall find again, contrary to the decrees of fate; but before his feet have borne him from these abysses, he may not turn round to look at her, for eternal loss will result from a single glance.

> I ordain it so. Now in my kingdom make, o ministers, my will known, so that Orpheus hears it and Eurydice hears it, and nobody shall hope to change it.

A stunned and amazed chorus celebrates the incredible. Literally, my friends, a snowball has survived in Hell. They sing, "Pity and love today have triumphed in Hades."

(musical example)

From their quiet, almost stunned beginning to their celebratory ending, this is a moment like no moment that has ever existed, and we should all be aware of that.

A word about Pluto's conditions: This guy did not get to be king of the underworld because he was a dummy. He knows something that the rest of us might not know. "What's really up?" we should ask. Are the conditions really so tough, that Orpheus not turn around? Can Pluto afford to set a precedent here? Can he afford to send a dead woman back up? No, he can't. He is counting on something that he would be aware of as a god, that we as an audience might not be aware of. And that is Orpheus's Achilles heel, his weak point, the one thing that is his downfall—his vanity. His vanity. Let's proceed, please.

A spirit sings, "Here is the gentle singer, who leads his wife to the skies above." We will hear a *ritornello* then—an instrumental chunk of music, which is joyful, walking music. It has a steady walking rhythm—dum, dum…dum, dum…dum, dum—and we can sense the physical activity of

Orpheus' walking. By the way, we hear that walking music in the strings. It's taking us away from the fearful brass of the underworld.

Orpheus starts to sing. While I read you Orpheus's song, ask yourself, what is he singing about? Is he singing about his love for Eurydice? Is he singing about his gratitude to Proserpina, or perhaps Pluto? Is he singing about his extremely good luck? No. What is he singing about?

> What honor is worthy of thee, my omnipotent lyre, that you have, in the infernal realm, been able to overcome every hardened spirit?

He would seem right now rather proud of himself. He continues.

> You will find a place among the most beautiful images of Heaven.

He's still talking to his lyre, my friends.

> You will find a place among the most beautiful images of Heaven, and to your sound the stars will dance in circles, now slowly, now quickly.

He sounds a little arrogant. Another verse:

> I, made perfectly happy through you, (my lyre,) will see the beloved brow. On the white breast of my lady I shall rest today.

As I asked before, where is Orpheus's gratitude to Pluto, his affection for Eurydice? It's nowhere to be found. He arrogantly congratulates himself and his lyre, even as he's leading Eurydice out of the underworld back to the overworld. This vanity, this self-centeredness is about to have dire consequences. He continues, and suddenly, I would tell you, that walking music stops:

> But while I am singing, alas, who will assure me that she is following? Who keeps the beloved eyes hidden from me? Perhaps pierced by envy the gods of Avernus forbid, so that my happiness

will not be complete, to look at you, blessed happy lights that can make others blessed with one glance alone.

Yes, doubt begins to assail him. He should keep his mind on his business. But now, he is thinking, "Maybe someone wants to get back at me because I'm so good, because I've done such a good job." Orpheus, who won the heart of the haughty Eurydice, who lulled Charon to sleep, who conquered the king and the queen of the underworld with nothing but his voice and his lyre, is losing control of himself.

"What do you fear, my heart? What Pluto forbids, Cupid commands." Cupid? Cupid? "A more powerful divinity, who conquers men and gods, I must obey." Cupid? He's saying, "Even though Pluto says don't turn around, Cupid says I should"? And he's using this as a justification to turn around? My goodness. He's dumber than we thought. And of course, Pluto sets it up. There's a noise behind Orpheus as he's walking and that's the killer. It's almost unfair to make this noise, but they make a noise, almost to force him to turn around to see what's behind him.

"But what do I hear, Ohimè? Do the Furies arm themselves to hurt me, madly desiring with such frenzy to rob me of my beloved? And I allow it?" Of course, we're saying to ourselves at this point, "Don't do it! Don't do it! Stupid! Don't do it!" But of course, he does it. He turns around and there she is. "O sweetest lights, I can indeed see you, I can, but what eclipse, alas, obscures you?" And, even as he looks at her, she begins to fade.

Let's listen from the point at which he says, "What do you fear, my heart? What Pluto forbids, Cupid commands."

(musical example)

Yes. "But what eclipse, alas, obscures you?" Bad, bad Orpheus. You did a bad thing. Third spirit says, "You have broken the law and are unworthy of mercy." Then the pathetic Eurydice, dissolving before his very eyes, speaks to him.

> Ah, sight too sweet and too bitter—

Listen for the extraordinary dissonance in her voice and the harmonies beneath her voice:

> So by too much love you thus lose me? And I, poor one, lose the happiness of returning to light and life, and lose at the same time you, dearest of all possessions, my husband.

First spirit breaks in:

> Return to the shades of death, unhappy Eurydice, hope no more to see the stars again, for henceforth to thy pleas Hell will be deaf.

Orpheus finally realizes what he has done:

> Where are you going, my life? Behold, I follow you, but who, alas, prevents me? Is it a dream? What hidden power drags me from my beloved against my will, and leads me to the hateful light?

The brass cut in, and we know that Hell has been triumphant.

(musical example)

All in all, for Orpheus it has been a very bad trip south. The act concludes with a vigorous chorus of spirits, who sing this.

> Virtue is a ray of heavenly beauty, prize of the soul, where alone it is valued. The devastation of time it does not fear; in man the years make its splendor brighter. Orpheus overcame Hell and was overcome by his own passions. Eternal fame is deserved only by him who will have victory over himself.

Act Five is almost an unnecessary tag-on. Let me just briefly tell you what happens in Act Five before we wrap up. We meet a grieving and despairing Orpheus who has returned to the light. He is now by himself on the stage. When this opera began back in Act One, the stage was covered with various people; nymphs, shepherds and so forth. Now, it is only Orpheus alone. In later opera, we would call this a perfect aria situation or an aria opportunity, a chance for Orpheus to reflect upon the catastrophe of the last day. But, the concept of aria—that is, of stopping time and expressing one's feelings through melody as well as through words—doesn't exist for Monteverdi. Only recitative exists for Monteverdi. Recitative forces action. It happens in real time, not contemplation. As a result, self-awareness eludes Orpheus. Striggio and Monteverdi did not have the means to give Orpheus an opportunity to reflect upon his nature. All he does is moan and groan.

> These are the fields of Thrace, and this is the spot where my heart was pierced by sorrow at the bitter news. Now that I have no longer any hope of recovering by praying, weeping or sighing, my lost happiness, what else remains for me but to turn to you, gentle woods, once comfort to my torments, as Heaven in pity for me let me languish in my languishing,

and so forth and so on. He seems to have learned nothing about himself and he seems unaware of his role in the events that just passed. Yes, grieving rhetoric utterly lacking in personal insight and any transcendent self-awareness. The selfish, narcissistic Orpheus can only react as recitative is bound to words. There is no abstract, purely musical means by which he can transcend his words and through music, again to quote T. S. Eliott, "touch that fringe of indefinite extent of feeling, which we can only detect out of the corner of the eye and on which we cannot completely focus, those feelings which only music can express."

The remainder of the opera is, for me, dramatically disappointing. Of course, I told you in the original story Orpheus was torn to shreds by a bunch of very drunken Furies. This doesn't happen in Monteverdi's opera, though it would have been rather interesting staging, had it. Rather, we have something called "divine intervention," *deus ex machina.* Orpheus's dad, Apollo, sees how unhappy his kid is, and he comes floating down on a device from the top of the stage to the bottom, and basically bawls out Orpheus for kind of blowing it down in Hades, but says in compensation, "Come with me to the stars. I will make you a god, and there you can see the face of Eurydice in the sky every night." This appeals to Orpheus, this idea of godhood, relieving him of his mortal and pathetic grief. He takes Apollo up on his offer. The opera ends with them being pulled up to the ceiling and the roof above the top curtain, tootling away—the only duet, really, of the entire opera. They apotheosize together.

Dramatically unconvincing or not, Monteverdi's *Orfeo* succeeds at every level; as a synthesis of all the genres and compositional techniques that were extant in 1607, as a brilliant example of the power of recitative to embody and magnify the power of words, and as a marriage of drama and music—the whole greater than the parts. In Monteverdi's *Orfeo,* the Greek ideal of the power of music, as described by *la Musica* in the prologue, has been reclaimed, redefined and reinvented. Remember what she said, "I am Music who, with sweet sounds, knows how to calm every troubled heart, and now to noble anger, now to love, can kindle the most icy souls." Indeed, this is what Monteverdi's music does. With Monteverdi's *Orfeo,* the history of opera has well begun. Thank you very much.

The Growth of Opera, the Development of Italian Opera Seria, and Mozart's *Idomeneo*
Lectures 9–12

The earliest operas were a synthesis. ... We tend to treat the word "synthetic" today as something bad; if something is synthetic, it's not made out of real stuff. But in terms of music, the word "synthesis" is an important and a good word, because it indicates various different styles and types of music combined, where the whole hopefully is greater than the parts.

We will begin by reviewing the birth of opera and its early history, and then we will move on to discussion of the invention of the aria. The earliest operas were a synthesis of old and new musical and dramatic genres and compositional techniques. Four elements were inherited from the Renaissance: stage scenery and machinery, dance/ballet episodes, popular songs/ballads, and madrigal-style choruses. These early operas also included the recitative element, which was new. Monteverdi's *Orfeo* was the first successful work to combine all these elements into a singularity greater than the parts.

Recitative was the essence of Monteverdi's operatic art. It was used for everything: action, narrative, dialogue and description of feelings. Because of the non-reflective and ever forward-moving nature of recitative, time cannot stop for consideration and reflection. For example, Orfeo's reaction to Euridice's death is recitative, and in it, he does not stop to reflect. There was little emotional depth in this genre at this point in its development. The concept of aria, in which music is divorced from words and creates a whole expressive world of its own, had not yet been realized. Moreover, recitative focuses on words, not music, which further limits emotional depth. A musical example in *Orfeo* is Orpheus' response.

In considering aria, we begin with the musical example of "Chiamo il mio ben cosi" from Christoph Willibald von Gluck's *Orfeo ed Euridice* (1762). In an aria, the words and music are on an equal footing. Additionally, real time stops. Orpheus can experience and express in music a depth of feeling far beyond that of words alone. The use of music as an expressive vehicle, which began with the earliest arias, is revolutionary. Gluck's operas mark the starting point for the modern opera repertory.

The period between Monteverdi (1567–1643) and Gluck (1714–1787) is sometimes called both the golden age of opera and the dark age of opera (a period which runs from 1640 through 1750). This period was very secular in terms of philosophy and science. It saw logical thought as transcendent. This development influenced music, resulting in a hugely expanded musical language. The harmonic system came into its own. Instrumental music became as popular as vocal music, and with the development of instrumental music there came a self-sufficient, pure, abstract musical language. This was Gluck's inheritance: a musical language that could create what could not be expressed in words alone.

> **The period between Monteverdi (1567–1643) and Gluck (1714–1787) is sometimes called both the golden age of opera and the dark age of opera (a period which runs from 1640 through 1750).**

The first phase of this period ran from 1640 through 1700. During this phase, the first public opera houses were opened. Also, opera quickly became a ubiquitous public entertainment in Italy. Huge numbers of operas were created and produced. The popularity of opera during this era can be compared with the popularity of television for modern audiences. Singing style and stage design developed rapidly. Opera captured the exuberant, expressive spirit of the Baroque. The quality of libretti declined in order to meet the growing public demand for spectacle, situation, and virtuosic singing (a situation again comparable with much contemporary television programming). Opera pulled further away from the Greek ideal. Choruses were used less and less as the demand for virtuoso soloists grew. Despite their number and fame, however, Baroque operas are seldom produced, due to their dramatic stupidity and strange, often bizarre content; thus the dark age of opera.

By the late 17th and early 18th centuries, literary devotees of opera were determined to reform the medium and return to it a degree of literary and dramatic substance. These reforms characterized the second phase of the golden/dark age of opera, which ran from 1700 through 1760.

Chief among the reformers of this phase was Pietro Metastasio (1698–1782). He was the great librettist of the first half of the 18th century. He standardized his libretti into a formulaic dramatic procedure (comparable with today's television sitcoms).

In opera developed during the second phase of the golden/dark age of opera, dry recitative (accompanied only by a harpsichord and, sometimes, a cello) alternated with arias. The principal characters had to sing one or two arias in each act. Subsidiary singers were only permitted one or two arias in the course of the entire opera. Every opera had three acts. No two successive arias could use the same singer, mood, or orchestration; and choruses, duets, and other ensembles were very rare, except for the final number, when all principal singers had to line up for an ensemble in block harmony.

Plots were based on mythological characters and ancient history. This is the formula for Italian opera seria. Metastasio formularized arias into a structure called the da capo aria: A-B-A form. As a musical example we consider "Mi rivedi" from Alessandro Scarlatti's *La Griselda* (1721).

Arias became classified into standard types. There are many different types, including the five we will describe here. First, the aria cantabile showcases all of the singer's lyrical ability. The aria di portamento is a dignified aria designed to show off the singer's breath and tone control. The aria di mezzo caratere is a compromise between the aria cantabile and the aria di bravura. The aria parlante (patter aria) demonstrates the singer's agility, and the aria di bravura (or aria d'agilità) is highly florid and designed to show off the singer's agility and extraordinary vocal compass.

As a result of the predictability of the Metastasian operatic formula, singers and vocal virtuosity increasingly became the focal points of reform opera. Singers embellished the written notes and improvised solo passages at the ends of arias. These embellished and extended cadences became known as cadenzas. The greatest vocal abuses were promulgated by the *castrati*. For a musical example, we will review "Siam navi all'onde" from Antonio Vivaldi's *L'Olimpiade* of 1734.

We now turn to a discussion of voice types. Basic voice classifications include soprano, alto, tenor, and bass. The soprano is the highest female voice, and the coloratura soprano is the highest of the soprano voices. The term coloratura refers to virtuosic singing, not vocal range. Coloratura sopranos are distinguished by their range, clarity, and agility as exemplified in the Queen of the Night's aria, "Der Hölle Rache" from Mozart's *The Magic Flute* of 1791 (musical example).

The lyric soprano is a fairly light, warm, and flexible voice. The dramatic soprano on the other hand is a heavier, darker, and larger voice than lyric. The spinto soprano is a voice lying between a lyric and a dramatic soprano, and the mezzo-soprano is heavier, darker, and lower than a true soprano, approaching the alto voice. The contralto (alto) is a female voice of exceptionally low focus.

The tenor is the highest male voice. The lyric tenor is a light, clear, and flexible voice, while the dramatic tenor is a more forceful, powerful voice, capable of greater volume and endurance. As a musical example, please consider Otello's entrance from Act 1 of Verdi's *Otello* (1886). The baritone is slightly lower in range, heavier, and fuller in sound than the tenor, and the bass is the lowest male voice. It is a rich, dark, heavy, and powerful voice that is not particularly agile. A good musical example is Charon's song from Monteverdi's *Orfeo*, Act 3 (1607).

We now return to Christoph Willibald von Gluck (1714–1787) and a consideration of his reforms. Gluck was Bohemian by birth. He split his mature career between Vienna and Paris and was a brilliant composer of Italian-style operas.

Gluck's operas were along the lines of traditional opera seria. They distinguished themselves, however, in their dramatic viability. Gluck believed strongly in telling a good story. To do so, he used his orchestra much more flexibly. He also simplified and streamlined his arias to reduce singers' abuses and to restore the dramatic integrity of his operas. His operas became models for the next generation of opera composers.

Wolfgang Amadeus Mozart's (1756–1791) *Idomeneo, Re di Creta* (*Idomeneo, King of Crete*) is the greatest opera seria. The libretto is by G. B. Varesco. Mozart is one of the few great opera composers not to have been an opera specialist. He wrote operas in all the styles popular in his time: opera seria, Gluck's reform-style opera, opera buffa, and Singspiel. His first opera was *La finta semplice* (*The Pretended Simpleton*) of 1768.

Mozart, whose *Idomeneo* is the greatest opera seria, transcending the formulas and predictability of the genre.

Idomeneo is the transcendent opera seria. In its story, Ilia (lyric soprano), the daughter of Priam, King of Troy, is in love with Idamante, who is also in love with her. He (soprano or tenor; the part was originally written for a castrato) is the prince and heir to the Cretan throne. Half-mad Greek princess Elektra is also in love with Idamante. Idomeneo is the King of Crete and father of Idamante. The action takes place on Crete, ten years after the end of the Trojan War. Idomeneo, in order to survive a shipwreck, promises to sacrifice to Neptune the first person he sees on landing in Crete. This turns out to be Idamante, his son and heir. Idomeneo desperately tries to find a way to avoid keeping his oath to Neptune.

In Act 2, the momentum builds to a tremendous degree as Mozart employs every device he can to avoid the formulaic and predictable dramatic action typical of opera seria. Each vocal number merges with the next. The use of a trio was rare in Mozart's day. He uses one in this act to break the predictable pattern. He also uses recitative for Idomeneo's monologue "Eccoti in me, barbaro Nume!" He knew that an aria at this point would have slowed the pace and killed the dramatic momentum. Musical examples abound and include Elektra's recitative, "Parto, e l'unico" and no. 14 (march); Elektra's recitative "Sidonie sponde"; the No. 15 (chorus), "Placido è il mar"/Elektra's aria, "Soavi zeffiri" and Idomeneo's recitative, "Troppo t'arresti"; the No. 16 (trio) from "Deh cessi il scompiglio"; the No. 17 (chorus), "Qual nuovo terrore!"; Idomeneo's recitative, "Eccoti in me, barbaro nume!"; and the No. 18 (chorus), "Corriamo, fuggiamo."

In conclusion, we note that the seamlessness of this music takes *Idomeneo* out of the category of traditional opera seria. The non-seria elements are as follows: The recitatives are accompanied, recitatives and arias do not automatically alternate, the use of a trio is unusual, flexible use is made of the chorus, and the orchestra transitions smoothly from one section to the next. ∎

The Growth of Opera, the Development of Italian Opera Seria, and Mozart's *Idomeneo*, I
Lecture 9—Transcript

Welcome to "How to Listen to and Understand Opera." This is Lecture 9, the first of a four-lecture set entitled "The Growth of Opera, the Development of Italian Opera Seria, and Mozart's *Idomeneo*." We would begin with a necessary review of the invention of opera, something discussed at length in the last two lectures but something that deserves to be talked about a little more. Then we will move on and talk about that most important invention of the aria; but first, just a review of the invention of the opera, please.

The earliest operas were a synthesis, and that's an important word. We tend to treat the word "synthetic" today as something bad; if something is synthetic, it's not made out of real stuff. But in terms of music, the word "synthesis" is an important and a good word, because it indicates various different styles and types of music combined, where the whole hopefully is greater than the parts. Indeed, early opera was a synthesis of many old aspects of music and theater, but with one essentially new aspect; so I would review that synthesis, to start with.

The earliest operas brought together any number of pre-existing musical genres, compositional techniques, and theatrical aspects. For example, the stage scenery and machinery—and when I say "machinery," I'm referring to the moving elements one would see on stage as opposed to the stationary scenic elements—in any case, the sometimes spectacular stage scenery and machinery that we see in early opera was inherited from Renaissance theater. So, here's an aspect of "old." Another older aspect that is synthesized into the new opera is the dance and balletic episodes, which were also inherited from Renaissance theater, ballet, and the masques. I haven't talked about masques yet, but I will when we get to a discussion of French opera. Another old element of Renaissance theater and music adapted to become part of the new operatic experience were the popular songs and ballads of the Renaissance, based on simple, rhymed poems. The madrigal-style choruses also come to us from the Renaissance, which were used, like the ancient Greek theatric choruses, to comment on the progress and the drama of the opera in which they were contained.

What was new and what made opera work was recitative; and this is very new, invented around the year 1600. The invention of recitative allowed opera to come into existence. Recitative captured what the early opera composers believed was what the ancient Greeks had done, and that is, combine the rhythm and articulation of the spoken word—that is, of speech, of oratory—to combine that rhythm with the rise and fall of pitch, as in song. Recitative is, at its basic level, a combination of the spoken articulation of words—that is, we would sing words the way we would speak them, with the same rhythms and the same articulation. There can be no doubt that the composers of early opera were convinced that they had created in recitative an infinitely more powerful mode of expression than just speech alone.

Combining the elements of scenery, dance, pop-style songs, madrigal and recitative into a smooth, coherent whole was the great artistic challenge of early opera. Monteverdi's *Orfeo* of 1607 was the first operatic work to successfully combine all of these parts into a singularity greater than the parts. Recitative in Monteverdi—really, recitative in all early opera—was kind of like olive oil, if you'll excuse me; it was used for everything. Recitative was used for action, for narrative, for dialogue and to describe feelings. It was a kind of all-in-one musical gesture. Here's the important point, and it brings us back to where we finished in our previous lecture; because of the non-reflective, ever-forward-moving nature of early recitative—and this includes Monteverdi's extraordinary recitative—because of the non-reflective and ever-forward-moving nature of recitation, time can nowhere stop for consideration, reflection, and change. That is such an important statement that I'm going to make it again. Because of the non-reflective, ever-forward-moving nature of recitative, time can nowhere stop for consideration, for reflection, and for change. Recitative, by its nature, occurs in real time, the way a conversation occurs in real time.

I've got to illustrate this point, because it's a very important point. Let's go back to one of the great recitatives we listened to when studying Monteverdi's *Orfeo*. This is the Act Two, Orpheus's response. This is the moment when Orfeo finally responds, after having been struck dumb, to the information of

Eurydice's death. Here's what Orpheus—excuse me, I keep saying "Orfeo" for one moment and then "Orpheus" the next, it's the same guy—this is what Orpheus says when he finally finds his tongue, having been informed of the catastrophe of Eurydice's snakebite and subsequent death.

He says,

> You are dead, my life, and I am breathing? You have left me, never to return, and I remain? No, no, if my verses have any power at all, I will surely go down to the deepest abysses, and, having softened the heart of the King of the Shadows; lead you back with me to see the stars; or, if impious fate denies me this, I shall remain with you in the company of death. Farewell earth, farewell sky and sun, farewell.

Now, this is Orpheus's soliloquy-like response to Eurydice's death, his immediate response to her death. I want us to examine the tenses. I mean, what are the tenses—past, present, future—that we hear in this particular bit of soliloquy?

"You are dead, my life, and I am breathing?" Pure present tense. Here and now. "You have left me, nevermore to return, and I remain?" Again, present tense.

"No, no, if my verses have any power at all, I will surely go down to the deepest abysses, and, having softened the heart of the King of the Shadows; lead you back with me to see the stars;" future. This is the action that I will do, and this will happen in the future. "Or, if impious fate denies me this, I shall remain with you in the company of death." He's anticipating another possible future scenario.

"Farewell earth, farewell sky and sun. Farewell." Back to the present. "Goodbye, addio, I'll see ya. If I get back, great; and if I don't, at least I'm with her in Hades." Now this is action music; there's no reflection here. There's no chance to think about who she was and what her death means to him. This is all action-oriented. "You are dead and I remain. No, if I can do this, I will do this; otherwise, I will still be here." "I am and I will—that's

165

what we're hearing in this signal moment of contemplation, that is, this particular recitative. Everything is happening in real time.

Let's play it. Let's refresh our memory of how it sounds, and please, be aware that everything is happening in the present or the future. This is action music happening, again, in real time.

(musical example)

As we talked about when we heard this in the previous lecture, we talked about it as a magnificent example of Monteverdi's art of recitative. Orpheus is impassioned, he is powerful, he's a man of action. "This is what has happened and this is what I will do." But my question to all of us is, how deep, how deep are our insights into Orpheus's feelings? I mean, what of Orpheus do we know, having heard this very special and signally important moment in this opera? I mean, do we understand the depths of his grief? Do we get a sense of his memories of his beloved? As an audience, can we share in his anguish? Do we hear anger, do we hear rage, do we hear acceptance, do we hear resignation? What do we hear? Very little of this emotional depth comes through in recitative.

I've got to make a point, and we all understand, that this is infinitely more expressive on a personal level than a madrigal would be; but still, it's not nearly as expressive as an aria would be. Because in Monteverdi, the words equal the music; the words give us all the musical rhythms; the words tell us. Because of the emphasis on articulation in recitative, the words create the music; the music is not influencing the words. There is not a musical line here that goes deeper and beyond the mere words to create a whole new emotional place; that concept doesn't exist yet. The concept of aria—where music itself, divorced from words, creates a whole expressive world—that concept doesn't exist yet.

So, if we can imagine in our mind's eye a big pendulum, and on one side of the pendulum the word "words," and on the other side of the pendulum the word "music;" certainly the pendulum is way up in Monteverdi's, as in any early opera, toward the word "words;" because the words determine the rhythm and the nature of the expression, because these are pieces based on recitative which is "word." It is left to the subsequent madrigal chorus, if you recall, to ponder Eurydice's tragic death. And we have that public mourning, that moment of ritual grief. But again, it wasn't personal; it wasn't personal.

Let's jump forward and talk about aria ,and compare this recitative to an aria; and you'll see exactly what I mean when we add that extra musical element to the word. We move forward 155 years to Christoph Willibald Gluck's opera *Orfeo ed Euridice*. So, another operatic version of the Orfeo and Eurydice story.

Let me set the scene for you. We're right near the very beginning of the opera. Eurydice has just been buried. This opera starts out rather more quickly than does Monteverdi's. She's already dead and buried, or being buried, when the opera begins.

During the funeral itself, Orpheus has wailed Euryidice's name three times. I mean he is absolutely disconsolate, "Euriiidice, Euriiidice!" I mean, real breast-beating stuff. The funeral ends, and Orpheus asks to be left alone. So he's left alone on stage very, very early in the opera. I would remind you that in Monteverdi's *Orfeo* we did not see Orpheus alone on the stage until the fifth act. But right away, here, in the first act, he's alone on the stage, silent, contemplative. These are the words he sings, supplied by the librettist Raniero de' Calzabigi.

> Thus I call upon my love at break of day and at its fading. But—alas, how vain my sorrow!—my heart's idol answers me not. Eurydice, Eurydice, beloved shade, alas, where are you hidden? Your faithful spouse in anguish calls you ceaselessly in vain, begs your return of the gods and vainly scatters to the winds his tears and his lamentations. Thus I seek my love upon these sad shores where, alas, she died! But to my grief Echo alone replies, for she knew love. Eurydice! Eurydice! Oh, our shores know that name and the woods have learned it of me!

He continues, and goes on and on. I've read about half the text for this extraordinary aria; that is Orpheus's first aria in Gluck's *Orfeo ed Euridice*.

Joseph Kerman writes,

> After the chorus has departed, Orpheus begins this first aria, '*Chiamo il mio ben cosi.*' The elegy is sung by Orpheus in this opera, not by the chorus as in Monteverdi's. Orpheus is equal to it. His previous inarticulate wailing is transformed to a tranquility, to a tranquility, beyond anything that Monteverdi could achieve. Orpheus is shown to pull himself together to a point where grief is viewed and understood, no longer lived but not shunned either. He transcends his sorrow by controlling it into music, into song, into an aria. The message in this piece is in the music, not in the words. The tranquility that Orpheus feels is in the melody and the harmony, not in the words. The words and music here in Gluck are complementary. The music functions on its own level, providing an emotional underpinning and sensibility beyond just what the words say.

This, my friends, is an aria.

Let us please listen, and I would point out that despite the fact that, as we know, Orpheus is a male, you will be hearing a woman sing this. This is because Gluck originally wrote this part for a—male soprano, but that's a euphemism. We'll talk more about what it's a euphemism for later in this course. Let's just say that these were the men without beards who were the great and famous singers of the seventeenth and eighteenth centuries. Today we will usually hear a woman sing this role, a mezzo-soprano or even a soprano, with the understanding that in Gluck's time this would have been a male soprano. Please, listen, and what I want you to think about while you hear this aria is how is this aria different from the equivalent recitative that we heard in the Monteverdi version just moments ago.

Gluck. (musical example)

Is this action music? Is this "I am and I will?" No, it's not. It's very different sort of music. We sense that time has stopped. We're living in psychological time right now; we're living within the mind of Orpheus, and we're feeling his feelings and contemplating his ideas and emotions. Why is this happening?

Why does it feel that way? Because the music is now so interesting and so full unto itself and complete, that the musical experience now is adding tremendous depth to the words and to the emotions. The musical experience has put the skids on the action and now we are in stopped time. We are no longer moving forward dramatically; rather we're contemplating, with the aid of music, the content of these words and, even more importantly, the feeling behind these words.

Joseph Kerman continues, "This art of control was what had been learned, the art of the aria after recitative, the second of the fundamental elements of operatic dramaturgy. Composers could now take a momentary sentiment and project it as realized emotion rather than as an impulsive flash of passion in the manner of Monteverdi."

You see, if we take that pendulum again, which was way up towards "words" in the early operas of the early 1600s, by now in 1760, that pendulum is dead in the middle, between "words" and "music." You see, in the Gluck, words and music are on an equal footing. Together they create that—again, back to T. S. Eliot's quote—"that indefinite feeling, which we can only detect out of the corner of our eye."

Now, I would take one minute—perhaps two, but I will discipline myself to keep this short—and discuss some of the things that have happened historically and musically between the time of Monteverdi and the time of Gluck, because that would be the era we call the "Baroque" era, that runs from about 1600, with the invention of opera, to around 1750 or so. The Baroque was a great era of codification and investigation. It's a very secular age in terms of philosophy and science. It's an era that sees logical thought as being transcendent. The world could be explained and understood if we simply understand the formulas and science behind things.

The effect of this philosophical view of the world on music was profound. Music was exposed to the same investigation, the same scientific attitude that every other aspect of the world was exposed to. As a result, we see the musical language expand hugely during the Baroque, particularly during the seventeenth century. For example, the art of harmony, what we call the functional harmonic system, really comes into its own in the 1600s.

Instrumental music, as a genre of music unto itself, comes into its own in the 1700s. By the time we begin the 1700s, by the time we begin that era of Bach, which would be the first half of the eighteenth century, instrumental music is at least as popular and at least as common as vocal music, and for this reason: The parts of the musical speech—rhythm, harmony, melody, instrumentation—have become developed enough that instrumental music by itself can create an emotional, expressive experience.

Please think about this for a second. What would be the most abstract art you can think of? Would it be painting? Would it be sculpture? I mean, what's real abstract art? Might I suggest to you the ultimate abstract art is instrumental music? We don't have words to explain what the music is all about, and we know that music exists in the ether; it's not something we can hold onto. A score, after all is nothing but a graph. It doesn't tell us what anything sounds like; we have to hear the music in performance. So, instrumental music, lacking concrete body and lacking words to explain why something goes up or something goes down, is completely abstract. Until the musical language is substantial enough to create a full experience, abstractness notwithstanding, we won't have an instrumental tradition.

I bring all of this up because we've got to understand that opera is evolving, even as all of these other aspects of the musical language are evolving also. By the time we get to Gluck's operas during the Classical era, past the Baroque era, we've got a whole musical language available to Gluck that was not available to Montiverdi. The abstract musical language has, by Gluck's time, evolved to a point where it alone can create complex emotional responses and impressions. So Gluck, like any opera composer, will use pure music—harmony and melody—to create a depth of expression beyond that which the words can. Aria could not be invented until the abstract musical experience was invented. That happened around 1650, 1660, but after the time of Monteverdi.

Aria represents temporary detachment from action, detachment from real time. It is true musical soliloquy. Aria represents opera's psychological time. I would tell you as an aside, but it's an important aside and we'll get back to Gluck again in a future lecture, that the arias of Gluck were revolutionary in their starkness and in their emotional directness. I would also tell you that

Gluck's operas mark the point where the modern opera house repertoire begins. I'll say that again because that's important. Gluck's operas mark the point where the modern opera house repertoire begins, which makes us wonder. Well, I mean, if this opera was from 1760 or so, how about the 160 years worth of operas that preceded Gluck? That's what we must now start talking about—this age of the Baroque opera, sometimes called the golden age of opera and sometimes called the dark age of opera. It's very paradoxical for reasons we will discuss.

The period between Monteverdi and Gluck is, as I said, sometimes called the golden age, and let's talk first the good stuff. Why should it be a golden age? Well, almost everywhere between about 1640 and 1760—and I'm using 1640 as a beginning of this golden/dark age period because this is pretty much when opera became a public rather than a private entertainment, around 1640—almost everywhere between 1640 and 1760 music meant opera. If you can imagine a huge blackboard behind me and imagine at the bottom corner of that blackboard, off in the bottom right-hand side, the words "everything else," and then across the great span of the board the word "opera." That is how music would have been conceived during the Baroque. There was opera, and then there was everything else. We don't think that way today. We know about the music of Handel and Scarlatti and Bach and all these great dead German dudes who wrote all this wonderful music that was not opera. But believe me, at that time, opera was by far the most celebrated music, way outweighing the other genres that existed.

Back to the Baroque opera. The number of operas created and produced was stunning. Everything was instantly staged, cheered, plundered for the next seasons and then thrown away and something else composed in its place. Singing style and stage design saw incredible development during both the seventeenth and early eighteenth centuries. Opera, as Vernon Lee demonstrated in his studies of the eighteenth century in Italy, caught the spirit of the Baroque age better than any other art form. I quote Vernon Lee: "The bold blend of music and poetry, and scene, the ornate dramatic convention, the pomp and the splendid abandoned theatricality, the fierce singleness of operatic passions, the moving architecture in and out of the ballet, all of this sums up with characteristic extravagance the very aspirations of the Baroque."

However, there's another side to this rosy operatic picture, and I would quote Joseph Kerman: "The period between Monteverdi and Gluck can also be called the dark ages of opera. In spite of all its extent and fame, and in spite of much musicological research, Baroque opera is very little known today. It is seldom produced and when it is, the nearly always bizarre productions seem designed to distract the audience from one basic fact, that modern directors find it all of unparalleled dramatic stupidity."

All right. We've got to talk about Baroque opera. We've got to investigate this golden/dark age of opera. For ease of study, we'll divide this operatic golden/dark age into two equal chunks of time: 1640 to 1700, and then from 1700 to 1760. Let's begin then with the golden/dark age of opera phase one, 1640 to 1700. This golden/dark age of opera fittingly begins with the opening of the first public opera house in Venice, Italy in 1637.

Let's contemplate this for a moment, and we'll try to not to be too rude either to the public, or to our modern-day public. Let's contemplate what happens when something becomes increasingly public and increasingly profitable. Yes, opera becomes, first in Venice—and by the way, this first phase of the golden/dark age of opera, this 1640 to 1700, this is the Venetian phase. This is when the city of Venice, or at least composers trained in Venice, dominates Italian and European opera. So, this is the great age of Venetian opera. Anyway, opera became, first in Venice and then in all of Italy, a public and popular entertainment. By the way, we cannot say that of most other countries. There's still a sense of aristocracy, even to this day, at the opera house, for reasons again that we'll talk about later when we talk a little about the sociology of opera. But suffice it to say for now, Italy has always embraced opera, at least since the mid-seventeenth century, as a public, not an aristocratic or private, entertainment.

Often I compare opera to TV and I think it's an apt comparison. Here we have a medium of fabulous potential that is increasingly debased in an ever-widening search for larger audiences. How do we get larger audiences, my friends? We lower the standards. The denominator goes down and down. When we think we've hit the bottom of the barrel, we find a whole new barrel underneath that, and underneath that. I think every generation has said, apropos of some genre of art or entertainment, "How low can we get? We've gotten as low as we can." No, no, no. There seems to be no bottom line for the depths of wonderful depravity we can experience. In any case, the point is obvious. When something goes public and there is a profit motive involved, what's important is putting people in seats, not any necessary aesthetic, literary, or musical quality. Donald Grout wrote: "The court operas, like Monteverdi's *Orfeo*, of the early seventeenth century had always kept a certain reserve, a refinement of form and content. After 1640, as opera became increasingly a public spectacle, changes were sadly inevitable."

The popularity of the new form of entertainment at Venice was amazing. Between 1637 and the end of the century, 388 operas were produced in 17 theaters in Venice itself, and probably at least as many more by Venetian composers in other cities. We're talking about at least 800 operas being written just by Venetian composers in that period from about 1640 to 1700. Nine new opera houses were opened during this period. After 1650, never fewer than four were in operation simultaneously. For the last two decades of the seventeenth century, this city of 125,000 people, that's all, 125K, not a big town by any means, supported six opera companies continuously, the usual season filling from 12 to 30 weeks of the year. Citizens were admitted on payment of about 50 cents, and wealthy families rented loges by the season.

Let's compare this to our modern day. There's two comparisons that come right to mind: first of all, the multiplex movie theater. Every strip mall in every suburban area is going to have at least one or two or three movie theaters that people can go to. They pay, I don't know, they pay more than 50 cents, sadly we do, to go to the movies these days. Nevertheless, it's the same thing. The movie house is for us what the opera house was for the Venetians: cheap, easy, quick, and fun entertainment.

There's another equivalent that comes to mind in today's world, because certainly, rich people do not rent loges at the opera house or at the movie theater today, but they do rent loges, skyboxes, luxury suites at the stadiums, the baseball stadiums and the football stadiums. It's a place to entertain people, to have dinner while you watch the game, to do business while you watch the game. This was very much the sociology in the early opera houses, by the way. They served food and gambled and did all kinds of things; again, stuff that I'll talk about later in the course. The concept of sitting still and quiet in the opera house is a very twentieth-century thing. I suppose as we spend more and more money for those seats, we want to actually hear what's going on, on the stage, bang for the buck and all of that. We should understand that while we don't necessarily treat the opera house this way in our culture, we do treat the movie theater and the sports stadium this way. This was the role of the opera house, first in Venice and then across Italy in the seventeenth century.

Needless to say, the quality of the opera libretti increasingly declined in order to meet the growing public demand for spectacle and situation. Mistaken identity was a dramatic stock in trade. The Aristotelian unities gave way to a bewildering succession of scenes, one after the other after the other. Sometimes as many as 15 or 20 scenes in a single operatic act, full of strong feelings and suspense abounding in the sharpest contrasts, and special effects of all kinds. Again, this should be sounding like the movie theater. Lavish scenic backgrounds added to the spectacle. Pastoral idylls, dreams, oracles, incantations, spectral apparitions, descents of gods, shipwrecks, sieges, and battles filled the stage. This is sounding more and more like movies every second.

In particular, the machines—the ingenious mechanical devices for the sudden and miraculous appearances and changes and supernatural events that took place on stage—attained a degree of sophistication never since surpassed. This is true, if you look at these wonderful books with these fabulous line drawings from the Baroque of how these machines were operated. We've seen opera houses, we've seen these theaters that have over the stage these huge five- and six-story boxes. That is, the area above the stage in an opera house is always much higher than the area above the auditorium and that's because of all of the rigging and all of the workings, and then there are all of the trap doors and false doors under the stage. Truly, the machines that they created at this time have never been surpassed because the resources and workpersonship was pretty unlimited at that time. Even with our lasers and even with our special effects, in the opera house we can't do what they used to do. Of course, we can in the movie theater, but not in the opera house.

The chorus, after about 1645, rapidly disappeared. It was replaced instead by balletic, that is, dance episodes. There was a growing view that the chorus belonged in the Church, it didn't belong in the opera house. By the way, we should see this as another signal. As we move into the public domain of popular entertainment, opera pulls further and further away from that Greek ideal, from the ideal as defined by Greek drama, and starts defining itself. The disuse of the chorus is part of that aspect of opera now defining itself. We no longer use a chorus. We no longer use a chorus in the Greek style of commentary; rather, we do something else. I'd like to feel that there was a good artistic reason for canceling out the chorus, but frankly, it was also an economic one. Opera house managers just loved the idea of not having to have so many singers on retainer all the time. "Look at the money we could save." No one in the audience really cares anyway; they'd rather go to church to hear a chorus.

The other reason why the audience didn't care about losing the chorus was because the decline of the chorus was followed immediately by the rise of the virtuoso solo singer, who became the great secular hero, the superstar of the Baroque world. Let me read you some contemporary reactions to seventeenth-century Venetian opera. By the way, we should understand that Venice did not have a monopoly on opera in the latter half of the seventeenth century, but it was pre-eminent, especially in Italy. Of course, there was always a special glamour, especially for foreign visitors, to go see an opera in Venice. It's kind of the way the theater is now in New York and London. Certainly there's theater all over the world, but when we go to London or go to New York, you've got to see a play. You just have to. It's part of the shtick; it's part of the experience. So, of course, in the seventeenth century any foreign visitor would go to see an opera in Venice.

I've got a couple of wonderful accounts written by two foreigners of what they saw in the opera house during this period. Let's start with a gentleman named John Evelyn, an Englishman, a very nice Englishman, who wrote this in 1645 apropos of a stay in Venice. "This night, having taken our places, we went to the opera where comedies and other plays are represented in recitative music by the most excellent musicians, vocal and instrumental, with a variety of scenes painted and contrived with no less art of perspective and machines for flying in the air and other wonderful motions. Taken together, it is one of the most magnificent and expensive diversions the wit of man can invent. The history was, that night, *Hercules in Lydia*. The scenes changed 13 times." So our Englishman, Mr. Evelyn, had a wonderful time. He was very impressed, and I would add, by the way, the English have always been the best musical fans on the planet.

English fan clubs helped to support Beethoven and Mozart and have always—when a composer comes to visit England, when Dvorak went to England, when Handel went to England, I mean fame and glory—the English have always embraced all kinds of German and Italian music, in particular. We shouldn't be surprised that Mr. Evelyn had a darn good time in Venice and was willing to write about it.

However, the next account is rather different. In 1680, the French traveler, Limojon de St. Didier, reported as follows, and of course, the French are a much tougher crowd. "At Venice the theaters are large and stately, the decorations noble, and the alterations of them, good. But they are very badly illuminated. The machines are sometimes passable and as often, they are ridiculous. These operas are too long, yet they would divert the four hours, which they last, if they were composed by better poets that were a little more conversant with the rules of theater. The ballets or dancings between the acts are generally so pitiful that they would better be omitted. For one would imagine these dancers wore lead in their shoes, yet the assembly bestow their applauses on them, which is merely for want of having seen better. The charms of their voices do make amends for these other imperfections. The men without beards (that is, the *castrati*) have delicate voices"—yes, Mr. St. Didier refers to them as "des voix argentine," the silver voices— "besides which they are admirably suitable to the greatness of the theater. They commonly have the best woman singers in all of Italy. Their airs are languishing and touching. The whole composition is mingled with agreeable songs that raise the attention. The symphony (that is, the orchestra) is awful, inspiring rather melancholy than gaiety. It is composed of lutes, therobos and harpsichords."

I kind of like this Frenchman's vision, his description, because it's probably a bit more realistic than Mr. Evelyn's. John Evelyn sounds like a tourist, in fact he sounds like someone who is kind of gawking—"Wow! Hoo-hoo! Woo, look at those operas!" Mr. St. Didier is coming in with a rather more critical eye, and frankly, history supports his critical French eye. These operas were often fatuous, with ridiculous machinery, bad dancing; what did make them work was the singing. The singing.

Who were the composers of these pre-1700s operas? Let me read some names of the most important composers of this age and see if you recognize any of them: Pier Francesco Caletti-Bruni, Pietro Antonio Cesti, Antonio Sartorio, Giovanni Legrenzi, Pietro Andrea Ziani, Giovanni Domenico Freschi, Carlo Francesco Pollarolo, Carlo Pallavicino, Alessandro Stradella. Between them, these gentlemen created over 300 operas. How many of these names have we recognized? Well, none, obviously, because these operas are almost never done today.

In conclusion, we have good and bad. We have golden and dark. I think I will save a kind of point-counterpoint argument because I'm going to present two points of view, one scholar who believes this was a golden age and one scholar who believes this was a dark age. I think I'll save that particular debate for the beginning of our next lecture. I thank you and we will continue immediately upon our return. Thank you.

The Growth of Opera, the Development of Italian Opera Seria, and Mozart's *Idomeneo*, II
Lecture 10—Transcript

This is Lecture 10, the second lecture of a four-lecture set entitled "The Growth of Opera, The Development of Italian Opera Seria, and Mozart's *Idomeneo*." At the end of the last lecture I promised you a kind of point-counterpoint, two different points of view regarding the first phase of the so-called golden/dark age of opera; that is, two different estimates of the quality and nature of this opera written essentially in or out of Venice between 1640 and 1700. Here are these two counter evaluations.

First, the good news, the upside, the golden age stuff. I will allow Donald Grout to tell us his positive opinion, his good spin on this opera:

> The Venetian opera of this period was scenically and musically splendid. Admittedly, the plots were a jumble of improbable characters and situations, a sometimes irrational mixture of serious and comic scenes; and served mainly as pretext for pleasant melodies, beautiful solo singing and striking stage effects, such as clouds bearing a large number of persons, enchanted gardens, and other such transformations.
>
> Vocal virtuosity had not yet reached the heights it attained in the eighteenth century. The orchestra had little to do, except accompany the singers, and the recitatives were of only slight musical interest. Indeed, the aria reigned supreme. Its victory, in one sense, marked the victory of popular taste over the aristocratic refinement of the original Florentine recitative, which had been so intimately connected with the rhythms and moods of the text.

Again, Grout says, "The Venetian opera of this period was scenically and musically splendid." Okay, the upside. Now, the downside. The bad news. Joseph Kerman is rather more unkind in his critical summary of Venetian opera:

Seventeenth-century Venetian opera had thrown dignity into the canals and was busy encrusting Latin history with a scandalous picaresque confusion of plot. It had completely debased recitative in favor of rather primitive arias and had completely eliminated the chorus. It was the worst period in Italian opera history.

If you'll excuse me, this reminds me of a joke. It's an old joke; it's not a great joke, but it's completely applicable so I will tell it. It's the one about that platoon of soldiers trapped on a farm far behind enemy lines. The sergeant gets up and says, "Men, I've got good news and bad news. What do you want first?" "Tell us the bad news, Sarge." So the sergeant begins, "All right, we're trapped far behind enemy lines on this farm. We could be here for weeks. We could be here for months. Who knows? It's dangerous. Every day could be the end. It could mean discovery and prison, if not being shot. And all we've got to eat for the time we're here is cow dung." So, the soldiers look at each other and say, "Oh, boy." So finally one of them says, "Well, what's the good news?" And the sergeant says, "There's lots of it!"

What does this have to do with seventeenth-century Venetian opera? Well, here we have opera based on fatuous, ridiculous stories with unreal characters, an amazing amount of stupid machinery and scenes, which might have nothing to do with the drama whatsoever. Basically, song and dance and dog acts parading as opera. What's the good news? There's lots of it.

Let's continue. We'll talk about seventeenth-century French opera during a later lecture, but it's necessary for us to continue now in the mainstream, which means Italian opera. It's now necessary to talk about that second phase of Baroque opera, the second phase of the golden/dark age of opera; that is, phase two, from about 1700 to 1760. In talking about this opera, we will talk about the creation of Italian opera seria.

By the end of the seventeenth century and the beginning of the eighteenth century, literary devotees of opera were determined to reform the medium and return to it at least some degree of literary substance, to what had become, of course, a bastardized medium, dominated by music and singers, the stories having become fatuous and almost incidental to what happened on stage. Chief among these literary reformers were the poets, Carlo Goldoni, who lived from 1707 to 1793, Apostolo Zeno, who lived from 1668 to 1750, and most importantly, Pietro Metastasio, who lived from 1698 to 1782.

This operatic reformation was brought to fulfillment by Pietro Metastasio, the guiding genius of eighteenth-century Italian opera and a literary figure of such stature that I would tell you that his compatriots seriously compared him with Homer and Dante. Metastasio's 27 *drame per musica*, that is, dramas for music, and other theater works were given—and get this—they were given over 1000 different musical settings during the eighteenth century. Some of Metastasio's libretti were set to music as many as 70 times. We have no equivalent in our modern world today. This is as if 70 different composers set to music Stephen Sondheim's lyrics to *West Side Story*; each time different music, different composer. This is only understandable when we keep in mind that in a pre-electronic age in which there was little or no sense of repertoire. You could only hear opera live, and most likely the operas you heard would have been composed specifically for that season at that city at that opera house. Recycling good libretti was the rule rather than the exception, and ultimately, it was a good idea, because a good libretto was hard to come by; and if no one had heard it in the city, why not use it.

According to Donald Grout, "A modern reader is apt to find Metastasio's plays mannered and artificial." Dante or Homer he is not.

> Elegant rather than powerful, his characters seem more like eighteenth-century courtiers than ancient Romans. Sentimental quandaries made up most of his situations and amorous and political intrigue followed. There is almost always a *lieto fine*, a happy ending. The stock figure of the magnanimous tyrant is typically in evidence. Yet, in spite of all of this, if one is willing to allow for the dramatic conventions of the time, some of Metastasio's plays might still be read with pleasure. His achievement—

and this is the important thing, my friends—

> consisted in the creation of a consistent dramatic structure, conforming to the rationalistic ideals of the period, but incorporating

lyric elements suited well for musical setting in such a way as to create an organized, organic, literary whole.

That means something with literary integrity; that is, a formula for creating a coherent operatic storyline.

What Metastasio basically did was create a formula, was to standardize his libretti into a veritable formulaic procedure. I will let the wonderful opera scholar, William Mann, describe this process, this procedure. Again, as I read this prescription I want you to contemplate, as I'm asking you to do much in the previous lecture and in this lecture, compare this to what in our culture today this is equivalent to. We have lots of stock literary procedures. We have the half-hour sitcom, which inevitably follows a certain formula. We have the one-hour cop or detective show. We have the one-hour hospital drama; the typical emergency room thing, whether it's Dr. Kildare all the way through to whatever emergency thing is on the tube right now. We've got all kinds of literary genres that are predictable and formulaic. Indeed, they break the formula here and there, and that's what makes that particular episode interesting. But we have an expectation; we have a formula, and the writers work within that expectation. So we have equivalents in our culture to what I'm about to point out.

> "The various characters would enter one by one and converse in dry recitative"—that means, very simply, accompanied recitative, accompanied typically by a harpsichord and maybe a cello playing the bass notes;
>
> during which some trait of character or dramatic incident would be revealed. After the event had occurred, whatever it was, the most involved person would sing an aria, which summed up the situation, and then would leave the stage. The aria, which had been carefully designed to exhibit the singer's best vocal qualities, might be one of several kinds: charming, angry, imperious, rapid patter, brilliant, smoothly wheedling, or some no-man's-land in between all of these.

The principal characters had to sing one or two arias in each act, the subsidiary persons, one or two in the course of the three-act opera; and it was always a three-act opera. No two successive arias could use the same singer, the same mood or the same orchestration. After the exit of the aria's soloist, those left on the stage would continue in secco recitative, perhaps joined by others bearing dramatic news. Other arias would follow until everyone had sung an aria and made an exit.

By the way, I would tell you that servants could leave without being granted an aria.

> Then there was a change of scene and the procedure would be resumed. Duets, trios, quartets and other ensembles were very, very rare, except in the final number, labeled "coro," which means "chorus;" when, there being no real chorus, all the principal singers would line up and sing a bright, brisk, concluding ensemble, usually in what we call "block harmony."

Klunk, klunk, klunk, everyone singing together with the same rhythms.

When we put all of this together, the predictable sequence of recitative and aria, the fact that most of these plots are based either on ancient history or on mythological people, when we consider the magnificent stage sets and the almost invariably serious content of these operas, we realize that what Metastasio has done is formularize and standardize a whole school of opera, which today we call Italian opera seria, serious opera. So when we talk about *seria*, or this so-called serious opera, we're talking about the Metastasian ideal, the ideal of recitative followed by aria, on and on and on, plots based on mythological or ancient history that deal with serious if not extremely overblown emotional content.

As a result of this formulaic and predictable alternation of recitative and aria, we get in Metastasio's libretti a subsequent alternation of—if it's recitative and aria, we're getting an alternation of words and music, of movement in real time, and of repose in stop time. It's a back and forth—something happens, we stop and contemplate it; something happens, we stop and contemplate it. Endlessly repeated patterns of tension and release.

Recitatives building emotional tension, which finds outlet in the arias. I love the way Willy Fleming put it in his book, *Opera*, "The recitative loads the gun and the aria fires it." That's exactly what happens. Clearly, these arias become the central musical events in these Metastasian reform operas, and these arias themselves become as standardized and as formularized as the libretti in which they are contained.

John Brown in his *Letters on the Italian Opera*, which was published in London in 1791, mentions five traditional aria types; that is, the arias become standardized and we have certain types. Let me quote John Brown's book from 1791, "Type one: The *aria cantabile*"–*cantabile* means singing,

> by pre-eminence so-called as if it alone were song. It gives the singer an opportunity of displaying at once and in the highest degree, all his powers. The proper subjects for this air are sentiments of tenderness. Aria type two: The *aria di portamento*, chiefly composed of long notes, such as the singer can dwell on.

By the way, I'm just going to put in an aside here. Singers love long notes. Singers have spent their life developing their voice and learning to achieve tone; and you've got to give singers some big, fat, long notes so they can take a deep breath and show you this wonderful breath and tone control. If you don't, they'll be angry with you, and frankly you don't want singers angry with you. They say illogical things. But we'll get to the nature of singers in a few minutes. In any case, back to *aria di portamento*,

> chiefly composed of long notes, such as the singer can dwell on, and have thereby an opportunity of more effectually displaying the beauties and calling forth the powers of their voices. The subjects proper to this air are sentiments of dignity. Type three: The *aria di mezzo caratere*, of medium character, a species of air, which though expressive neither of the dignity of the *aria di portamento* nor the pathos of the *aria cantabile*, is, however, serious and pleasing. Type four: The *aria parlante*, the speaking air is that which admits neither long notes nor ornaments of execution. The rapidity of motion of this type of aria is proportioned to the violence of the passion,

which is being expressed by it. This species of aria goes sometimes by the name *aria d'emota e parola* and likewise, *aria agitata*.

As I proceed—because I'm going to read you the last one, darn it; we have one more to do and we'll do it—we should be becoming aware that the act of writing an opera is not some inspirational act where the composer sits down and looks at the libretto and just sees how they feel. No, no, no. The act of composition is much closer to what an architect does when designing a building. You sit down, you decide what the scope is going to be, what the size of the lot is, what kind of building it's going to be, because form and function must be married. Then, based on your budget and all of the realities you face, you design something that fits the needs of the client. That's exactly how composers work, especially opera composers, who have to turn out a tremendous amount of material very quickly.

Working with the librettist, the librettist says, "You know, I think it's time for something that really shows some real deep pathos; let's do an *aria cantabile*." Or, the composer looks at a libretto and says, "There's lots of words here, I think this is going to be one of those patter-type arias," or what we here call an *aria parlante*. First, you go through the libretto labeling everything and saying it will be this type or that type, and this is what I'm going to write here and this is what I'm going to write there. This is a very logical and a very workpersonlike approach to the act of musical composition. It's not some random act of inspiration; if it was, no one would ever get anything on paper. The act of inspiration can only come after you've decided what your parameters are, what your restrictions are; and then you can afford to be inspired. We should understand that these aria types were givens, were understoods. When a contemporary listened to an opera, they would immediately say, "Ah, that's one of those," or "Ah, that's one of those."

Our fifth aria type, at least according to Mr. Brown, "The *aria di bravura*, *aria d'agilità*, is that which is composed chiefly, indeed too often, merely to indulge the singer in the display of certain powers of execution,"—yes, *bravura* means virtuosity—"particularly extraordinary agility or compass of voice." This is just one of many extant aria classifications. There are many other tracts, many other letters, many other writings to classify other aria types dependent on the writer.

Metastasio had a lot to do with the creation of a structural formula for the arias themselves, and this is very important, so let me repeat. Metastasio had much to do with the creation of a structural formula for the arias themselves, and this is the so-called *aria da capo* or *da capo* aria. Let me explain. A *da capo* aria is one in which we have one strophe or one phrase, and we'll call that *A*. *A* is sung pretty straight; I mean *"bing, bang, bung."* Then typically in a *da capo* aria we have another strophe, another phrase, and that is given new music, different music, contrasting music; so we'll call it *B*. Having sung the contrasting phrase, we return to the original. We go back to the cap, back to the top—that's called the *da capo*—and we sing the original phrase again, *A*.

Now, the singer is given license, as is the composer. We don't want to repeat ourselves exactly. Isn't it tiresome when we're talking to someone and we realize we told this person the exact same story yesterday? It's an embarrassing moment when that realization strikes, so we suddenly add a flourish. We try to make a change; we try to alter it a little bit so that this person does not think we are an early Alzheimer's victim. In any case, the same thing might be true here in the *aria da capo*. When we return to the *da capo*, the composer will embellish and the performer is expected to further embellish the notes of the *da capo* so that it sounds like a return, but it also sounds like a development at the same time. More than anyone else, it is Metastasio who is responsible for creating this *da capo* procedure. By the way, he wrote his arias in his libretti, because this is how he structured them, as A-B-As.

As an example of a *da capo* aria, we're going to listen to one by Alessandro Scarlatti. This is not Domenico Scarlatti; this is Alessandro Scarlatti, who lived from 1660 to 1725, and this is an opera called *La Griselda*. It dates from 1721, and it's an aria named "Mi rivedi," which means, "You see me again." Let me give you a little background on this story and we'll dive in. Griselda has been the queen of Sicily for 15 years, but she's just been repudiated, rather unceremoniously kicked out by the king, Gualtiero. We can imagine he is now in search of that perfect trophy queen. So, poor Griselda must return home to her humble origins, and this aria reflects her mixed feelings. On one hand, she is very sorrowful and very hurt and very upset at having been dumped and so disdained. That will be heard in the *A* sections, *A* and the *da capo*, what we call *A'* (A prime), and these sections will be in c-minor, a relatively dark-sounding key, which is meant to resonate with the relatively dark emotions portrayed therein. However, she is also happy to be back home and happy to be away from the intrigues and the "bull" that characterized the court. The *B* section will be much brighter-sounding music in e-flat major.

Let us read the text. *A*: "You see me again, o shady forest, but no longer queen and bride; unfortunate, disdained, a shepherdess." *B*: "Yet, there is my homeland's mountain and here is still the friendly fountain; there is the meadow and this is the river; and only I am not the same." Then back to the top, the *da capo*. The same words but slightly different music. "You see me again, o shady forest, but no longer queen and bride; unfortunate, disdained, a shepherdess."

The libretto is by Apostolo Zeno. Zeno was one of those three poets I talked about before, who were so active in creating the reform movement in early eighteenth-century opera. Let us listen to this piece and I will point out these phrases as we hear them. First, of course, will be *A*, but I will point out *B* and then the *da capo*, *A'*.

(musical example)

Unfortunately, the overwhelming emphasis on arias in these Metastasian *opere serie*—and *serie* would be the plural of *seria*—and the stiff, unyielding formula of these arias, which are almost invariably in this *aria da capo* form, led to tremendous abuses on the parts of the singers. Again, I have to remind you that the virtuoso singer was to the eighteenth century what the solo pianist was to the nineteenth century, what the conductor and the movie star and the professional athlete are to the twentieth century—that is, the transcendent, media hero.

Singers arbitrarily demanded changes in their parts. They demanded substitutions of arias, despite the fact that the substituted aria might have nothing to do with the dramatic content of that particular opera. They added embellishments and cadenzas that went far beyond good taste, they went far beyond bad taste, if you want to know the truth, to become mere vocal display. Please think about it. Sadly, Metastasio had the opposite effect he wanted to have. If you create a dramatic formula, after a couple of years everyone's going to know what's going to happen in a story. If all the arias have the same form, there's no real surprise in the arias either. Where is there dramatic interest, where will there be danger and the unknown? Only in how the singers sing the arias. The singers knew they were powerful, and their demands for ever more notes or for substituting arias were a reflection of their growing power within this Metastasian reform.

The principal of absolute dominance of the aria entailed the absolute dominance of the singer in performance. In their submission to this, audiences, composers and poets allowed excesses on the parts of singers, which would never have been endured in another age. Only rarely was even an autocrat like Handel—who had the incidental advantage of being both composer and manager in one person—only rarely was even Handel able to control his singers, and only then by an extraordinary combination of tact, patience, humor, force, and the constant threat of physical violence. Handel was a big man and he was not unknown to actually hang a singer out the window, which by the way, apparently was a form of execution in medieval Germany, to simply drop someone out of the upper level of a house.

Yes, indeed. Metastasio might insist all he pleased that poetry should be the dictator of opera, and he complained about the mutilation of his dramas. Now I quote Metastasio, "By those ignorant and vain vocal heroes and heroines, who, having substituted the imitation of flutes and nightingales to human affections, render the Italian stage a national disgrace." Of course, Metastasio was powerless to alter a situation that he, with his own works, had so mightily helped to create. Thus, Metastasio continues to rail,

> The singers of the present times wholly forget that their business is to imitate the speech of man with numbers and harmony. On the contrary, they believe themselves more perfect in proportion as their performance is remote from human nature. When they have played their symphony with the throat, they believe they have fulfilled all the duties to their art; hence, the audience keeps their

hearts in perfect tranquility and expect the performers merely to tickle their ears.

Indeed, the technique of singing would seem to have reached heights in the eighteenth century that has never since been equaled. In the nature of things, it's difficult for us really to understand or to know what the singers of the era were singing, because the singer's greatest display of virtuosity was improvised. Of course, it was impossible to record these, because there was no recording medium, and very few of these improvisations were written down. So, we really don't know exactly what Metastasio is talking about.

In general, however, it could be said that there were two related practices that the singers of this era, of this second phase of the dark/golden age of opera, indulged in. One thing they indulged in is called "coloratura," and that is embellishing a given melodic line and making it very, very, very "notey" and highly ornamental. Coloratura. The other practice they indulged in was improvising passages at the very conclusion of an aria. These passages would be called "cadenzas." Let me quickly explain what a cadenza is. The Italian word for this (piano example) is cadenza, the English word for that is cadence. A cadence is a musical punctuation mark. (piano example) That, of course, is what we would call a "final cadence" or a "closed cadence," because we hear in its solidity a sense of closure. If that was a punctuation mark, it would be a period.

What singers would do is, between the third-to-last and second-to-last chord, they would ask the orchestra to "Shut up, and I'm just going to do something." (piano example with stop at third-to-last chord) Warble, warble, warble, warble, sing, sing, sing, sing, plumb heights and depths of virtuosity and self-indulgence. (piano example of second-to-last chord) End with a trill, then properly resolve. These solos taken at the cadence came to be known by the name of cadence, or cadenza. So these are the two brands of embellishment singers most often indulged in, coloratura, that is ornamenting a preexisting melodic line, or stretching out the ending of a piece, sometimes painfully so, in what we call a cadenza.

I would tell you that the greatest vocal abuses were promulgated by the *castrati*, that's plural for *castrato*. Music historian Charles Burney traveled through Italy in the early 1770s:

> I inquired throughout Italy at what place boys were chiefly qualified for singing by castration, but could get no certain intelligence. I was told at Milan that they only did this at Venice. In Venice, I was told they only did it at Bologna, but at Bologna, the fact was denied and I was referred to Florence; from Florence to Rome, and from Rome I was sent to Naples. The operation is most certainly against the law in all these places as well as against nature, and all the Italians are so much ashamed of it that in every providence they transfer it to some other.

None of the Italian cities want to own up to the fact that they use castrated boys, who of course grow into castrated men, who have voices very different from any other homo sapiens. Denials not withstanding, Burney heard that there were gelding parlors across Italy bearing this sign, "*Qui se castrono ragazzi*," "Here are boys castrated." One wonders what sort of neon icon one would hang outside of that particular shop.

According to Grout, "There are many references to the presence of eunuchs among the singers of Italian and German chapels during the sixteenth century." That would be during the 1500s.

> They are found at Florence in 1534, in the papal chapel at Rome in 1562. By the end of the seventeenth century, they were a usual feature in Italian churches, despite periodic pronouncements by the popes against the custom.

> They came into opera first in Monteverdi's *Orfeo*. Seventeenth century Italian operas made use of them to almost the total exclusion of women. Castrati singers flourished, especially during the period from 1650 to 1750, both male and female roles in the opera being entrusted to them. Their popularity began to decline in the latter part of the eighteenth century; and the last Italian opera castrato [that is, someone who was surgically snipped] died in 1861.

> Their extraordinary vogue was due in part to the shortage of women singers after the first few years of the seventeenth century, coupled with the fact that for a long time,

and this was true especially in Rome—

> women were forbidden to appear on the public stage. Even where women did take part in opera, for example, in France, where there were no castrati singing, women in opera were generally regarded as morally outside the pale of respectable society. The castrati held their own, even in the eighteenth century when there was no dearth of really good female singers. The reasons? The reasons are clear, by reason of the sheer superiority of their art. These castrated boys would have been educated in the conservatories of Italy from the moment after the castration at the age of 7 or 8 years old, 10 or 12 hours a day for 10 or 15 years. They developed the most unheard of techniques in the history of vocal singing.
>
> Their voices, known as the *voci bianchi*, or "the white voices," were more powerful, more flexible if less sweet and expressive than those of women, and this vocal quality in the castrati often remained unhindered for more than 40 years.

That's amazing, because other voices break down, my friends.

> So great were the rewards for a successful career that even the slightest sign of a promising voice was often sufficient to induce hopeful parents to offer up their son for emasculation.

Now, here's the rub, and boy, is it ever a rub. Even though the operation would obviously have to be done before puberty, these castrated boys would indeed have a voice change. All voices break at some point or another. They didn't keep a child's voice. It wasn't until puberty was reached and passed that one could really know what kind of voice this poor male would end up with, and in 99 out of 100 cases, the voice was not suitable for singing. The inevitable result was, as Charles Burney, again an eyewitness, tells us, that in every great town in Italy could be found numbers of "these pathetic creatures without any voice at all or at least without one sufficient to compensate for such a loss." Yes, indeed.

Of all of the Italian castrati, the most renowned was Carlo Broschi, who lived from 1705 to 1782. His stage name was Farinelli. He had a legendary career across Europe. He was brilliantly successful as a singer in virtually every country, the friend of princes and emperors, and for 24 years, the confidante of two successive Spanish kings and virtually prime minister of Spain, the hero of popular tales. My goodness, he was even the subject of an opera himself. He was a figure in the public imagination of the eighteenth century, comparable to Liszt or Paganini in the nineteenth century, or Marilyn Monroe or Mohammed Ali or Frank Sinatra or Elvis Presley here in the twentieth century.

I've got a wonderful anecdote to tell you. Some castrati were known for their power, others for their brilliance; and I would point out we're going to listen, after the lecture break, to a modern singer trying to sound like what a castrato might have sounded like, and you'll hear right away that a male soprano doesn't sound like a female soprano. It's a very different voice. It's high but it's got a body to it that's not the same sort of body that a woman would sing with; there's a little more depth and there's much more power. It's still a male voice. Some castrati were known for their power, others for their brilliance. Gasparo Pacchierotti was known for his heart-rending expressivity. In Rome, performing *"Arta versi"* by Bertoni, Pacchierotti came to his climactic line, "eppur son innocente;" "Yet, I am innocent." This line is followed by an orchestral exclamation. Pacchierotti sang the line with all of the pathos, power, and expressivity he could muster and then he waited for the orchestral explosion. Nothing. *Niente.* He turned in panic to the concertmaster, the first violinist, and said, "What is happening?" Of course, the reply, "We are all crying." I think that's sweet. Hey, if the singer can touch the orchestra, the singer can touch anybody. Tears notwithstanding, the castrati demanded ever more virtuosic and athletic arias with which to stun their audience and silence their many critics. Whether these arias had anything to do with the storyline of the opera in which they occur is often sadly immaterial.

I suppose for human reasons we can be glad that we can't really know what these male sopranos sounded like, because it would imply that we are still doing this and we are not, obviously. However, there are some modern male singers who sing in their falsetto range—as Groucho Marx would say, not to be confused with a false set of teeth. Anyway, there are some modern singers that sing in their falsetto range and have attempted to recreate both the sound and the virtuosic display of the castrati. We're going to listen to just such a singer, singing an aria entitled "We are like ships on the silver waves," from Antonio Vivaldi's opera, *L'Olimpiade*, of 1734. So what we have, typical of the Italian opera of this era, is a *da capo* aria preceded by a brief recitative.

Before we take our break, let's at least read through the text and talk about its nature. Then after the break, we will listen to the aria itself. By the way, this text was written by Pietro Metastasio.

Recitative: "Of all the many follies of which the world is full, who can deny that the greatest folly is anyone that is in love."

The aria, Phrase *A*: "We are like ships on the silver waves, drifting out of control; like capricious winds are our affections, every pleasure is a rock, the whole of life a sea."

B: "Like a steersman reason keeps good watch over us, but then on the swell of pride we let ourselves be carried away."

Da capo: "We are like ships on the silver waves, drifting out of control; like capricious winds are our affections, every pleasure is a rock, the whole of life a sea."

I've got to point out a couple of things right now. This aria is of a type; it is of the tempest type, a standard, storm-type aria in which the music illustrates the storm being sung about. For example, we have these endless roulades in the voice part. (piano examples) These roulades are meant to imitate the waves of the sea as they rise and fall and the blowing of the wind of the storm. Of course, nature here becomes a metaphor for human passions unleashed by love. I would also point out that this aria has been written for a tremendous vocal range. The lowest note in this aria is the a below middle c. (piano example) The highest note in this aria is a c over two octaves higher. (piano example) To make most male voices do that, you have to do terrible things to them, but of course, this would be written for a castrato; in fact, specifically it was written for Marianino Nicolini, who had this tremendous vocal range and, of course, who had the technical know-how to sing this aria.

I think we should all be primed and ready. Let us take our lecture break here and when we return, we will listen to Antonio Vivaldi's *L'Olimpiade*, the aria " Siam navi all'onde algenti" as an example of the great art of the castrato. Thank you.

The Growth of Opera, the Development of Italian Opera Seria, and Mozart's *Idomeneo*, III
Lecture 11—Transcript

Welcome back to "How to Listen to and Understand Opera." This is Lecture 11, which is the third lecture in a four-lecture set entitled "The Growth of Opera, the Development of Italian Opera Seria, and Mozart's *Idomeneo*."

Where we left off was we were about to listen to, and we are indeed about to listen to, a fabulous aria by Antonio Vivaldi written for a castrato by the name of Marianino Nicolini. A point I would make quickly before we go on: We should understand that opera composers almost always knew, and indeed those who write opera today almost always know, the singers for whom they're writing the particular parts. Just to write a part without knowing who's going to sing it is useless. What a composer wants to do is bring out the best and sometimes the worst in their singers (if they don't like them), by supplying a part that feeds into what they can do really well.

Of course, as history continues other singers will sing a part written for this person, but you should understand that a composer really wants to know what the vocal qualities are and the acting abilities of a particular singer before they sit down and actually start composing. This idea of tailoring a vocal part is really important and quite preferable than just sitting down and writing for a voice. Voices are so variable, human beings are so different on stage, that we really need both the aural, A-U-R-A-L, image of their voice and the visual image of their body and face before we can really sit down and get a sense of what the music should sound like.

In any case, this aria, written for Marianino Nicolini, is here in our performance being recreated by a male soprano, a modern male soprano, singing in his falsetto range. Most importantly, though, this performance seeks to exploit the kind of embellishment and ornamentation that a contemporary Baroque castrato might have used. Let me point out that at the end of the *B* section—because this is a *da capo* aria as almost all would have been from the 1720s and 1730s and 1740s, and so forth—the last two words of *B* are *lascia trasportar*; please note the cadenza, the added material the singer is going to insert at that moment. And at the close of the *da capo*, at the close of the aria at *un mar*, please note the even longer cadenza that the singer is going to insert. This is typical of what we would have heard at the time, and it's also typical of a tremendous virtuosity performed by this particular singer.

In any case, let's listen. What I want you to be most aware of in this recitative followed by *da capo* aria is that despite the fact that this is in the soprano range, this does not sound like a female soprano. This is something otherworldly to our ears. It's a voice type we are not accustomed to hearing but one that someone who lived in seventeenth and eighteenth century would be very accustomed to, the male soprano.

(musical example)

While I was preparing this course, my daughter came down at my studio and I didn't tell her who or what was singing this, I simply put it on and let her listen. At its conclusion she shook her head and she said, "Like, freaky." Indeed, it is like, freaky. The music is freaky and the voice is a voice the likes of which we are not accustomed to hearing. One word, I would love to tell you who this singer is but The Teaching Company is contractually forbidden by the licensing agency we use to reveal the names of the performers on the recordings you're hearing. That's why I don't stand here on the air and say, "This is such and such, and that is so forth and so on." We cannot, but it would be a most interesting experience for all of you to go out and buy all of the male sopranos you can and try to find this guy, because that's a very interesting voice, is it not?

This seems as good a time as any for me to get into the various classifications of voice types. Any course on opera has got to deal with the voice types sooner or later, so let's do it now. First, just a couple of words about singers, please. Singers, my friends, are not like other musicians, and opera singers are not like other singers; they've a very special breed. The cynic would say, not a happy breed of human being at all, but they are a special breed and we have to accept them as such. An opera singer, unlike a flute player, unlike a choral singer, is always on stage, is always the soloist; and therefore, they are always exposed. Opera singers by their nature have to have huge egos.

They have to be that batter who wants to be up in the bottom of the ninth, with two men on and two men out, ready to hit the ball. This has to be the person who wants it at that moment, in front of everyone who could witness their failure if they don't pull it off.

For this kind of singer, their body is their instrument. If they have a cold, if they have a sore throat, if stress is doing to their body what stress does to all of ours, it comes out in their singing. They can't hide behind an instrument. Everything that is wrong with them becomes wrong with their music. Like athletes, singer's bodies break down. There's a limited time that a singer can sing at the top of their game, after which they will teach but remember the glory of those moments, which tends to create a degree of unhappiness if not bitterness.

I would also point out that an opera singer must know how to move and act, even while they are singing this extraordinarily difficult repertoire all from memory. We're asking them to do a tremendous amount. Can we imagine asking a pianist to play on and off for four hours and somehow act and mug and move while they're performing? They'll say, "Hey, it's enough to press the levers." But not for a singer. It's not enough, not if you're an opera singer. You've got to be a really good actor, you've got to move well, and you've got to be able to perform the music.

You may call me a speciesist, that's fine. As far as I'm concerned, the most beautiful sound on the planet is the sound of the female human voice. There is nothing as profound to me as a gorgeous voice holding a perfect tone. There's just something about it. It's the immediacy of our own species speaking to us that the voice brings that no other instrument, for me, can deliver. Let's go through the voice classifications and talk a little bit about vocal quality. Human singing voices—indeed, we're not talking about humpback whales here—human singing voices are divided into four general categories: soprano, alto, tenor and bass.

Soprano means highest, and indeed a soprano voice, whether owned by a girl, woman, boy, or one of these unfortunate snipped men, is the highest classification. Alto means high, and an alto is a woman whose voice is pitched below a soprano's, lower than a soprano's. A tenor is a high male voice, and by the way, not always the most pleasant of human beings. I would read a wonderful anecdote, which comes to us from the 1880s. The great Wagnerian conductor, Klaus von Bülow, praised a certain tenor, who charity will keep nameless for now, in front of the critic and writer Henry Kraabel. Kraabel disagreed vehemently, saying that the singer lacked virility. Von Bülow's response is a classic, "But my dear fellow. A tenor isn't a man; it's a disease," a view shared by more than one conductor and producer, I would add. Bass or basso means lowest and refers to the lowest male voice.

Let's talk about these divisions one by one. First, soprano. The very highest soprano is the so-called coloratura soprano, the highest of all soprano voices. The term "coloratura" itself only refers to virtuoso singing, not to any particular vocal range. There have been coloratura tenors and coloratura altos and even coloratura basses. However, because of its agility, it is the soprano voice that is most often given a coloratura part. The distinguishing features of a coloratura soprano are as follows; her range will be up to an octave higher than the other sopranos, so an almost topless upper end. She will typically have a clear, often bell-like vocal quality and incredible agility, for which composers have written some of the most extraordinarily virtuosic music. We just heard, in that Vivaldi aria, a coloratura voice, but of course, it was a coloratura male soprano.

Let's listen to another coloratura aria, shall we, because this is one of the most famous in the repertoire. This is the "Queen of the Night" from Mozart's *The Magic Flute* of 1791. This part was originally sung by Josepha Hofer, who was born Josepha Weber. This is Mozart's sister-in-law. The part of Queen of the Night includes the incredible coloratura aria "Der Hölle Rache," the wrath of Hell. Among its many difficulties, the aria features a handful of high f's. A high f is up here (piano example). To squeeze out that sound a whole bunch of times, to leap into that pitch, oh boy! To step into it is hard enough, and, of course, you are taught by singers who are unhappy with you that if you want me to sing high, I've got to step into it. To leap into a high pitch, that's dangerous, my friends. If you miss, you miss, and it sounds terrible. Mozart has our soprano leaping into those f's as if they were two octaves lower. In any case, this is where the Queen of the Night shows her true mettle. Spitting fire and brimstone, she viciously tells her daughter, Pamina, that her daughter must kill Sarastro, the priest of the Sun.

The queen sings this: "The wrath of hell within my breast I cherish; death, desperation prompt the oath I swore. If by your hand Sarastro does not perish, then as my child I shall know you nevermore. Abandoned be forever, forsaken be forever, and shattered be forever all the force of nature's tie, if not through you Sarastro's like be taken! Hark! Gods of vengeance, hear a mother's cry!" Ho, ho, ho, ho! Some mom!

Let's listen to this as an example of brilliant, coloratura writing for the soprano.

(musical example)

Yes, there's a classic case of "sing at your own risk."

The next general dividing line for sopranos is between lyric and dramatic sopranos. A lyric soprano is a typically light voice, a very flexible voice. For example, the voice we heard singing "La musica," the prologue from Monteverdi's *Orfeo*, was a perfect example of a lyric soprano, a fairly light and flexible soprano voice. A dramatic soprano will be a singer with a heavier, darker, and larger voice. We talk about a big voice as being simply one that takes up more space than a lyric one; Electra from *Idomeneo*. We heard her sing "Of Orestes and Ajax." There was a little coloratura in there, but that particular singer that we heard was a good example of a dramatic soprano, a very big and powerful soprano voice. The dividing line between lyric and dramatic sopranos is often not clear. Of course, we're talking about small gradations here and this is very subjective. A voice lying between lyric and dramatic with qualities of both is sometimes called a "spinto," S-P-I-N-T-O.

Lying between the soprano and alto voices is the middle female voice known as the mezzo or mezzo-soprano; "mezzo" meaning middle. A mezzo has what we would call a very big chest, excuse me; that's not as bad as it sounds. A singer's chest register is their low register. What sets a mezzo apart from a regular soprano is that a mezzo will have a big chest; that is, she will be able to get three, four, maybe even five notes lower than your typical lyric soprano. Many dramatic sopranos have this chest register and they can sing mezzo parts as well as soprano parts, although generally a singer will sacrifice either their high end or their low end, depending on what repertoire they sing and how they practice and train. Believe me, learning to sing is the same kind of training as an athlete would go through—tremendous physicality, tremendous power involved, and tremendous time spent in practice. You're usually one or the other by dint of the fact that you need to practice the chest if you want it to be there, and you need to practice the top if you want it to be there, but they are generally exclusive of each other. A mezzo can approach very near an alto voice, and where a mezzo leaves off and an alto begins is again subjective. For example, in Verdi's day a voice that he would have considered a mezzo we would probably simply call an alto. Again, there is a lot of gray area here; it's very subjective.

Be she coloratura, lyric, dramatic, spinto, or mezzo the soprano is generally the diva, my friends, the goddess, the first lady of the theater, the prima donna; and she knows it. Oh, she knows it.

Ethan Mordden tells us this marvelous anecdote:

> A soprano on tour in Mexico was captured by bandits who turned out to be music lovers unwilling to molest a daughter of art. They agreed to let her go if she proved that she was indeed the prima donna she claimed to be. "Well, how can I do that?" she asked. "Sing for us," they responded. "What! What! Sing in a cavern? Sing before rabble, without footlights, make-up, costumes? No lords in the boxes, no critics in the pit, no bouquets hurled at the curtain? No money in the box office?" "Let her go," sighed the bandit chief. "She's a prima donna all right."

The alto or contralto—it's the same thing. The term contralto can either refer to an ordinary alto or a female voice of exceptionally low compass, not unlike the voices of former female East German female weight lifters. A counter-tenor is an exceptionally high male voice singing in the same range as a female alto. Any one of us, my friends, can be a counter-tenor simply by wearing wet leather boxer shorts and allowing them to dry in the sun.

Tenors. Like sopranos, tenors are classified as lyric or dramatic, depending on the quality of their voice. A lyric tenor would have a light, clear flexible voice. A perfect example of a lyric tenor would be Monteverdi's *Orfeo*. A dramatic tenor would be one with a bigger, more forceful and powerful voice capable of much more volume and much more endurance. Your classic dramatic tenor roles are Otello in Verdi's *Otello*, and Tristan in Wagner's *Tristan and Isolde*. By the way, the Germans don't call Tristan a dramatic tenor. They call him a heroic tenor, a "Heldentenor," but it's the same thing—a very big male voice capable of huge endurance.

Otello's first-act entrance in Verdi's *Otello* is one of the most magnificent and dramatic moments in all of opera. He's just survived a vicious storm; he's on board ship. As he arrives, he triumphantly disembarks and sings of his victory over the Turkish fleet. This is what Otello says at the moment of his entrance: "Rejoice! The Mussulman's pride is buried in the sea; ours and heaven's is the glory! After our arms the storm defeated him." Near the end of this brief but moving little aria, Verdi asks our tenor to go up to a high b, that's as high as he gets, (piano example) seven notes above a middle c. That is one note short of about the highest you can ask a tenor to go. You don't want to ask a tenor to go higher than this c, (piano example) because if you do, they could break all kinds of internal organs that they need for various functions.

Let's listen to this extraordinary entrance of Otello, and let's be aware, at least in the back of our minds, of how high he gets near the end of this brief aria.

(musical example)

That's a big voice. If we compare in our mind's ear that voice and the voice we heard in Monteverdi's *Orfeo*, we realize that they might both be tenors. This is a much bigger voice capable of much more power.

One more comment about that high c, that theoretical upper range of the male voice. Another wonderful anecdote; this one features Otto Klemperer, the famous twentieth-century conductor. Before I tell you the anecdote, I would tell you that many singers "mark" at rehearsals. That means they sing with half a voice. They save the voice so that they don't give much wear and tear on it. The problem with a singer who marks in rehearsal is you're not quite sure what you're going to hear in performance until the performance, and by then, it might be too late to do something about it.

In any case, during a rehearsal Klemperer was screaming at his tenor, who again will remain nameless, "Sing!" The tenor would not. Klemperer would say "Sing!" The tenor would not, until finally Klemperer yelled out "Sing I tell you, you fool! Sing!" The tenor walked to the edge of the stage and said to Klemperer, "Herr doctor, I have two high c's left. Do you want to hear them now, or do you want to hear them tonight at the performance?" And that was it. We don't know Klemperer's response, but I imagine he grunted and grumbled and left the tenor alone. One does not have an unlimited number of high c's if you're a tenor, and you must marshal them very carefully.

A baritone is a voice lower in range than a tenor, and fuller and more heavy in sound. A baritone is to the tenor and bass of the men's voices what a mezzo-soprano is to the soprano and alto of female voices. It's the in-betweeny voice, a little of each. And again, you can have a lyric or a dramatic baritone. We've also heard a baritone in this course, the singer who sang *"Ging Heut Morgen Übers Feld,"* from the *Songs of a Wayfarer* was a baritone.

Lastly, the bass; the lowest male voice, a rich, dark, heavy and powerful voice though not a particularly agile voice. The term "basso profundo" is often used to describe an unusually deep voice. These are the lowest of the singers; and I can assure you, you hear a good basso profundo, they will shiver the timbers under the very seats in which we sit. We've heard a basso profundo; Charon the boatman from Monteverdi's *Orfeo* has such a voice. Please, I would refresh your ears of what he sounded like. "Give up thy foolish intention, into my boat will I never admit a bodily being, for the ancient outrages again awaken in my soul bitter memories and just anger." And when he finishes his aria, Charon is singing this note, (piano example) a low e, very low in the male compass.

(musical example)

We can't expect men to get much lower than that. They'll get down to a c, two notes lower than that, and beneath that everything just starts to fall apart.

These would be the extremes of the ranges, and this is as much as we have time to investigate today; so by no means has this been an inclusive survey of voice types. But we've done as well as we could. We've not discussed, for example, the types of voices conventionally assigned to certain types of roles, because that changes. In Italian opera, tenors are almost always heroes and basses are either always older men or villains. In Russian opera, it's the other way around: the bass is the heroic voice and the tenor often the villainous one. Neither have I discussed children's voices; and thankfully, believe me, it's a rare boy soprano who can get within a country mile of the pitch that's been notated on the page. We've discussed enough about voices that we'd have a common vocabulary, and that's what's important.

Thus armed, back to our discussion regarding opera seria, the golden/dark age, phase two, 1700 to 1760. The predictable, dramatically overblown nature of opera seria plots coupled with the extraordinary liberties and vocal excesses opera singers indulged in made opera seria a big, fat, juicy, ripe target for satire. Indeed, it was satirized all the time.

Perhaps the most famous satire is Marcello's *Teatro a la Moda*, *The Fashionable Theater*, which first appeared in 1720. Marcello's work appears in the form of friendly advice offered to everyone connected with opera, from poets and composers down to stagehands and the singing teachers. Thus, Marcello says that the composer, and now I quote, "will hurry or slow down the pace of the aria according to the caprice of the singers and will conceal the displeasure with which their insolence causes him by the reflection that his reputation, his solvency and all his interests are in the singer's hands.

> The director will see that all the best songs go to the prima donna, and if it becomes necessary to shorten the opera, he will never allow her arias to be cut, but rather, he will cut entire scenes.
>
> If a singer has a scene with another actor whom he is supposed to address when singing an aria, that singer should take care to pay no attention to that other singer, but will bow to the spectators in the loges, smile at the orchestra and the other players in order that the audience may clearly understand that he is the *Signor Alipi Forconi,* [master of music] and not the Prince Zoroaster who he is representing on stage. While the introduction of his aria is being

played, the singer should walk about the stage, take snuff, complain to his friends that he is in bad voice, that he has a cold and so forth.

And while singing his aria, he shall take care to remember that at the cadences, he may pause as long as he pleases and make runs, decorations and other ornaments according to his fancy. During which time the leader of the orchestra shall leave his place at the harpsichord, take a pinch of snuff and wait until it shall please the singer to finish. The singer should take a breath several times before finally coming to a close on a trill, which he will be sure to sing as rapidly as possible from the beginning, without preparing it by placing his voice properly, and all the time using the highest notes of which he is capable.

If a singer has a role in a new opera, she will, at the first possible moment, take all her arias, which in order to save time she has copied down without the harmonies, to her maestro, so that he may write in the passages, variations and beautiful ornaments. And the maestro, without knowing the first thing about the intentions of the composer either with regard to tempo or harmony or instrumentation, will write below them in the empty space of the bass staff, everything he can think of in the very greatest quantity, so that the virtuosa may be able to sing her song in a different way at every performance. And if her variations have nothing in common with the harmony or with the violins, which are supposed to play in unison with her or with the other instruments; even if they are not in the same key, that will be of no consequence since it is understood that the modern opera director is both deaf and dumb.

Yes, this is a satire but, my friends, I think it gets very, very, very close to the truth. Audiences, particularly in Italy, looked upon the formulaic, rapidly-written, dramatically fatuous opere serie as pure entertainment. This is a very important point. Contemporary audiences, far from regarding the opera as a serious dramatic spectacle as we might today, looked upon it as amusement. Charles DeBrosses reports that the performances in Rome began at eight or nine in the evening and lasted until midnight. Everyone of any consequence had a box, which became a social gathering place for friends, like these luxury boxes at the stadiums today.

I quote DeBrosses: "The pleasure these people take in music and the theater is more evidenced by their presence than by the attention they bestow on the performance." After the first few times, no one would listen at all except to a few favorite arias. The boxes were comfortably furnished and lit, so that the occupants could indulge in cards and other games. Again, Charles DeBrosses: "Chess is marvelously well adapted to filling the monotony of the recitatives, and the arias are equally good for interrupting a too-serious concentration on chess."

Charles Burney mentions the faro tables at the Milan opera house. At Venice, where the pit was usually filled with gondoliers and workmen, again to quote Burney, "There is a constant noise of people laughing, drinking, joking while sellers of baked goods and fruit cry their wares aloud from box to box." Get your red hots! Get your... Can you imagine at the opera house? It's a very different environment than the one we are accustomed to.

This brings us back to Gluck and his reforms. Christoph Willibald Gluck was born in 1714 and he died in 1787. He was Bohemian by birth, a brilliant composer in the Italian style. He splits his mature career between Paris and Vienna. Now, Gluck's operas are written along the lines of traditional opera seria. His stories are based on ancient history or mythology, and they are grand in scope and scenic scale. But Gluck believed powerfully in telling a good story, and to that end he used his orchestra much more flexibly and creatively. In particular, he made frequent use of what we call orchestrally-accompanied recitatives, recitative accompagnato or recitative stromentato, which did much to break up the monotony and the predictability of dry, that is, harpsichord-accompanied, recitative followed by an orchestrally-accompanied aria.

Even more importantly, my friends, Gluck simplified his arias in order to make them more emotionally and dramatically direct and to limit the indiscriminate liberties taken by the singers. Gluck wrote this in 1766, in the preface to his opera *Alceste*,

> My intention was to purify music from all of the abuses, which have crept into Italian opera through the vanity of the singers and the excessive compliance of the composers, and have made the most splendid and beautiful of all arts the most ridiculous and boring. I tried, therefore, to bring musicians back to the real task of serving the poetry, by intensifying the expression of emotion and the appeal of every situation without interrupting the plot or weakening it by excessive ornamentation.

Gluck succeeds in doing what Metastasio attempted to do and failed; that is, he succeeded in controlling the singers to the degree that drama starts returning, first to his operas but then to other operas written by other people in the style of Gluck.

Since the beginning of Lecture 9, we have made a full circle. Monteverdi's *Orfeo* creates an art form and Gluck's *Orpheus ed Euridice* redefines it. Both operas seek in their own way to balance words and music, expression and emotion. Martin Cooper wrote in 1935 about this constant pendulum swing of operatic emphasis on words or music, on excess and reform. I quote Martin Cooper:

> Opera is constructed of three elements: the musical, the literary and the spectacular. And at different times, each of these three elements has, in fact, gained an undue supremacy over the others. For this reason the history of opera is the history of a series of reformations and counter-reformations, no two countries and no two epics agreeing on the role of each element and how they should ideally play in the constitution of the whole. Neither evolutionary nor unified, it is the history of perpetually recurring schools of thought, one never victorious over the other, though occasionally gaining the majority of popular opinion.

Gluck's operas, as I said before, are the first operas or the oldest operas that are still repertoire in the modern opera house. His operas also become the essential models for the next generation of opera composers. Of course, the greatest opera composer of the next generation is Johannes Wolfgang Christian Crysostomus Gottlieb Mozart, born 1756, died 1791. Mozart's

Idomeneo, Re de Crete, Idomeneo, The King of Crete, of 1780 is, for my money, the greatest opera seria of the eighteenth century, and it owes a great debt to Gluck. The libretto, written by Giambattista Varesco of Salzburg, is one of the old Metastasian types. It's built on a classical subject with amorous intrigues, but it includes within it some choruses in the newer style of Gluck. What makes *Idomeneo* really work is Mozart, and how Mozart treats these time-honored but no longer useful traditions of opera seria.

A few more words about Mozart and then we will take our break, wholly prepared to deal with *Idomeneo*. Mozart was one of the few great opera composers who was not an opera specialist. He lived at a very good time and place, because there were many different opera styles popular when Mozart was alive. For example, the old style opera seria, the reformed-style Italian opera of Gluck, the new comic Italian style called opera buffa, and even the German-language opera, singspiel, was evolving at this time. Mozart wrote operas, brilliant, superb operas, in all of these extant styles.

His first opera was *La Finta Semplice, The Pretended Simpleton*. It dates from 1768, when he was 12. At the age of 14, he composed his first opera seria, *Mitridate, King of Pontus*. Two years later he wrote another opera seria, *Lucio Silla*, which was also produced in Milan. By the way, both of these early opera seriae by Mozart were based on libretti by Metastasio. The opera buffa, *La Finta Giardiniera, The Pretended Gardner*, followed in 1775; Mozart would have been 19. The opera seria, *Il Re Pastore, The Shepherd King*, libretto by Metastasio, followed again in 1775. His next opera *Idomeneo*, written five years later at the age of 24, is Mozart's first great operatic masterwork.

When we return we will talk quickly about the story, the voice character of the main players and then we will sample a bit of Act Two of *Idomeneo* so that we can see: (a) where good opera seria can go, (b) if it's in the hands of someone like Mozart.

Thank you very much

The Growth of Opera, the Development of Italian Opera Seria, and Mozart's *Idomeneo*, IV
Lecture 12—Transcript

Welcome back to "How to Listen to and Understand Opera." This is Lecture 12, the fourth lecture in a set entitled "The Growth of Opera, the Development of Italian Opera Seria, and Mozart's Idomeneo." That is indeed exactly where we left off. We've worked our way up through the growth of opera, the development of opera seria, and now we are about to talk about Mozart's Idomeneo. A limited discussion indeed, but enough that we can get an idea why this is such a transcendently good opera compared to so much of the dross that passes for opera seria. So, we will call Idomeneo "opera seria transcendent."

Quickly, the outlines of the story: The action takes place in Crete, ten years after the conclusion of the Trojan War. First, let's talk about the love triangle. We meet Ilia at the very beginning of this opera. Ilia is the daughter of King Priam, king of Troy, who was sent to Crete as a prisoner. On arriving in Crete, Ilia was shipwrecked and she was rescued in one of those marvelous little serendipitous things that always happen in opera but rarely in real life: She was rescued by Idamante, the prince and heir to the Cretan throne. Now despite Ilia's hatred for the Greeks—and she should hate them; they destroyed her homeland, they destroyed her family, they kept her prisoner—despite her hatred for the Greeks, she has fallen in love with Idamante, which has filled her with tremendous guilt and self-loathing.

Ilia is about 19 or 20 years old and she is a soprano, generally a lyric soprano. A point I should make; singers sometimes have smaller voices versus larger voices. We could say that a certain singer, for example, someone like Maria Callas—a very famous dramatic soprano—we could say generally everything she's going to sing would be a dramatic soprano voice. However, we could also say that certain roles are lyric roles and certain roles are dramatic roles. The role of Ilia is a lyric role. Mozart reserves some of his most graceful and melodic music for her, whereas for Electra, some of the most, if you'll excuse me, electrifying and dramatic music. The role itself defines the way the singer will sound, not just the inherent qualities of the singer's voice. The role of Ilia is essentially a lyric soprano role. Idamante, the young prince who rescued her, is about 21 or 22 years old, and his part was originally written for a castrato named Vincenzo dal Prato. So, Idamante is also a soprano.

Electra is the third member of our love triangle. She's living in Crete and is still grieving for her father and her brother. She is vindictive, hysterical and, as we know, very close to insanity. She is also in love with Idamante. Of course, when this piece was originally performed in Munich in 1780 there would not have been a problem figuring out the genders of everyone, despite the fact that all three members of this triangle are sopranos, because the male soprano would simply sound different from the other sopranos. By the way, if you wanted a male to sound young, that's why you would have a male soprano. Ideally this would be a youngish male part. However, on a modern recording, this is going to be a problem because, let's say we have a female soprano singing the part of Idamante, which is common. Who's who on a recording? You don't have the advantage of seeing someone on stage dressed as a man. Instead we're just listening to three sopranos, all singing about how they love each other and blending into each other, and it's hard to keep track.

By the way, I should mention, there's such a thing as a "trouser role." That's a phrase we hear here and there, "trouser role." A trouser role is a part being sung by a woman that was created for a man, so she's wearing trousers when she sings it. Idamante is such a part. If it's sung by a woman today, she'll be dressed as a man. It's a trouser role. In the recording we're going to listen to, gratefully, Idamante is going to be sung by a tenor. This will happen as often as not in the opera house today, that the previously male soprano part will be sung an octave lower by a tenor and we won't have the gender problems, especially on a recording, that otherwise we would have. It can be very, very confusing.

Here's the situation on which the plot of the opera turns. Idomeneo, who is a dramatic tenor, is the king of Crete, and he's shipwrecked on his return from Troy. Like Snake Pliskin, everybody thinks he's dead. Idomeneo is not dead. He's made a bargain with Neptune, promising to sacrifice the first person that he, Idomeneo sees once he emerges from the surf and steps, once again, onto his beloved ground of Crete. Idomeneo, I would tell you, is filled with guilt and self-loathing over this dishonorable arrangement.

I imagine you've all guessed it already. Who's the first person that Idomeneo sees when he emerges from the surf? His own son, Idamante, who comes to comfort this shipwrecked soldier coming out of the water. They haven't seen each other for 20 years, really since Idamante was an infant, so there's no reason why either should recognize each other. When they finally do identify themselves, Idamante attempts to embrace his father: "Dad, Dad, you're alive!" Idomeneo, for his part, flees in horror. Like Abraham, he realizes he must sacrifice his own son to appease the gods. Idamante, for his part, is filled with guilt and self-loathing over whatever insult made his father run off from him. This is Freudian, my friends. Everybody hates themselves in this opera. It's most interesting.

Idomeneo dawdles. He doesn't want to have his son killed. Until finally, halfway through Act Two, he decides to renege entirely on his promise to Neptune. Get this, this is how he figures he's going to get out of the problem. He's going to put Idamante and Electra on a boat back to Electra's home country of Argos, way off on the Greek mainland. He'll spirit him away, and that way Neptune can't do anything to him. Please, think about this. He's going to put his son, whom Neptune, the god of the sea, wants dead, in a boat on the open sea. Veeeery clever, Idomeneo. That's real thinking. One wonders if Idomeneo left a couple of arrows from his quiver back in Troy. Obviously, this is not going to work; and it doesn't.

For her part, Electra is overjoyed. She doesn't know anything—neither does anyone else—about this pact that Idomeneo has made with Neptune. All she knows is that she's going to have Idamante on the proverbial slow boat to Argos, finally away from Ilia. Anything can happen on that boat, and she is just filled with joy. She can't wait. She is virtually quivering, she's so excited. She sings in this aria—and this doesn't sound like the crazed Electra we've already met. The crazed Electra is still in the future, when she completely loses out, but now she's filled with sexual and emotional anticipation.

> I leave, but will the one object I love and adore, o gods, come with me? Ah, there is not room in my heart for such great joy! Away

from my rival, I shall well succeed, with cunning and with flattery, so that the fire, which once I could not extinguish, will no longer burn for her, but instead will flame for me. Love that is close at hand will prove stronger than passion at a distance; love is more effective when one is near the beloved.

Yes indeed, she has every intention of making Idamante fall for her. With Ilia left on Crete, she on the boat with Idamante, anything can, and in her imagination, will happen.

We're going to start listening from the very conclusion of this aria when Electra is singing, "when one is near the beloved," *"s' è vicin l'amante cor,"* and then we're going to continue listening. Here's what will happen immediately as this aria concludes. As Electra reaches the conclusion, we hear a wind, brass, and percussion band playing the next number, a march, in the distance. Then Electra says, "I hear in the distance the sweet sound, summoning me to go aboard." She exits in great haste and great excitement. The band, march music, which we've been hearing from the distance, grows louder as the scene changes. We arrive with Electra and the new scene at a busy harbor populated by townsfolk, soldiers, and sailors. Then the band stops, and Electra bids farewell to Crete in a dry recitative: "Shores of Sidon, you were the cause of my tears of sorrow and of love! Oh cruel, inimical place…I leave you finally, and bid you my last *addio*, my last farewell."

This is what we will listen to, and here's what I want you to be aware of. We have an absolutely effortless, seamless segue. I will use that word a lot, "segue." I should make sure we all know where it comes from. It comes from the Italian *"seguire,"* which means to connect. A segue is a connection between two otherwise unlike parts. When we talk about segues, we talk about this sort of connection. I want you to notice the effortless, seamless segue from the end of Electra's aria overlapping with the march. The march gets louder, the scene changes. The march is continuous, so we've had a continuous bit of music through the scene change; and then her recitative. Nonstop music, everything carefully connected, none of it predictable. No apparent breaks in the musical fabric.

(musical example)

Immediately following the end of this recitative, we have a choral number; that is, the chorus comes in and sings, almost prayerfully, the following. "The sea is calm; Let us go, everything is reassuring, we shall have good fortune; now, let us leave quickly!"

Electra comes in and sings. "Sweet breezes, be the only ones to blow; calm the anger of the north wind; be kind with your gentle breezes, spread love everywhere." Is this our Electra? Yes, it is. It's when she still thinks she has a chance. Then the chorus comes back in and repeats its opening phrase. "The sea is calm; Let us go, everything is reassuring, we shall have good fortune; now, let us leave quickly." The peaceful calm of the sea is a thinly veiled metaphor for Electra's own very unaccustomed calm. This gentle and idyllic music is literally the calm before the storm. It's filled with inspired effects. Sustained flutes create gentle breezes when *zeffiri*, zephyrs, are evoked. We have a kind of rocking, triple meter, *dum-dum-dum, dum-dum-dum*, that's meant to invoke the gentle voyage on a calm and happy sea.

After this conclusion of this combination chorus and aria of Electra, we again have no break between segments. Suddenly an allegro, which means a fast outburst, accompanies the last line of the chorus. Idomeneo hurries forward and begins a dry recitative. He turns to Idamante, Idomeneo does, and says, "Go, prince." Idamante responds, "O heavens!" because he doesn't want to leave and he doesn't know why he's being forced to leave—I have to get on the boat with her? In any case, Idomeneo says, "You linger too long." He thinks if he shoves Idamante on the boat and gets that boat kick-started that somehow they're just going to avoid old Neptune. "Leave now, and let a thousand of your heroic exploits announce your return and your fame: If you wish to learn the art of ruling, begin by helping the unfortunate, and become more worthy of your father and of yourself." This Idomeneo was a blowhard, isn't he? "Become more worthy of your father." The father is not worthy of the son. But that's a different story entirely.

Having said all this, we're nevertheless going to go into a very long goodbye in the trio that follows. Again, I just want to listen to this segment: the chorus, followed with Electra, followed by the chorus again, and then that seamless merge into Idomeneo's dry recitative. By the way, the last chord of the recitative becomes the first chord of the trio that follows, so that will be segued into seamlessly also.

Let's listen to this and then I'm going to start drawing some quick conclusions about the nature of Mozart's opera seria.

(musical example)

On that final chord—that becomes the first chord of the following trio, which is where we cut it off. We will not listen to this following trio. I'll read through it. It's a long goodbye. It's very, very beautiful, but we're limited by our time together. Let's understand the important point now, because it should be forming in all of our minds. Where's the predictable pattern of recitative, aria, recitative, aria, that is opera seria? It sure is not here. Whatever Mozart's doing, it's going against the grain, and as a result we have a tremendous flexibility of different orchestral forces, different kinds of numbers, one piling on the other. A trio is very rare in opera seria. They're hard to write. They take time to write. They're hard to balance. It's not the kind of music we are accustomed to hearing in this more formulaic procedure. Mozart does it because, my friends, he can.

Idamante says, "Before leaving, allow me, o God, to place a kiss on the paternal hand."

Electra says to Idomeneo, "Let my lips express in parting the gratitude with which my heart is filled: farewell, noble king."

Idomeneo, maintaining this kind of formal behavior, "Go, good luck be with you; this is your destiny, my son. Fulfill our wishes, o heavens!"

Electra says, "How great are my hopes!"

And Idamante, "I go, but my heart remains here. Cruel destiny! O Ilia! O father! O departure!"

And then Idamante, Idomeneo and Electra say together, "O gods! What will happen?" That merges seamlessly into what happens next, which is the final moment of this second act. Suddenly and unexpectedly, *allegro con brio*, the music becomes stormy to indicate the emotions being felt and to presage what's about to come. We will pick up from the very end of the trio. This is more tempest music, like what we heard in that Vivaldi aria a lecture ago. Tempest music; that is, a storm in nature as a metaphor for an emotional storm in the hearts of people.

They all sing together, "Let this turbulence cease, Heaven's compassion will lend its hand." As they're about to embark on the boat, a storm suddenly springs upon them out of nowhere. Orchestral introduction, all hell breaks loose. Demonic rushing springs alternate with pulsing chords. We hear the piccolo screaming above our heads. This is not just a storm, my friends, it's a cataclysm. Quietly trembling strings are followed by an explosive entry by the chorus, who sings, "What new terror is this! What harsh roaring! The anger of the gods has made the sea violent. Neptune, have pity!" The ferocious orchestral storm, wide dynamic ranges, and huge chords fill the chorus with dreadful fear and energy.

The storm increases. We hear the sea rising in ever-higher melodic ideas, thunder and lightening. Then a terrible monster appears from out of the sea. It is Neptune's emissary. The chorus recognizes its appearance as a punishment intended for one or all of them; they don't know who. Only Idomeneo knows why this sea creature is there. The chorus sings, fearfully, "What hatred, what anger Neptune shows us; what is our fault, that the heavens become angry? Who is the guilty one?" Dramatically and repeatedly the chorus asks, "Who is the guilty one?"

That merges immediately into a recitative, but now accompanied by the full orchestra. No time to go back to just the harpsichord. It's Idomeneo, and he knows it's him, and he says, "You are after me, o cruel God! The guilty one! I alone sinned, punish me only, and let your anger fall on me. Let my death appease you; but if you insist on having a victim for my failing, I cannot give you an innocent one; you are unjust if you want him,…you have no claim upon him." For the first time in this opera, Idomeneo sounds powerful and heroic and utterly kingly. Finally, the wimpiness and fear that has characterized him to this point leaves, and he is once again a powerful monarch. I would tell you that this passage, this accompanied recitative, was originally intended by Varesco, the librettist, to be an aria. Mozart said, "No way. We need a recitative there." Aria would have stopped the action. Aria would have stopped the real-time continuity and forced the moment of reflection and repose. Mozart said, "No way." We do need action, we do need real time, we do need forward-moving music. It must be recitative. So recitative it is.

The orchestral storm continues. Meanwhile, the terrified chorus is frozen with fear. The storm rises inexorably around them. Their contrapuntal singing, weaving in and out, "*Corriamo, fuggiamo*," "Let us run, let us flee," seems to suggest huge waves breaking on the wharfs. Yes. "Let us run, let us flee from that pitiless monster! We are already prey! Ah, treacherous fate is more cruel than anything." Indeed, the people flee and as they do the storm fades into the distance. The act ends on a strangely quiet note, disturbingly quiet; as if, poof, it suddenly was gone. We know that monster's not gone yet.

We will listen, then, from the end of the trio, "Let this turbulence cease," through this sequence of extraordinary events; the coming of the storm, the explosion of the storm, the chorus's acknowledgement of the storm, the coming of the sea creature, Idomeneo's recitative, and then the chorus's final chorus, "Let us run, let us flee." Absolutely seamless, no breaks in the action, the momentum continuous, the music continuous. This is not, my friends, an opera seria.

(musical example)

Quiet and disquieting ending to this act notwithstanding, clearly Neptune has spoken. There will be no escape to Argos. Electra has been stymied and the beginning of her end is clear. Neptune's monster, instead, ravages the Cretan countryside until it is destroyed by, guess who? The young, brave prince, Idamante. Ultimately, both Idamante and Idomeneo will be pardoned by Neptune, but that is still far in the future of this opera.

I will leave the exact events that lead to that pardoning to you, for you to listen to this opera on your own, your hands glued to the translation of the libretto. It is a waste of time to put this music on in the background. Its pleasantries don't even approach the drama you can get and the joy you will receive if you read the translation while you listen. That's the point. Unless you are absolutely conversant in the rather stiff Italian that this opera is written in, I strongly recommend that you take that time and you sit down with the libretto. It's up to you to figure out why and how Idomeneo and Idamante get out of this fix.

Back to the second half of Act Two, which is what we've just been dealing with. Mozart has created a seamless, dramatic continuity, which seems to laugh in the face of opera seria convention. Where is the predictable pattern of dry recitative followed by *da capo* arias? Where is it? Well, it's not there. Instead, we get accompanied recitatives, which is something that Gluck, of course, showed Mozart how to do. We get orchestral transitions from scene to scene, like that march music. We get segues that pivot from the last chord of one set to the first chord of the next. We get a trio, very unusual in opera seria, and a very flexible use of the chorus.

This is really not behaving the way an opera seria should. In fact, really what makes *Idomeneo* a great, perhaps the greatest, opera seria, is that because of Mozart's music it doesn't behave like a dull, predictable opera seria. It's like celebrating a great cabernet by saying it doesn't taste like dishwater. Certainly, Mozart has taken a genre and has elevated it through his own music and his own inspiration. Of course, this is something that Mozart managed to do in almost every genre of music; that is, make it transcend what it was, due to his own actions and compositional gift.

In 1779, in reference to Italian opera seria, Samuel Johnson wrote this; the Italian opera is "an exotic and irrational entertainment." Well, thanks to Gluck and Mozart opera was no longer an exotic and irrational entertainment. The dark ages or the golden age, however you want to look at it, are now ended.

Onwards then to the rise of comic opera, opera buffa, and Mozart's *The Marriage of Figaro*, which will be Lectures 13 through 16. Before we pause, I have a soapbox to mount and just a brief discussion on the nature of opera and why we should listen to it.

Opera outside of Italy, and sometimes even within Italy, was essentially an aristocratic entertainment. It's something we talked about today. In our age of P.C. and proletariat diversity, some of us might ask ourselves, "Is this a good thing?" I mean, should we be listening to, celebrating, and reveling in this elitist, aristocratic music? I must share with all of you the following introductory paragraph I received as part of a proposal for a course on world music from a violinist, an earnest violinist that I know. Now, I quote:

> The classical tradition in Western music in Eurocentric culture is a dying, if not dead, tradition. The musical style of the standard repertoire grew out of a relentlessly dominating minority culture known as "imperialist Europe." Audiences and players are drawn to this essentially dead tradition as an escape from interactive values, interactive values which can properly be found in popular and world music cultures. We must reject the dead tissue of our elitist past and embrace the living traditions of the present, if we, as musicians and audiences, are to be relevant to our times.

This, *mes amis*, is a bunch of *merde*, of nonsense, of shoe-soiling doggy-doo, of garbage, Montezuma's revenge, a PC guilt-trip of the first order. When we marvel at the Parthenon, do we remind ourselves that it is the product of a patriarchal, femophobic, faux-democratic boys'-club regime? When we stand dumbstruck before Michelangelo's *Pietà*, do we ruminate upon the elitist, oppressive, Machiavellian, robber baron, mercantilistic ruling class that commissioned it? When we move and groove to really good down-and-dirty rock-and-roll, do we pause to reflect upon the grimy, stinking, tattooed, psychosexual drug-inspired environ that was its original milieu? When we stand in tears before the subtlety and power of a painting by Rembrandt, or Rubens, or Vermeer, do we give a rat's butt that this art "grew out of the relentlessly dominating minority culture known as imperialistic Europe?" No, we don't. We couldn't care less.

So why do some of us feel the need to flog and flay this marvelous and timeless musical heritage of ours because the circumstances surrounding some of its creation don't live up to our contemporary view of politically correct creational standards? We've got it backwards today. There's nothing wrong with the art—art created, incidentally, by middle class and working class individuals. There is clearly something wrong with some of us. If we as a culture, a civilization, cannot understand, and appreciate, and assimilate as our own, the crystalline life force and truth in the best art of our past, what does it say about us here today? Is Mozart's extraordinary insight into the human condition irrelevant to us because it was a product of imperialistic Europe? Or are some of us today just culturally and intellectually unworthy of it?

Let me put it this way: Let's pretend that in Josephine Vienna, between about 1780 and 1795, there was a PC movement to equalize the musical arts, to celebrate, let's say, beer-hall dance music at the expense of more elevated, elitist music. Wonderful. Today we would have scads of crummy, beer-hall dance music. Divorced from its social constituency, this repertoire would simply stand as a monument to drunkenness and bad taste. The great works of Mozart and Haydn and the young Beethoven might have gone unwritten for a simple lack of support and cultural interest. Not only would we today be denied this amazing legacy, but all the composers who've lived since the 1780s and 90s would have lacked the essential models for their own music; thereby altering profoundly, I fear for the much worse, the evolution of Western music.

If Mozart and Gluck and Wagner and Puccini and Monteverdi are dead art, I would suggest we've all forgotten how to properly live. In an age of talk shows that celebrate victims, some of us would actually seem to believe that we're the victims of a Eurocentric musical repertoire, iconographic of imperialism and repression. As if there's actually a cultural conspiracy out to get us. Makes you wonder where Oliver Stone stands on this. Of course, what should be important to us always is content, content, and content; and whether that content speaks to us.

Now back to opera. These works, these operas, these investigations through words and music into the hearts and souls of people are as relevant, as classic as the *Iliad*, as *The Canterbury Tales*, as *Tom Jones*—please, the book not the singer—*Catcher in the Rye*, and *Gravity's Rainbow*. I don't know about you, but their oppressive sins notwithstanding, I'm grateful to the aristocratic and clerical classes of Europe, and Asia, and Africa, and meso-America. Without them, much of the greatest art, music and architecture would simply never have been created. They had the time, they had the resources, they had the vision, for whatever selfish reasons, to cultivate and finance the work of great artists. I only wish that our financial aristocrats today were one-tenth as interested in our contemporary arts. There would be no crisis in the arts, as we know it today. The pluralism, which is central to our culture, would ensure that our new art would have a chance to become the province of the many, not just the few. Great opera, great art from the past is not elitist entertainment. It is for all of us, each and every one.

Off the soapbox. I thank you.

The Rise of Opera Buffa and Mozart's *The Marriage of Figaro*
Lectures 13–16

Comic opera—slapstick, satirical, often bawdy, and almost always irreverent—has had a very different history than that of serious opera or what we call opera seria. ... Comic opera has its roots in popular entertainment, and this is a huge and very enduring difference

Comic opera developed quite separately from opera seria, which was an entertainment of the aristocracy. Comic opera had its roots in popular entertainment. It grew out of comic musical entertainment that traveling musicians had staged since the Middle Ages. In 16th-century Italy, these developed into a tradition of traveling companies called commedia dell'arte. During the second half of the 17th century, comic interludes, drawn from the situations and characters of commedia dell'arte, were inserted between the acts of serious operas. By the end of the 18th century, the once lowbrow comic intermezzi had developed into the dominant operatic genre of opera buffa.

Comic opera/opera buffa grew out of the Enlightenment, with its emphasis on popular, nonelitist art and its spirit of dramatic and musical naturalism. The melodic content of the new opera buffa reflected the more natural, populist, melodic spirit of Classical-era Enlightenment music.

To understand opera buffa more fully, we will compare two musical examples: "Siam navi all'onde algenti" from Vivaldi's *L'Olimpiade* (1734) and "Non più andrai" from Mozart's *The Marriage of Figaro* (1786). Vivaldi's music is highly artificial and extreme in its use of embellishments and in its sentiments. Mozart's music is far more natural-sounding.

This new, Enlightenment-inspired music, with its focus on accessible melodies, is known as the Classical style. It is classical in the ancient Greek sense because of its clarity of line, balanced structures, emotional restraint, and elegance.

Opera buffa also was affected by the political conditions of its time. By the mid-18th century, Baroque opera seria came to represent the old, elite, aristocratic order. Its main elements were formulaic use of recitative and aria—they followed one another predictably; grandiose and expensive productions; libretti based on ancient history and mythology; stiff, overblown characters; and da capo arias, with very few ensembles and almost no choruses. The predictability of the arias led to abuses by the singers. Enlightenment philosophers and artists saw opera buffa—with its accessible melodies, small casts, and everyday dramatic situations—as the ideal opera for the new spirit of the Enlightenment. Jean-Jacques Rousseau (1712–1778) took the lead in this rejection of Baroque opera seria. He and his followers embraced Giovanni Pergolesi's *La serva padrona* as the new ideal for opera.

Almost by their nature … opera buffa plots were politicized in an era when class distinctions underwent profound reexamination.

La serva padrona (1733) is early opera buffa. It began as an intermezzo, although it was later performed as an opera. Typical of the early version of its genre, it features lively, catchy music in which no particular formulas are followed. It also features a cast of only three characters: Serpina (soprano), Uberto (bass) and Vespone (mute). The plot involves a simple ruse by which a servant (Serpina) tricks an old bachelor (Uberto) into marriage. A musical example is the recitative and aria, "Son imbrogliato io già."

Even as it evolved, opera buffa continued to use commedia dell'arte character archetypes. The most significant character division in opera buffa is between savvy, street-smart servants and members of the lower class, on the one hand, and blundering, pompous aristocrats, merchants, doctors, and lawyers, on the other. Almost by their nature, then, opera buffa plots were politicized in an era when class distinctions underwent profound reexamination.

Mozart wrote many operas buffa. In his youth he wrote *La finta semplice* (1768) and *La finta giardiniera* (1775). He created his best known and most esteemed works with librettist Lorenzo da Ponte, a brilliant and controversial figure. Da Ponte remains, along with Metastasio, Boito and Hofmannsthal, one of the great librettists in opera history. The works that he and Mozart developed together include *The Marriage of Figaro* (1786), *Don Giovanni* (1787), and *Così fan tutte* (1789).

We will look at *The Marriage of Figaro* in greater detail. Its basic story line is adapted from two plays by the French dramatist Pierre de Beaumarchais (1732–1799): *The Barber of Seville* (1772) and *The Marriage of Figaro* (1784). In *The Barber of Seville* we meet a young Count Almaviva, who, with the help of his former valet Figaro, wins and weds the young and cunning Rosina. This play concludes with the count's renunciation of his feudal right to deflower any maiden in his service on her wedding night. The *Marriage of Figaro* takes place three years later. The count has become a shameless philanderer. Rosina (the countess) is wise beyond her years. Figaro is to marry Susanna, whom the count intends to bed before her marriage. The action of the play (and opera) revolves around the count's determination to seduce Susanna, and Figaro and Susanna's determination to marry before he can force the issue.

Beaumarchais' play was a clear attack on the French aristocracy. The play was initially banned in France and permanently banned in Austria. Da Ponte's libretto removed much of what was politically offensive (although Mozart's music puts much of it back in!).

Our game plan in discussing this play will involve two components. First, we will meet the main characters and observe Mozart's incredible musical portraiture. Second, we will observe the quintessence of Mozart's dramatic craft by examining the Act 2 finale.

We will begin our discussion of Act 1 of *The Marriage of Figaro* by considering some musical examples. First, the overture; this is a perfect combination of great musical substance and great musical beauty. Also, the opera opens with a duet for Figaro and Susanna, "Cinque, dieci, venti," that is memorable for the way Mozart conveys perfect harmony between Susanna and Figaro by writing their music in thirds and sixths. Susanna tells her fiancé Figaro that Count Almaviva is planning to seduce her: no. 2 (duet), "Se a caso madama." In his recitative, "Bravo, signor padrone!" and his cavatina, "Se vuol ballare," Figaro shows his determination to outwit the count.

Dr. Bartolo and Marcellina are introduced. Dr. Bartolo is the former guardian of Rosina. He had planned to marry Rosina himself, but was thwarted by Figaro and Count Almaviva. (The role of Dr. Bartolo is sung by a bass, in the Italian tradition of assigning the bass voice to older men and villains.) Marcellina is Bartolo's former maid. She once lent Figaro money and this loan has now come due. Figaro promised to marry Marcellina if he could not repay the loan. Figaro and Susanna are planning to repay the loan with the dowry to be given them by the count. For their own personal reasons, Dr. Bartolo and Marcellina want Figaro to fail to repay the loan. The relevant musical example here is no. 4 (aria) "La vendetta."

We will now examine the ways in which the characters in *The Marriage of Figaro* are, and are not, archetypes of commedia dell'arte. First, the inspiration for Dr. Bartolo comes from Pantalone, a character who prides himself on being an expert on many subjects, but one who actually knows very little and is always being caught out. The character of Figaro on the other hand is based on harlequin, an athletic, graceful, cunning valet and ladies' man, who claims noble birth. Rosina's character comes from Colombina, a pretty, young girl with a sharp wit and an acid tongue. Marcellina is the only character not based on commedia dell'arte. She is an old, rapacious spinster, inspired by a character in classic Roman comedies.

Cherubino, an oversexed adolescent, is introduced. Mozart's depicts his character in an aria brilliantly evocative of a breathless, love-sick adolescent: no. 6 (aria) "Non so più cosa son." The predatory and unscrupulous Count Almaviva is also introduced with "Ah, no Susanna."

The count decides that Cherubino is getting in his way and tries to pack him off to the army. Figaro sings a satirical farewell to Cherubino. He paints a dire picture of life in the army in the hope of dissuading Cherubino from leaving. He needs the boy as an ally in his plan to thwart the count's designs on Susanna. Figaro's aria, "Non più andrai," (in rondo form) is what first made this opera a success.

In Act 2 of *The Marriage of Figaro*, the countess (Rosina) is introduced. Still very young, and wise beyond her years, she prays for the return of her philandering husband's affections in one of Mozart's most beautiful and moving arias, "Porgi amor." As a result of various intrigues, the count becomes convinced that the countess is having an affair. He is incensed and determined to learn the truth.

An opera buffa finale is itself conceived as a miniature comedy. Mozart's Act 2 finale is in eight distinct parts, 20 minutes (or so) of continuous music. In Part 1, the count is convinced that Cherubino and the countess have been having an affair and that Cherubino is hiding in the countess's closet. At this point there are two characters onstage: the count and countess. In Part 2, the count discovers, to his surprise, not Cherubino but Susanna in the closet. In Part 3, the mood completely changes as the count calms down and asks for his wife's forgiveness, and in Parts 4 and 5, Figaro enters and there are now four characters onstage. The mood grows quieter as the count tries to figure out what is going on. He questions Figaro about an anonymous note he received, but Figaro refuses to answer. In Part 6, Antonio, the gardener, enters the scene. We now have a quintet. Antonio unwittingly stirs up more trouble when he complains that someone jumped out of a window and ruined his flowerbed. This is followed by Parts 7 and 8, in which the comic confusion increases and the dramatic and musical tension comes to a climax with the entrance of Don Basilio, Dr. Bartolo, and Marcellina, who has come to claim Figaro as her husband! We now have seven characters onstage singing their own lines simultaneously in a variety of ensembles and solos.

The Act 2 finale is a brilliant continuous sequence of ensembles of increasingly long, separate musical lines, all coming together. Only a great writer of symphonies or string quartets could have written this finale, which is equally remarkable for its dramatic power. Mozart's music enhances dramatic momentum and creates a whole new drama of underlying subtleties and truths not revealed in the libretto.

Mozart's operas are not "easy-listening." They require our total involvement. Nor were they considered easy to listen to in Mozart's own time. His characters live and breathe; his music imbues them with an extraordinary range of moods, emotions, subtlety, unconscious motivation, and humanity. ■

Orfeo
(1607)
Claudio Monteverdi

Libretto by Alessandro Striggio

ACT TWO

Orfeo

Tu se' morta, mia vita, ed io
respiro? Tu se' da me partita per
mai più non tornare, ed io rimango?
No, che se i versi alcuna cosa
ponno, n'andrò sicuro a' più
profondi abissi, e, intenerito il cor
del re de l'ombre,
meco trarrotti a riveder le stelle;
o, se ciò negherammi empio
destino, rimarrò teco in
compagnia de morte.
Addio terra, addio cielo e sole,
addio.

Orpheus

You are dead, my life, and I am
breathing? You have left me,
nevermore to return, and I remain?
No, no, if my verses have any
power at all, I will surely go down
to the deepest abysses, and, having
softened the heart of the King of
Shadows; lead you back with me to
see the stars; or, if impious fate
denies me this, I shall remain with
you in the company of death.
Farewell earth, farewell sky and sun,
farewell.

Orfeo ed Euridice
(1762)
Christoph Willibald von Gluck

Libretto by Raniero da Calzabigi

ACT ONE

Orfeo

Chiamo il mio ben cosi
quando si mostra il di,
quando s'asconde.
Ma, oh vano mio dolor!
l'idolo del mio cor

Orpheus

Thus I call upon my love
at break of day
and at its fading.
But—alas, how vain my sorrow!—
my heart's idol

non mi risponde. Euridice! Euridice! ombra cara, ah, dove sei nascosta? Affannato il tuo sposo fedele invano sempre ti chiama, agli dei ti ridomanda, e sparge ai venti con le lagrime sue invan i suoi lamenti. Cerco il mio ben così in queste, ove morì, funeste sponde. Ma sola al mio dolor perchè conobbe amor, l'eco risponde. Euridice! Euridice! Ah! questo nome sanno le spiaggie, e le selve l'appresero da me! Per ogni valle risuona: in ogni tronco scrisse il misero Orfeo de mano tremolante: Euridice non è più, ed io vivo ancora! Dei, datele nuova vita, uccidetemi! Piango il mio ben così se il sole indora il dì, se va nell'onde. Pietoso al pianto mio va mormorando il rio, e mi risponde. Numi! barbari numi, d'Acheronte e d'Averno pallido abitator, la di cui mano avida delle morti mai disarmò mai trattener non seppe beltà nè gioventù,	answers me not. Eurydice, Eurydice, beloved shade, alas, where are you hidden? Your faithful spouse in anguish calls you ceaselessly in vain, begs your return of the gods and vainly scatters to the winds his tears and lamentations. Thus I seek my love upon these sad shores where, alas, she died! But to my grief Echo alone replies, for she knew love. Eurydice! Eurydice! Oh, our shores know that name and the woods have learned it of me! Through every valley it re-echoes: on every treetrunk the wretched Orpheus has writ with trembling hand: Eurydice is no more, whilst I yet live! Give her new life, you gods, kill me! Thus do I weep for my love, whether the sun makes golden the day, whether it sinks into the sea. Touched by my tears the river murmurs and answers me. Gods, barbarous gods, of Acheron and Avernus wan inhabitant, whose hand, greedy for deaths, nor youth nor beauty has ever known how to subdue or restrain,

voi mi rapiste	you have carried off
la mia bella Euridice—	my fair Eurydice from me—
oh memoria crudel!—	oh cruel remembrance!—
sul fior degli anni!	in the flower of her youth!
La rivoglio da voi,	I want her back from you,
numi tiranni!	tyrant gods!
Ho core anch'io	I, too, have the courage,
per ricercar sull'orme	following in the footsteps
de' più intrepidi eroi,	of the bravest heroes,
nel vostro orrore	to seek my wife, my sole delight,
la mia sposa, il mio ben!	in your horrid realm!

La Griselda
(1721)

Alessandro Scarlatti

Libretto by Apostolo Zeno

Griselda

A
Mi rivedi o selva ombrosa,
Ma non più Regina e sposa,
Sventurata, disprezzata
Pastorella.

B
È pur quello il patrio monte,
Questa è pur l'amica fonte,
Quello è il prato e questo è il rio;
E sol io non son più quella.

A' (da capo)
Mi rivedi o selva ombrosa,
etc.

Griselda

A
You see me again, o shady forest,
but no longer queen and bride;
unfortunate, disdained,
a shepherdess.

B
Yet there is my homeland's
mountain and here is still the
friendly fountain; there is the
meadow and this is the river;
And only I am not the same.

A' (da capo)
You see me again, o shady forest,
etc.

L'Olimpiade
(1734)
Antonio Vivaldi
Libretto by Pietro Metastasio

Recitative

Tra le follie diverse de quai ripieno
è il mondo chi pùo negar, che la
follia maggiore in ciascuno non sia
quella d'amore.

Of all the many follies of which
the world is full, who can deny
that the greatest folly in
anyone is that of love.

Aria

𝐴
Siam navi all'onde algenti
lasciate in impetuosi
venti i nostri affetti sono,
ogni diletto è scoglio,
tutta la vita un mar.
𝐵
Ben qual nocchiero in noi
veglia ragion ma poi
pur dal'ondoso orgoglio
si lascia trasportar.
𝐴' (da capo)
Siam navi all'onde algenti,
etc.

𝐴
We are like ships on the silver
waves, drifting out of control;
like capricious winds are our
affections, every pleasure is a rock,
the whole of life a sea.
𝐵
Like a steersman reason
keeps good watch over us, but then
on the swell of pride
we let ourselves be carried away.
𝐴' (da capo)
We are like ships on the silver waves,
etc.

Die Zauberflöte
The Magic Flute (1791)
Wolfgang Amadeus Mozart
Libretto by Emanuel Schikaneder

NO. 14 ARIA "Der Hölle Rache"

Königin	**Queen**
Der Hölle Rache kocht in meinem Herzen, Tod und Verzweiflung flammet um mich her! Fühlt nicht durch dich Sarastro Todesschmerzen, so bist du meine Tochter nimmermehr.	The wrath of hell within my breast I cherish; death, desperation prompt the oath I swore. If by your hand Sarastro does not perish, then as my child I shall know you nevermore.
Verstossen sei auf ewig, verlassen sie auf ewig, Zertrümmert sei'n auf ewig alle Bande der Natur, wenn nicht durch dich Sarastro wird erblassen! Hört! Rachegötter! Hört der Mutter Schwur! *(Exit.)*	Abandoned be forever, forsaken be forever, and shattered be forever all the force of nature's tie, if not through you Sarastro's life be taken! Hark! Gods of vengeance, hear a mother's cry! *(Exit.)*

Otello
(1886)
Giuseppe Verdi
Libretto by Arrigo Boito

ACT ONE

Otello	**Othello**
Esultate! L'orgoglio musulmano sepolto è in mar; nostra e del ciel è gloria! Dop l'armi lo vinse l'uragano.	Rejoice! The Mussulman's pride is buried in the sea; ours and heaven's is the glory! After our arms the storm defeated him.

Idomeneo

(1780)

Wolfgang Amadeus Mozart

Libretto by G.B. Varesco

ACT TWO

Recitative (accompanied)

Elettra

Parto, e l'unico oggetto ch'amo
ed adoro, o Dei! meco s'en vien?
Ah, troppo angusto è
il mio cor a tanta gioja!
Lunge della rivale farò ben io,
con vezzi, e con lusinghe, che quel
foco, che pria spegnere non potei,
a quei lumi s'estingua,
e avvampi ai miei.
Scaccierà vicino ardore dal tuo sen
l'ardor lontano; più la mano può
d'amore s' è vicin l'amante cor.

Electra

I leave, but will the one object I love
and adore, o gods, come with me?
Ah, there is not room
in my heart for such great joy!
Away from my rival, I shall well
succeed, with cunning and with
flattery, so that the fire,
which once I could not extinguish,
will no longer burn for her,
but instead will flame for me.
Love that is close at hand will prove
stronger than passion at a distance;
love is more effective when one is
near the beloved.

NO. 14 MARCIA

Odo da lunge armonioso suono, che
mi chiama all'imbarco, orsù si vada.
(She exits.)

I hear in the distance the sweet
sound, summoning me to go aboard.
(She exits.)

Recitative (secco)

Elettra

Sidonie sponde, o voi per me
di pianto e duol, d'amor!
Nemico crudo ricetto,
or ch'astro più clemente
a voi me toglie, io vi perdono,
e in pace allieto partir mio
alfin vi lascio e do l'estremo addio.

Electra

Shores of Sidon, you were the cause
of my tears of sorrow and of love!
Oh cruel, inimical place, now
that a more compassionate star
takes me from you, I forgive you,
and, departing in peace and
gladness, I leave you finally, and
bid you my last farewell.

NO. 15 CHORUS

Coro

𝐴
Placido è il mar;
andiamo, tutto ci rassicura,
felice avrem ventura,
sù, sù, partiamo or' or!

Elettra

𝐵
Soavi Zeffiri, soli spirate,
del freddo borea l'ira calmate,
d'aura piacevole cortesi siate,
se da voi spargesi per tutto amor.

Coro

𝐴'
Chorus sings a varied repetition of 1st verse

Chorus

𝐴
The sea is calm;
Let us go, everything is reassuring,
we shall have good fortune;
now, let us leave quickly!

Electra

𝐵
Sweet breezes, be the only ones to
blow; calm the anger of the cold
north wind; be kind with your
gentle breezes, spread love
everywhere.

Chorus

𝐴'
Chorus sings a varied repetition of 1st verse

Recitative (secco)

Idomeneo

Vatene prence.

Idamante

O ciel!

Idomeneo

Troppo t'arresti.
Parti, e non dibbia fama,
di mille eroiche
imprese il tuo
ritorno prevenga:
di regnare se l'arte
apprender vuoi, ora
incomincia a renderti
de'miseri il sostegno,
del padre, e di te stesso
ognor più degno.

Idomeneo

Go, prince.

Idamante

O heavens!

Idomeneo

You linger too long.
Leave now, and let a
thousand of your heroic
exploits announce your
return and your fame:
If you wish to learn the art
of ruling, begin
by helping the
unfortunate, and become more
worthy of your father and
of yourself.

NO. 16 TERZETTO

Idamante
Pria di partir, o Dio! soffri,
che un bacio imprima sulla
paterna man.

Elettra
Soffri che un grato addio sul
labbro il cor esprima: addio,
degno sovran.

Idomeneo
Vanne, sarai felice;
Figlio, tua sorte è questa.
Seconda i voti o ciel!

Idomeneo, Idamante, Electra
Seconda i voti o ciel!

Elettra
Quanto sperar mi lice!

Idamante
Vado, e il mio cor qui resta.

Idamante, Elettra, Idomeneo
Addio!

Idamante, Idomeneo
Destin crudel!

Idamante
(aside)
O Ilia! O padre! O partenza!

Idomeneo, Idamante, Elettra
O dei! Che sarà?
Deh cessi il scompiglio, del ciel
la clemenza sua man porgerà.

Idamante
Before leaving, allow me, o God,
to place a kiss on the
paternal hand.

Electra
Let my lips express in parting the
gratitude with which my heart is
filled: farewell, noble king.

Idomeneo
Go, good luck be with you;
this is your destiny, my son.
Fulfill our wishes, o heavens!

Idomeneo, Idamante, Electra
Fulfill our wishes, o heavens!

Electra
How great are my hopes!

Idamante
I go, but my heart remains here.

Idamante, Idomeneo, Electra
Adieu!

Idamante, Idomeneo
Cruel destiny!

Idamante
(aside)
O Ilia! O father! O departure!

Idomeneo, Idamante, Electra
O gods! What will happen?
Let this turbulence cease, Heaven's
compassion will lend its hand.

ORCHESTRAL INTRODUCTION

NO. 17 CHORUS

Coro	Chorus
Qual nuovo terrore!	What new terror is this!
Qual rauco mugito!	What harsh roaring!
De' Numi il furore ha il	The anger of the gods has made
mar infierito. Nettuno, mercè!	the sea violent. Neptune, have pity!
Qual'odio, qual' ira nettuno ci	What hatred, what anger Neptune
mostra, se il cielo s'adira, qual	shows us; what is our fault, that
colpa è la nostra?	the heavens become angry?
Il reo qual' è?	Who is the guilty one?

Recitative (accompanied)

Idomeneo	Idomeneo
Eccoti in me, barbaro Nume!	You are after me, o cruel God!
Il reo! Io solo errai,	The guilty one! I alone sinned,
me sol punisci,	punish me only,
E cada sopra di me il tuo sdegno.	and let your anger fall on me.
La mia morte ti sazi alfin;	Let my death appease you;
Ma se altra aver pretendi	but if you insist on having
vittima al fallo mio.	a victim for my failing,
Una innocente darti io non posso,	I cannot give you an innocent one;
e se pur tu la vuoi . . . ih giusto sei,	you are unjust if you want him, . . .
pretenderla non puoi.	you have no claim upon him.

NO. 18 CHORUS

Coro	Chorus
Corriamo, fuggiamo quel mostro	Let us run, let us flee from that
spietato! Ah, preda gia siamo!	pitiless monster! Ah, we are
Chi, perfido fato,	already prey! Who, treacherous
più crudo è di te?	fate, is more cruel than you?

L'Olimpiade
(1734)
Antonio Vivaldi
Libretto by Pietro Metastasio

Aria

Siam navi all'onde algenti	We are like ships on the silver
lasciate in impetuosi venti	waves, drifting out of control; like
i nostri affetti sono,	capricious winds are our
ogni diletto è scoglio,	affections, every pleasure is a rock,
tutta la vita un mar.	the whole of life a sea.

Le nozze di Figaro
The Marriage of Figaro (1786)
Wolfgang Amadeus Mozart
Libretto by Lorenzo da Ponte

No. 9 Aria

Figaro

A
Non più andrai,
farfallone amoroso,
notte e giorno d'intorno girando,
delle belle turbando il riposo,
Narcisetto, Adoncino d'amor.
B
Non più avrai questi bei pennacchini,
quel cappello leggero e galante,
quella chioma, quell'aria brillante,
quel vermiglio donnesco color!
Non più avrai, *etc.*
A
Non più andrai, *etc.*

Figaro

A
You'll go no more,
amorous butterfly,
flitting about, night and day,
disturbing ladies' rest,
little Narcissus, Adonis of love.
B
You'll wear no more these plumes,
that smart and jaunty cap,
those curls, that dashing air,
that pink, effeminate complexion!
You'll wear no more, *etc.*
A
You'll go no more, *etc.*

La serva padrona
The Maid-Mistress (1733)
Giovanni Pergolesi
Libretto by Gennaro Antonio Federico

Uberto
Or indovino, chi sarà costui!
Forse la penitenza farà cosi.
Di quant'ella
ha fatto al padrone;
s'è ver, come mi dice,
un tal marito la terrà fra
la terra ed il bastone.
Ah, poveretta lei!
Per altro io penserei . . .
ma ella è serva . . .
ma il primo non saresti . . .
Dunque, la sposeresti?
Basta . . . oh! no, no, non sia.
Su, pensieri ribaldi, andate via!
Piano, io me l'ho allevata:
sò poi com'ella è nata . . .
Eh! Che sei matto!
Piano di grazia,
eh non pensare affatto.
Ma io ci ho passione, e pur . . .
quella meschina . . .
Eh torna . . .
Oh Dio! . . . e siam da capo . . .
Oh . . . che confusione!

Son imbrogliato io già,
ho un certo chè nel core,
che dir per me non so,
s'è amore o sè pietà.
Sent'un che poi mi dice:
Uberto, pensa a te.
Io sto fra il sì e 'l no,

Uberto
Now I can guess who it will be!
Perhaps this will be her penance.
He will do to her what
she's done to me.
If what she told me is true,
a husband like him will keep her
between the earth and a stick.
Poor thing, she is!
Otherwise I might think of . . .
but she is a servant . . .
but I would not be the first . . .
Would you marry her, then?
Enough . . . oh no, no it can't be.
Irresponsible thoughts, get lost!
Control yourself, I raised her myself.
I know how she was born . . .
How crazy you are!
Easy now, please,
think no more about it.
Still, I feel a passion for her . . .
that rotten creature . . .
And yet . . .
Oh God! . . . here I go again . . .
Oh . . . what confusion!

I am all mixed up.
I have a certain ache in my heart.
Honestly, I cannot tell
whether it's love or pity.
Common sense tells me:
Uberto, think of yourself.
I am between yes and no, between

fra il voglio e fra il non	wanting her and not wanting her,
voglio, e sempre più m'imbroglio,	and I get more confused
ah misero infelice,	all the time, miserable fellow.
che mai sarà de me!	What ever will become of me!

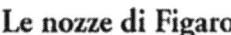

Le nozze di Figaro
The Marriage of Figaro (1786)
Wolfgang Amadeus Mozart
Libretto by Lorenzo da Ponte

ACT ONE

NO. 1 DUETTINO

A half-furnished room with a large armchair center. Figaro is measuring the floor; Susanna is trying on a hat in front of a mirror.

Figaro

Cinque... dieci... venti
trenta... trentasei... quarantatre.

Susanna

Ora sì, ch'io son contenta,
sembra fatto inver per me.

Figaro

Cinque...

Susanna

Guarda un po', mio caro Figaro...

Figaro

... dieci...

Susanna

... Quarda un po', *etc.*

Figaro

Five... ten... twenty
thirty... thirty-six... forty-three.

Susanna

Now I'm pleased with it, yes,
it seems made just for me.

Figaro

Five...

Susanna

Take a look, my dear Figaro...

Figaro

... ten...

Susanna

... Take a look, *etc.*

Figaro

... venti, *etc.*

Susanna

Guarda adesso il mio cappello, ...

Figaro

... quantantatre.

Susanna

Guarda un po', mio caro Figaro,
guarda adesso il mio cappello.

Figaro

Sì, mio core, or è più bello,
sembra fatto inver per te.

Susanna

Guarda un po', ...

Figaro

Sì, mio core, *etc.*

Susanna

... Ora sì, ch'io son contenta, *etc.*

Figaro

Sì, mio core, *etc.*

Susanna, Figaro

Ah! il mattino alle nozze vicino,
quant'è dolce al mio/tuo tenero
sposo questo bel cappellino vezzoso
che Susanna ella stessa si fe'.

Figaro

... twenty, *etc.*

Susanna

Look at my hat now, ...

Figaro

... forty-three.

Susanna

Take a look, my dear Figaro,
look at my hat, now.

Figaro

Yes, sweetheart, now it's much
prettier, it seems made just for you.

Susanna

Take a look, ...

Figaro

Yes, sweetheart, *etc.*

Susanna

... Now I'm pleased with it, yes, *etc.*

Figaro

Yes, sweetheart, *etc.*

Susanna, Figaro

Ah! The wedding morn is nigh,
how dear to my/your tender
bridegroom is this charming little
hat which Susanna made herself.

Recitative

Susanna

Cosa stai misurando,
caro il mio Figaretto?

Figaro

Io guardo se quel letto,
che ci destina il Conte,
farà buona figura in questo loco.

Susanna

In questa stanza?

Figaro

Certo, a noi la cede
generoso il padrone.

Susanna

Io per me te la dono.

Figaro

E la ragione?

Susanna

La ragione l'ho qui.

Figaro

Perchè non puoi far,
che passi un po' qui!

Susanna

Perchè non voglio.
sei tu mio servo,
o no?

Figaro

Ma non capisco perchè
tanto ti spiacia, la più
comoda stanza del palazzo.

Susanna

What are you measuring,
my darling Figaro?

Figaro

I'm seeing if that bed
which the Count is giving us
will look well in this corner.

Susanna

In this room?

Figaro

Of course, the master has
generously given it to us.

Susanna

Then you may have it all to yourself.

Figaro

What's your objection?

Susanna

I have my reasons.

Figaro

Why won't you share them with
me?

Susanna

Because I don't wish to.
You are my humble servant,
aren't you?

Figaro

But I don't understand why
you turn up your nose at the most
comfortable room in the castle.

Susanna

Perch'io son la Susanna,
e tu sei pazzo.

Figaro

Grazie, non tanti elogi;
guarda un poco, se potria
meglio stare in altro loco.

Susanna

Because I am Susanna
and you are an idiot!

Figaro

Thank you—you're too kind;
tell me now, do you know of any
other room to suit us better?

NO. 2 DUETTINO

Figaro

Se a caso madama
la notte ti chiama
din, din, din, din,
in due passi da quella puoi gir.
Vien poi l'occasione
che vuolmi il padrone,
don, don, don, don,
in tre salti lo vado a servir.

Susanna

Così se il mattino
il caro Contino
Din, din, din, din,
e ti manda
tre miglia lontan
din, din, don, don,
a mia porta il diavol lo porta
ed ecco in tre salti...

Figaro

Susanna, pian, pian,...

Susanna

Ed ecco,...

Figaro

... pian, pian,...

Figaro

Supposing one night
my lady should call you
ting, ting, ting, ting,
you can go to her in a trice.
Then it may happen
that the master wants me
dong, dong, dong, dong, and I'm
with him in a hop, skip and jump.

Susanna

Suppose some morning
your precious Count
ting, ting, ting, ting,
should send you on an errand
three miles away
ting, ting, dong, dong,
the devil brings him to my door
and in a hop, skip and jump...

Figaro

Susanna, softly, I pray you,...

Susanna

And in...

Figaro

... softly, softly,...

Susanna

... in tre salti ...

Figaro

... pian, pian, ...

Susanna

... din, din, ...

Figaro

... pian, pian, ...

Susanna

... don, don!

Figaro

... pian, pian.

Susanna

Ascolta!

Figaro

Fa presto!

Susanna

Se udir brami il resto,
discaccia i sospetti,
che torto mi fan.

Figaro

Udir bramo il resto,
I dubbi, i sospetti
gelare mi fan.

Susanna

Discaccia i sospetti, *etc.*

Figaro

I dubbi, i sospetti, *etc.*

Susanna

... a hop, skip and jump ...

Figaro

... softly, softly, ...

Susanna

... ting, ting, ...

Figaro

... softly, softly, ...

Susanna

... dong, dong!

Figaro

... softly, softly.

Susanna

Listen to me!

Figaro

Quickly, then!

Susanna

If you wish to hear the rest,
dismiss your suspicions
which do me wrong.

Figaro

I must hear the rest,
though I am chilled with
doubts and suspicion.

Susanna

Dismiss your suspicions, *etc.*

Figaro

Though I am chilled, *etc.*

Susanna
Or bene, ascolta e taci.

Figaro
Parla, che c'è di nuovo?

Susanna
Il signor Conte,
stanco d'andar cacciando
le straniere bellezze forestiere,
vuole ancor nel castello,
ritentar la sua sorte;
n'è già di sua Consorte,
bada bene, appetito gli viene.

Figaro
E di chi dunque?

Susanna
Della tua Susannetta.

Figaro
Di te?

Susanna
Di me medesma, ed ha speranza
ch'al nobil suo progetto
utilissima sia tal vicinanza.

Figaro
Bravo! Tiriamo avanti.

Susanna
Queste le grazie son,
questa la cura ch'egli prende di te,
della tua sposa.

Figaro
O guarda un po',

Susanna
Now listen quietly.

Figaro
Tell me what is happening.

Susanna
My lord,
weary of pursuing
beauties from far and near
wishes to try his luck
once again in the castle.
But his appetite is not whetted
by his wife, make no mistake.

Figaro
Who is it, then?

Susanna
Your little Susanna.

Figaro
You?

Susanna
Myself, and he hopes
to further his noble plan
by having us near him.

Figaro
Bravo! Tell me more.

Susanna
Hence the gracious concern
which he lavishes on you
and your bride-to-be.

Figaro
Well, well,

che carità pelosa.

Susanna

Chetati, or viene il meglio;
don Basilio, mio maestro di canto
e suo factotum, nel darmi la lezione
mi ripete ogni dì questa canzone.

Figaro

Chi! Basilio? oh birbante!

Susanna

E tu credevi,
che fosse la mia dote
merto del tuo bel muso?

Figaro

Me n'era lusingato.

Susanna

Ei la destina per ottener da me
certe mezz'ore
che il diritto feudale . . .

Figaro

Come! ne' i feudi suoi
non l'ha il Conte abolito?

Susanna

Ebben, ora è pentito,
e par che tenti riscattarlo
da me.

Figaro

Bravo! mi piace;
che caro signor Conte!
Ci vogliamo divertir,
trovato avete . . .
(A bell rings.)

a sprat to catch a mackerel!

Susanna

Hush, now comes the best part;
Don Basilio, my singing teacher and
his factotum, during lessons informs
me daily of the Count's desire.

Figaro

Who! Basilio? The rogue!

Susanna

And did you believe
that my dowry was the
reward for your handsome face?

Figaro

I flattered myself I deserved it.

Susanna

His object is to claim from me
those half-hours of pleasure
which feudal privilege . . .

Figaro

What! Has not my lord
abolished such rights on his estates?

Susanna

He regrets it now, it seems,
and is trying to redeem his right
from me.

Figaro

Bravo! I like that!
How kind of my lord!
We'll have some fun out of this!
You've found . . .
(A bell rings.)

Figaro
Chi suona? la Contessa.

Susanna
Addio, addio, Figaro bello.

Figaro
Coraggio, mio tesoro.

Susanna
E tu, cervello.
(Susanna kisses him and goes off.)

Figaro
Who rang? It's the Countess.

Susanna
Goodbye, goodbye, sweet Figaro.

Figaro
Courage, my treasure.

Susanna
And you, use your brains.
(Susanna kisses him and goes off.)

Figaro
Bravo, signor padrone!
Ora incomincio a capire
il mistero, e a veder schietto
tutto il vostro progetto.
A Londra, è vero?
Voi ministro, io
corriero, e la Susanna,
segreta ambasciatrice.
Non sarà, Figaro il dice.

Figaro
Bravo, my master!
Now I'm beginning to understand
the mystery, and see your plan
quite plainly.
We're off to London, are we?
You as ambassador, I as
your courier, and Susanna
as "secret attaché."
Never, says Figaro here and now.

NO. 3 CAVATINA

A
Se vuol ballare, signor Contino,
Il chitarrino le suonerò, sì.
Se vuol venire nella mia scuola,
La capriola le insegnerò, sì.
Saprò, ma piano piano
Meglio ogni arcano
Dissimulando scoprir potrò.

B
L'arte schermendo,
L'arte adoprando,

A
If you wish to dance, my dear Count
I'll play the guitar, oh yes!
If you'll come to my school
I'll teach you to scheme
I'll deal with you . . . but softly . . .
by pretense I shall be better able
to discover every secret.

B
But parrying artfulness
with artfulness,

Di qua pungendo, di là scherzando,	now pricking, now feinting jokingly
Tutte le macchine, rovescierò.	I shall upset all his intrigues.
ℜ'	ℜ'
Se vuol ballare, *etc.*	If you wish to dance, *etc.*
(He goes off.)	*(He goes off.)*

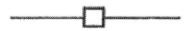

(Bartolo and Marcellina enter.)	*(Bartolo and Marcellina enter.)*
	Recitative
Bartolo	**Bartolo**
Ed aspettaste il giorno	And you wait till the day
fissato per le nozze,	fixed for the marriage
a parlarmi di questo?	to speak to me of this?
Marcellina	**Marcellina**
Io non mi perdo, dottor mio,	I'll not lose heart, doctor.
di coraggio, per romper de' sponsali	To break up a planned marriage at
più avanzati di questo,	an even more advanced stage than
bastò spesso un pretesto; ed egli	this a mere pretext has sufficed
ha meco, oltre questo contratto	before now.
certi impegni . . . so io . . . basta!	And besides this contract
Conviene la Susanna atterrir,	he has obligations to me, never fear!
convien con arte impuntigliarla	But we must frighten Susanna
a rifiutare il Conte;	and artfully induce her
egli per vendicarsi	to refuse the Count;
prenderà il mio partito,	he, out of spite,
e Figaro così fia mio marito.	will take my part
	and so Figaro shall be my husband.
Bartolo	**Bartolo**
Bene, io tutto farò.	Very well. I'll do all I can.
Senza riserve, tutto a me palesate.	Tell me all without reserve.
(Aside)	*(Aside)*
Avrei pur gusto di dar in moglie	I should relish marrying off
la mia serva antica,	my former servant
a chi mi fece un dì	to the man who, that time,
rapir l'amica.	engineered my ward's elopement.

NO. 4 ARIA

La vendetta, oh, la vendeta	Vengeance, ah, vengeance
e un piacer servato ai saggi.	is a pleasure reserved for the wise;
L'obliar l'onte, gli oltraggi	to forget affronts and outrage
è bassezza, è ognor viltà.	is ever baseness and cowardice.
Coll'astuzia, coll'arguzia	With cunning and acumen,
col giudizio, col criterio	with common sense and discretion,
si potrebbe,	it can be satisfied.
il fatto è serio;	A difficult matter.
ma credete si farà.	But believe me, it shall be done.
Se tutto il codice	If I have to turn inside out
dovessi volgere,	the legal code,
se tutto l'indice	if I have to read
dovessileggere, con un equivoco,	the whole index with some
con un sinonimo,	ambiguity, some synonym,
qualche garbuglio si troverà.	I'll find a way to confound him.
Tutta Siviglia conosce Bartolo,	All Seville knows Bartolo.
il birbo Figaro vinto sarà.	That knave Figaro shall be outwitted.
(Bartolo goes off.)	*(Bartolo goes off.)*

———□———

(Cherubino enters.)   *(Cherubino enters.)*

Cherubino
Susanetta, sei tu?

Cherubino
Dear Susanna, is it you?

Susanna
Son io, cosa volete?

Susanna
'Tis I. What do you want?

Cherubino
Ah, cor mio,
che accidente!

Cherubino
Ah, my sweetheart,
what a misfortune!

Susanna
Cor vostro? Cosa avvenne?

Susanna
Your sweetheart? What's happened?

Cherubino
Il Conte ieri, perchè

Cherubino
Yesterday, because the Count

trovommi sol con Barbarina,
il congedo mi diede;
e se la Contessina,
la mia bella comare,
grazia non m'intercede,
io vado via, io non ti vedo più,
Susanna mia.

Susanna

Non vedete più me? Bravo!
Ma dunque non più per la Contessa
secretamente il vostro cor sospira?

Cherubino

Ah, che troppo rispetto
ella m'ispira!
Felice te, che puoi
vederla quando vuoi,
che la vesti il mattino,
che la sera la spogli,
che le metti gli spilloni,
i merletti . . .
ah! se in tuo loco . . .

NO. 6 ARIA

Non so più cosa son,
cosa faccio, or di foco,
ora sono di ghiaccio, ogni
donna cangiar di colore,
ogni donna mi fa palpitar.
Solo ai nomi d'amore di diletto,
mi si turba, mi s'altera il petto,
e a parlare mi sforza d'amore
un desio ch'io non posso spiegar.
Non so più, *etc.*
Parlo d'amor vegliando,
parlo d'amore sognando, all'acqua,
all'ombra, ai monti,
ai fiori, all'erbe, ai fonti,
all'eco, all'aria, ai venti,

found me alone with Barbarina,
he decided to send me away;
and if my beautiful godmother
the Countess does not
intercede on my behalf
I shall go away and never
see you again, my Susanna.

Susanna

You won't see me again. Bravo!
But does your heart sigh no more
in secret for the Countess?

Cherubino

Ah, she inspires me with
too much respect!
Happy you, who can
see her when you wish,
you dress her in the morning,
help her to undress at night,
busy yourself with her pins
and her lace . . .
ah! If I were in your place . . .

I no longer know what I am,
what I'm doing, now I'm
feverish, now I'm chilled; every
woman makes me change color,
or makes me tremble with emotion.
The very words "love" and "delight"
excite me and make my heart race.
And I am forced to speak of love
by a desire that I cannot explain.
I no longer know, *etc.*
I speak of love waking,
I speak of love dreaming, to the
water, the shadow, the mountains, to
the flowers, the grass, the fountains,
to the echo, the air, the winds

che il suon de' vani accenti	which waft away with them
portano via con se . . .	the sound of my fruitless words . . .
Parlo d'amor, *etc.*	I speak of love, *etc.*
E se non ho chi m'oda,	And if no one is there to listen,
parlo d'amor con me.	I speak of love to myself.

Recitative

Cherubino

Ah, son perduto . . . il Conte!

Cherubino

Ah, I'm lost . . . the Count!

Susanna

Oh, me meschina!
(The Count comes in as Cherubino hides behind the chair.)

Susanna

Oh, poor me!
(The Count comes in as Cherubino hides behind the chair.)

Count Almaviva

Susanna, come sembri
agitata e confusa.

Count Almaviva

Susanna, how agitated
and confused you seem.

Susanna

Signor, io chiedo scusa, ma,
se mai qui sorpresa . . .
per carità partite.

Susanna

My lord, I beg your pardon, but
if we were to be surprised here . . .
Go, I beg you.

Count

Un momento e ti lascio.
Odi.

Count

A moment and I'll leave you.
Listen.

Susanna

Non odo nulla.

Susanna

I cannot.

Count

Due parole: tu sai che ambasciatore
a Londre il Re mi dichiarò.

Di condur meco Figaro destinai.

Count

Two words. You know that the
King has appointed me ambassador
to London. I have decided to take
Figaro with me.

Susanna

Signor, se osassi . . .

Count

Parla, mia cara, e con quel dritto
ch'oggi prendi su me, finchè tu
vivi chiedi, imponi,
prescrivi.

Susanna

Lasciatemi, Signor,
dritti non prendo,
non ne vo', non ne intendo.
Oh, me infelice!

Count

Ah, no, Susanna,
io ti vo' far felice!
Tu ben sai quant'io t'amo;
a te Basilio tutto già disse.
Or senti, se per pochi
momenti meco in giardin,
sull'imbrunir del giorno. . . .
Ah, per questo favore io pagherei.

Susanna

My lord, if I dared . . .

Count

Speak, my dear, and with that right
which you have from me, while you
live, ask, command and dispose
of me.

Susanna

Leave me, my lord,
I claim no rights,
nor wish nor understand them.
How unhappy I am!

Count

Ah, non, Susanna,
I want to make you happy!
You know how much I love you,
Basilio has already told you.
If you would only, for a few
moments meet me in the garden
at dusk,
Oh, I would pay for such a favor.

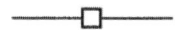

Cherubino

Perdono, mio Signor!

Count

Nol meritate.

Susanna

Egli è ancora fanciullo.

Count

Men di quel che tu credi.

Cherubino

Forgive me, my lord.

Count

You don't deserve it.

Susanna

He's only a child.

Count

Less so than you think.

Cherubino

È ver, mancai;
ma dal mio labbro alfine . . .

Count

(Hastily interrupting him)
Ben, bene; io vi perdono;
anzi farò di più: vacante è un posto
d'uffizial nel reggimento mio;
io scelgo voi, partite tosto,
addio.

Susanna, Figaro

Ah, fin domani sol.

Count

No, parta tosto.

Cherubino

A ubbidirvi, Signor,
son già disposto.

Count

Via, per l'ultima volta
la Susanna abbracciate.
(Aside)
Inaspettato è il colpo.
(The Count goes off.)

Figaro

Ehi, capitano, a me pure la mano.
(Aside to Cherubino)
Io vo' parlarti pria che tu parta.
(Aloud)
Addio piccolo Cherubino!
Come cangia in un punto
il tuo destino!

Cherubino

I was at fault;
but never from my lips . . .

Count

(Hastily interrupting him)
All right, all right, I pardon you;
I'll do more: there is a vacancy
for an officer in my regiment:
it is yours. You leave at once.
Goodbye.

Susanna, Figaro

Oh, let him stay until tomorrow.

Count

No, he leaves at once.

Cherubino

My lord, I am ready
to obey your command.

Count

Come, for the last time
kiss Susanna.
(Aside)
An unexpected blow for them.
(The Count goes off.)

Figaro

Well, captain, give me your hand.
(Aside to Cherubino)
I want to speak to you before you go.
(Aloud)
Goodbye little Cherubino!
How your destiny changes
in a mere moment!

NO. 9 ARIA

A
Non più andrai,
farfallone amoroso,
notte e giorno d'intorno girando,
delle belle turbando il riposo,
Narcisetto, Adoncino d'amor.
B
Non più avrai questi bei pennacchini,
quel cappello leggero e galante,
quella chioma, quell'aria brillante,
quel vermiglio donnesco color!
Non più avrai, *etc.*
A
Non più andrai, *etc.*
C
Fra guerrieri, poffar Bacco!
Gran mustacchi, stretto sacco,
schioppo in spalla, sciabola al fianco,
collo dritto, muso franco,
o un gran casco o un gran turbante,
molto onor, poco contante.
Ed in vece del fandango,
una marcia per il fango,
per montagne, per valloni,
colle nevi e i sollioni,
al concerto di tromboni,
di bombarde, di cannoni,
che le palle in tutti i tuoni,
all'orecchio fan fischiar.
Non più avrai, *etc.*
A
Non più andrai, *etc.*
C' (coda)
Cherubino alla vittoria,
All gloria militar!

A
You'll go no more,
amorous butterfly,
flitting about, night and day,
disturbing ladies' rest,
little Narcissus, Adonis of love.
B
You'll wear no more these plumes,
that smart and jaunty cap,
those curls, that dashing air,
that pink, effeminate complexion!
You'll wear no more, *etc.*
A
You'll go no more, *etc.*
C
Among warriors, by Jingo!
Bushy mustaches, tight tunic,
shoulder arms, saber at your side,
neck straight, serious-faced,
a big helmet or a big turban,
much honor, but little money.
And instead of the fandango,
a forced march through the mud,
over hill and dale,
in snow and scorching sun,
to the accompaniment of
trombones, mortars and cannons,
and cannonballs whistling
and whining in your ears.
You'll wear no more, *etc.*
A
You'll go no more, *etc.*
C' (coda)
Cherubino, march to victory
and military glory!

END OF ACT ONE

ACT TWO

NO. 10 CAVATINA

Countess

Porgi amor, qualche ristoro,
al mio duolo, a' miei sospir!
O mi rendi il mio tesoro,
o mi lascia almen morir!
Porgi amor, *etc.*

Countess

Grant, o Love, a cure
for my grief and sighing!
Bring my darling back to me,
or at least let me die.
Grant, o Love, *etc.*

Recitative

Countess

Vieni, cara Susanna,
finiscimi l'istoria.

Countess

Come, dear Susanna,
finish your story.

Susanna

È già finita.

Susanna

It's already finished.

Countess

Dunque volle sedurti?

Countess

So he wanted to seduce you?

Susanna

Oh, il signor Conte non fa tai
complimenti colle
donne mie pari;
egli venne a contratto di danari.

Susanna

Oh, my lord does not pay such
compliments to
women of my station;
he made a business proposition.

Countess

Ah! il crudel
più non m'ama.

Countess

Ah! The cruel wretch
no longer loves me.

Susanna

E come poi è geloso di voi?

Susanna

Why, then, is he jealous of you?

Countess

Come lo sono i moderni mariti,
per sistema infedeli,

Countess

He is like all modern husbands,
willfully unfaithful,

per genio capricciosi, e per orgoglio
poi tutti gelosi. Ma se
Figaro t'ama, ei sol potria . . .
(Enter Figaro singing)

Figaro
La la la la la la . . .

Susanna
Eccolo.

naturally capricious and yet
proudly jealous. But if Figaro
loves you, he alone could . . .
(Enter Figaro singing)

Figaro
La la la la la la . . .

Susanna
Here he is.

NO. 11 CANZONA

Cherubino

Voi che sapete
che cosa è amor,
Donne, vedete s'io l'ho nel cor.
Quello ch'io provo vi ridirò,
è per me nuovo,
capir nol so.
Sento un affetto pien di desir,
ch'ora è diletto,
ch'ora è martir.
Gelo, e poi sento
l'alma avvampar
e in un momento torno a gelar;
ricerco un bene fuori di me,
non so ch'il tiene,
non so cos'è, sospiro
e gemo senza voler,
palpito e tremo senza saper.
Non trovo pace notte nè di,
ma pur mi piace languir così.
Voi che sapete, *etc.*

Cherubino

You ladies who are acquainted
with love,
tell me if I have it in my heart.
What I experience, I repeat,
is something new to me which
I cannot understand.
I feel a strange desire
which in turn delights
and tortures me.
One moment I freeze,
the next I'm all aflame
then in a second I'm freezing again.
I seek a pleasure outside of me
I know not who can give it
or what it is, I sigh
and mourn for no good reason,
I shiver and shake, I know not why.
I know no peace, night and day,
and yet I love my languishing.
You ladies who are acquainted, *etc.*

Countess

Bravo, che bella voce, io non sapea
che cantaste si bene.

Susanna

Oh, in verità, egli fa tutto ben
quello ch'ei fa. Presto a noi,
bel soldato; Figaro v'informò . . .

Cherubino

Tutto mi disse.

Susanna

(measuring herself by him)
Lasciatemi veder; andrà benissimo:
siam d'uguale statura—
giù quel manto.

Countess

(to Susanna)
Che fai?

Susanna

Niente paura.

Countess

E se qualcuno entrasse . . .

Susanna

Entri, che mal facciamo?
La porta chiuderò,
ma come poi acconciargli i capelli?

Countess

Una mia cuffia prendi nel
gabinetto, presto!
(Susanna goes out.)
Che carta è quella?

Countess

Bravo, you've an attractive voice, I
never knew you could sing so well.

Susanna

Oh, truly, everything he attempts
he does well. Come, brave soldier,
I imagine Figaro told you . . .

Cherubino

He told me all.

Susanna

(measuring herself by him)
Let me see; it will be just right:
we're exactly the same height—
off with that coat.

Countess

(to Susanna)
What are you doing?

Susanna

No need to worry.

Countess

But if someone should come in . . .

Susanna

Let them, what harm are we doing?
I'll close the door.
But what can we do about his hair?

Countess

Fetch one of my bonnets from
my closet. Quickly!
(Susanna goes out.)
What is that document?

Cherubino
La patente.

Countess
Che sollecita gente!

Cherubino
L'ebbi or da Basilio.

Countess
Della fretta obliato hanno
il sigillo!

Susanna
(returning)
Il sigillo di che?

Countess
Della patente.

Susanna
Cospetto! Che premura!
Ecco la cuffia.

Countess
Spicciati; va bene;
miserabili noi se il
Conte viene!

Cherubino
My commission.

Countess
They're in a great hurry!

Cherubino
I received it just now from Basilio.

Countess
In their hurry, they've forgotten
the seal.

Susanna
(returning)
What seal?

Countess
On the commission.

Susanna
Mercy! What haste!
Here is the bonnet.

Countess
Hurry; yes, that's right;
what a plight we should be in if
my lord came in now!

NO. 12 ARIA

Susanna
Venite inginocchiatevi,
restate fermo lì.
Pian piano or via giratevi.
Bravo! va ben così.
La faccia ora volgetemi.
Olà, quelgli occhi a me.

Susanna
Come, kneel down
and keep quite still
Now turn slowly round.
Bravo! That's it.
Now turn your face towards me.
No, look at me.
etc.

Susanna, Cherubino
... Le porte, son serate,
Che mai sarà?

Cherubino
Qui perdersi non giova.

Susanna
V'uccide, se vi trova.

Cherubino
Veggiamo un po' qui fuori:
Dà proprio nel giardino.

Susanna
Fermate Cherubino, fermate,
per pietà!

Cherubino
Qui perdersi non giova.

Susanna
Fermate, Cherubino!

Cherubino
M'uccide, se mi trova.

Susanna
Tropp'alto per un salto, ...

Cherubino
Lasciami, ...

Susanna
... fermate, per pietà!

Cherubino
... lasciami!
Pria di nuocerle
nel foco volerei.

Susanna, Cherubino
... The doors are locked,
whatever is to be done?

Cherubino
I must find a way out.

Susanna
He'll kill you if he finds you.

Cherubino
What about the window?
It looks on to the garden.

Susanna
Stop, Cherubino, stop,
for pity's sake.

Cherubino
I must find a way out.

Susanna
Stop, Cherubino!

Cherubino
He'll kill me if he finds me.

Susanna
It's too high to jump, ...

Cherubino
Leave me alone, ...

Susanna
... stop, for pity's sake!

Cherubino
... leave me alone!
Before I'd harm her,
I'd leap into the fire.

Abbraccio te per lei.
Addio!
(He kisses Susanna.)
Così si fa.
(He jumps out of the window.)

Susanna

Ei va a perire, o Dei!
Fermate, per pietà!
Fermate, fermate!
(She runs to the window and looks out after Cherubino)
Oh, guarda il demonietto
come fugge!
È già un miglio lontano; ma non
perdiamci invano;
entriam nel gabinetto;
venga poi lo smargiasso,
io qui l'aspetto.

Give her this kiss from me.
Goodbye!
(He kisses Susanna.)
This is how to do it.
(He jumps out of the window.)

Susanna

He'll kill himself, O heavens!
Stop for pity's sake!
Stop, stop!
(She runs to the window and looks out after Cherubino)
O, look at the little rogue,
how he runs!
He's a mile off already; but there's
no time to lose;
into the closet;
then let the braggart come,
I'm waiting here for him.

ACT TWO

NO. 15 FINALE

Part I: Allegro, E-flat Major

Count

(screaming at the closet door)
Esci ormai, garzon malnato!
Sciagurato, non tardar!

Countess

Ah! signore, quel furore
per lui fammi il cor tremar.

Count

E d'opporvi ancor osate?

Count

(screaming at the closet door)
Out you come, you ill-bred brat,
quickly now, you little wretch!

Countess

Ah, my lord, your rage
makes my heart tremble for him.

Count

And do you still dare to oppose me?

Countess	**Countess**
No, sentite.	No, but hear me.
Count	**Count**
Via parlate.	Speak and quickly.
Countess	**Countess**
Giuro al ciel ch'ogni sospetto e lo stato in che il trovate, sciolto il collo, nudo il petto . . .	I swear before heaven that any suspicion and the state in which you find him, his collar undone and his chest bare . . .
Count	**Count**
Sciolto il collo! nudo il petto! Seguitate.	Collar undone! Chest bare! Go on.
Countess	**Countess**
Per vestir femminee spoglie . . .	To dress him up as a young woman . . .
Count	**Count**
Ah! comprendo, indegna moglie, mi vo' tosto vendicar.	Ah, I understand, unworthy wife, I will soon be revenged.
Countess	**Countess**
Mi fa torto quel trasporto, . . .	This fury does me wrong . . .
Count	**Count**
Ah! comprendo, indegna moglie, . . .	Ah! I understand, unworthy wife, . . .
Countess	**Countess**
. . . M'oltraggiate a dubitar; . . .	. . . you outrage me by your doubting.
Count	**Count**
. . . Mi vo' tosto vendicar; . . .	. . . I will soon be revenged.
Countess	**Countess**
Mi fa torto quel trasporto, *etc.*	This fury does me wrong, *etc.*

Count

Ah, comprendo
indegna moglie, *etc.*
... Qua la chiave.

Countess

Egli è innocente!

Count

Qua la chiave!

Countess

Egli è innocente!
Voi sapete.

Count

Non so niente!
Va lontan dagli occhi miei.
Un'infida, un'empia sei,
e mi cerchi d'infamar.

Countess

Vado, sì, ma ...

Count

Non ascolto.

Countess

Ma ...

Count

Non ascolto.

Countess

Non son rea!

Count

Vel leggo in volto!
Mora, mora!

Count

Ah! I understand,
unworthy wife, *etc.* ...
... Give me the key.

Countess

He is innocent!

Count

Give me the key!

Countess

He is innocent!
You know he is.

Count

I know nothing of the sort!
Away out of my sight.
You are faithless and wicked,
and seek to disgrace me.

Countess

I'll go, yes, but ...

Count

I'll not hear you.

Countess

But ...

Count

I'll not hear you.

Countess

I'm not guilty!

Count

I can read it in your face!
Die, die!

Countess
ah! la ciece gelosia . . .

Count
Mora, mora!

Countess
. . . qualche eccesso gli fa far.

Count
Mora, mora e più non sia, . . .

Countess
Ah! la cieca gelosia, . . .

Count
. . . ria cagion, . . .

Countess
. . . qualche eccesso gli fa far!

Count
. . . ria cagion del mio penar! . . .
. . . Ah! comprendo! . . .

Countess
Mi fa torto . . .

Count
. . . Indegna moglie, . . .

Countess
. . . quel trasporto!

Count
. . . mora, *etc.*

Countess
Ah! Blind jealousy . . .

Count
Die, die!

Countess
. . . will goad him to some desperate deed.

Count
Die, die and be no more, . . .

Countess
Oh, blind jealousy . . .

Count
. . . deceitful cause, . . .

Countess
. . . will goad him to some desperate deed!

Count
. . . deceitful cause of my suffering! . . .
. . . Ah! I understand! . . .

Countess
This fury, . . .

Count
. . . Unworthy wife, . . .

Countess
. . . wrongs me!

Count
. . . die, *etc.*

Countess

Ah! la cieca gelosia, *etc.*
(The Count draws his sword, opens the door . . . and finds Susanna standing there.)

Count

(astonished)
Susanna!

Countess

(equally astonished)
Susanna!

Countess

Ah! Blind jealousy, *etc.*
(The Count draws his sword, opens the door . . . and finds Susanna standing there.)

Count

(astonished)
Susanna!

Countess

(equally astonished)
Susanna!

Part II: Molto Andante, B-flat Major

Susanna

Signore!
Cos'è quel stupore?
Il brando prendete,
il paggio uccidete,
quel paggio malnato,
vedetelo qua.

Count

(aside)
Che scola!

Countess

(aside)
Che storia è . . .
. . . mai questa, . . .

Count

La testa . . .

Susanna

My lord!
Why so dumbfounded?
Take your sword,
and put the page to death,
that ill-bred page,
you see him here before you.

Count

(aside)
What sly minxes!

Countess

(aside)
What fantasy . . .
. . . can this be, . . .

Count

My head . . .

Susanna

(aside)
Confusa han la testa,
non san come va. ...

Countess

... Susanna v'è là ...

Count

... girando mi va. ...
... Sei sola?

Susanna

Guardate! qui ascoso sarà.

Count

Guardiamo!

Count, Susanna

Guardate!/Guardiamo!
qui ascoso sarà.

Susanna

(aside)
They are so bewildered,
they're quite at a loss. ...

Countess

... Susanna is there! ...

Count

... is reeling ...
... Are you alone?

Susanna

Look! Perhaps he's hidden here.

Count

Let us see!

Count, Susanna

Look!/Let us see!
Perhaps he's hidden here.

Part III: Allegro, B-flat Major

Countess

(aside to Susanna)
Susanna, son morta,
il fiato mi manca.

Susanna

(aside to Countess)
Più lieta, più franca,
in salvo è di già.

Count

(to Countess)
Che sbaglio mai presi.
Appena lo credo.

Countess

(aside to Susanna)
Susanna, I'm half dead,
I can hardly breathe.

Susanna

(aside to Countess)
Put your mind at ease and be gay,
he's safe by now.

Count

(to Countess)
To think I made such a mistake.
I can scarcely believe it.

Se a torto v'offesi,
perdono vi chiedo,
ma far burla simile
è poi crudeltà.

Countess, Susanna

Le vostre follie
non mertan pietà.

Count

Io v'amo!

Countess

Nol dite!

Count

Vel giuro!

Countess

Mentite!
Son l'empia, l'infida
che ognora v'inganna.

Count

Quell'ira, Susanna,
m'aita a calmar.

Susanna

Così si condanna
chi può sospettar.

Countess

Adunque la fede
D'un anima amante
sì fiera mercede
doveva sperar?

Count

Quell'ira, Susanna, *etc*.

If I wronged you,
I ask you pardon,
but to play such a trick
was cruel.

Countess, Susanna

Your follies
do not deserve forgiveness.

Count

I love you!

Countess

Do not say it!

Count

I swear it!

Countess

You are lying!
I am the faithless, wicked wife
who is always deceiving you.

Count

Susanna, help me
to calm her anger.

Susanna

Thus are punished
those who are suspicious.

Countess

Must the constancy
of a loving heart
such harsh reward
expect?

Count

Susanna, help me, *etc.*

Susanna
Così si condanna, *etc.*
(to Countess)
Signora!

Count
Rosina!

Countess
Crudele!
Più quella non sono.
Ma il misero oggetto
del vostro abbandono
che avete diletto
di far disperar.

Susanna, Count
Confuso, pentito, è/son
troppo punito, ...

Countess
Crudele! crudele! soffrir sì
gran torto, ...

Susanna, Count
... abbiate pietà, abbiate pietà!

Countess
... quest'alma non sa, ah, no,
quest'alma non sa!

Count
Ma il paggio rinchiuso?

Countess
Fu sol per provarvi.

Count
Ma i tremiti, i palpiti?

Susanna
Thus are punished, *etc.*
(to Countess)
My lady!

Count
Rosina!

Countess
Cruel one!
I'm no longer your Rosina,
but the miserable object
of your abandon
whom you have been pleased
to make suffer.

Susanna, Count
Confused, repentent, I've/he's
been punished enough, ...

Countess
Cruel one, my heart
cannot bear ...

Susanna, Count
... have pity, have pity!

Countess
... the great wrong you
do me!

Count
But you said the page was
shut in there?

Countess
It was only to test you.

Count
But your trembling, your anxiety?

Countess
Fu sol per burlarvi.

Count
Ma un foglio sì barbaro?

Susanna, Countess
Di Figaro è il foglio,
e a voi per Basilio.

Count
Ah, perfidi. Io voglio . . .

Susanna, Countess
Perdono non merta
chi agli altri nol dà.

Count
Ebben se vi piace,
comune è la pace.
Rosina inflessibile
con me non sarà.

Countess
Ah, quanto Susanna,
son dolce di core!
Di donne al furore
chi può crederà?

Susanna
Cogli uomin, signora,
girate, volgete,
vedrete che ognora
si cade poi là.

Count
Guardetemi!

Countess
Ingrato!

Countess
It was only a joke.

Count
But such a heartless note?

Susanna, Countess
The note was from Figaro,
and Basilio delivered it.

Count
Ah, the villains. I'll . . .

Susanna, Countess
He deserves not forgiveness
who forgives not others.

Count
Well then, if you wish,
let us make peace all round.
Rosina will not be adamant
with me.

Countess
Ah, Susanna, how
soft-hearted I am!
How can a woman's wrath
ever be taken seriously?

Susanna
With men, my lady,
whatever you do, and wherever you
turn, you will see that always
you end up like that.

Count
Look at me!

Countess
For shame, sir!

Count

Guardatemi, ho torto,
e mi pento.

Susanna, Countess, Count

Da questo momento,
quest'alma a conoscer la/mi/vi
apprender potrà, *etc.*

Count

Look at me, I was wrong,
and I am sorry.

Susanna, Countess, Count

From this moment,
he/I will be able to learn
to appreciate her/me/you, *etc.*

Part IV: Allegro, G Major

(Figaro enters.)

Figaro

Signore, di fuori
son già i suonatori:
le trombe sentite,
i pifferi udite;
tra canti, tra balli
de' vostri vassalli,
corriamo, voliamo
le nozze a compir.

Count

Pian, piano, men fretta.

Figaro

La turba m'aspetta.

Count

Pian, piano, men fretta,
un dubbio toglietemi
in pria di partir.

Susanna, Countess, Figaro

La cosa è scabrosa, . . .

(Figaro enters.)

Figaro

My lord, the musicians
are already outside:
hear the trumpets
and the pipes.
Mid the singing and dancing
of your retainers,
let us run, let us haste
to the wedding.

Count

Hush, hush, less hurry.

Figaro

The crowd awaits me.

Count

Hush, hush, less hurry;
relieve me of a doubt
before you go.

Susanna, Countess, Figaro

A delicate situation, . . .

Count
Con arte . . .

Susanna, Countess, Figaro
. . . Com'ha da finir? *etc.*

Count
. . . le carte convien qui scopir, *etc.*

Count
I must . . .

Susanna, Countess, Figaro
. . . how will it end? *etc.*

Count
. . . play my cards carefully, *etc.*

Part V: Andante, C Major

Count
Conoscete, Signor Figaro,
questo foglio chi vergò?

Figaro
Nol conosco!

Susanna
Nol conosci?

Figaro
No!

Countess
Nol conosci?

Figaro
No!

Count
Nol conosci?

Figaro
No!

Susanna, Countess, Count
Nol conosci?

Count
Do you know, Master Figaro,
who wrote this letter?

Figaro
I do not.

Susanna
You do not know?

Figaro
No!

Countess
You do not know?

Figaro
No!

Count
You do not know?

Figaro
No!

Susanna, Countess, Count
You do not know?

Figaro
No! No! No!

Susanna
E nol desti a Don Basilio?

Countess
Per recarlo.

Count
Tu c'intendi?

Figaro
Oibò, oibò!

Susanna
E non sai del damerino . . .

Countess
. . . Che stasera nel giardino . . . ?

Count
Già capisci?

Figaro
Io non lo so.

Count
Cerchi invan difesa
e scusa,
il tuo ceffo già t'accusa,
vedo ben che vuoi mentir.

Figaro
Mente il ceffo, io già non mento.

Susanna, Countess
Il talento aguzzi invano, . . .
. . . Palesato abbiam l'arcano, . . .

Figaro
No! No! No!

Susanna
Didn't you give it to Don Basilio?

Countess
To deliver it.

Count
You remember?

Figaro
Oh dear, oh dear!

Susanna
And what about the page . . .

Countess
. . . Who tonight in the garden . . . ?

Count
Do you understand now?

Figaro
No, I don't.

Count
You look in vain for defense
and excuse,
your face is giving you away,
I can see you are lying.

Figaro
My face, then, is lying, I am not.

Susanna, Countess
In vain you sharpen your wits, . . .
. . . we've told everything, . . .

Figaro
Mente il ceffo, io già non mento.

Susanna, Countess
... Non v'è nulla da ridir.

Count
Che rispondi?

Figaro
Niente, niente!

Count
Dunque accordi?

Figaro
Non accordo!

Figaro
My face, then, is lying, I am not.

Susanna, Countess
... You've nothing left to repeat.

Count
What's your answer?

Figaro
Nothing, nothing!

Count
You confess, then?

Figaro
No, I don't!

Part VII: Andante, B-flat Major

Antonio
Vostre dunque saran queste
carte che perdeste.

Count
Olà, porgile a me.

Figaro
Sono in trappola.

Susanna, Countess
Figaro, all'erta!

Count
Dite un po', questo foglio cos'è?

Figaro
Tosto, tosto, n'ho tante,
aspettate.

Antonio
Sarà forse il sommario dei debiti?

Figaro
No, la lista degli osti.

Count
(to Figaro)
Parlate.
(to Antonio)
E tu lascialo.

Susanna, Countess
Lascialo e parti, *etc.*

Figaro
Lasciami e parti . . .

Antonio
These, then, will be your
papers you lost.

Count
Here, give them to me.

Figaro
I'm trapped.

Susanna, Countess
Figaro, beware!

Count
Tell me, what is this paper?

Figaro
Just a moment, just a moment,
I have so many, wait.

Antonio
Perhaps it's a list of your debts.

Figaro
No, a list of innkeepers, more likely.

Count
(to Figaro)
Speak up!
(to Antonio)
And you leave him alone.

Susanna
Leave him alone and go! *etc.*

Figaro
Leave me alone and go! . . .

Antonio

Parto sì, ma se torno a trovarti, *etc.*

Figaro

... Vanne,
non temo di te!, *etc.*
(Antonio goes off.)

Count

(opening the papers)
Dunque?

Countess

(aside to Susanna)
Oh ciel, la patente del paggio!

Count

Dunque?

Susanna

(aside to Figaro)
Giusti Dei, la patente!

Count

Corragio!

Figaro

O che testa!
Quest'è la patente
che poc'anzi il fanciullo
mi diè.

Count

Per che fare?

Figaro

Vi manca ...

Count

Vi manca ...

Antonio

I'll go, but if I catch you again, *etc.*

Figaro

... Be off with you,
I'm not afraid of you! *etc.*
(Antonio goes off.)

Count

(opening the papers)
Well?

Countess

(aside to Susanna)
Heavens, the page's commission!

Count

Well?

Susanna

(aside to Figaro)
Heavens, the commission!

Count

Come now!

Figaro

Oh, what a head!
It's the commission
which the boy gave me a
little while ago.

Count

What for?

Figaro

It needs ...

Count

It needs ...

Countess
(aside to Susanna)
Il suggello.

Susanna
(aside to Figaro)
Il suggello.

Count
Rispondi!

Figaro
È l'usanza . . .

Count
Su via ti confondi?

Figaro
È l'usanza di porvi il suggello.

Count
Questo birbo mi toglie . . .

Susanna
Se mi salvo da . . .

Count
. . . il cervello, . . .

Susanna
. . . questa tempesta, . . .

Countess
Se mi salvo da . . .

Figaro
Sbuffa invano e . . .

Countess
. . . questa tempesta, può non havvi naufragio per me, . . .

Countess
(aside to Susanna)
The seal.

Susanna
(aside to Figaro)
The seal.

Count
Answer!

Figaro
It's usual . . .

Count
Come . . . you're confused?

Figaro
It's usual to seal the document.

Count
This knave will turn . . .

Susanna
If I weather . . .

Count
. . . my head, . . .

Susanna
. . . this storm, . . .

Countess
If I weather . . .

Figaro
He blusters in vain and . . .

Countess
. . . this storm, there will be no more shipwreck for me, . . .

Count
... Tutto, tutto è un mistero per me, ...

Figaro
... la terro calpesta! Poverino, ne sa men di me, ...

Susanna, Countess
... Se mi salvo, *etc.*

Count
... questo birbo, *etc.*

Figaro
... Sbuffa invano, *etc.*
(Marcellina, Basilio and Bartolo enter.)

Count
... It's all, all a mystery for me, ...

Figaro
... stamps his feet! Poor fellow, he knows less about it than me, ...

Susanna, Countess
... If I weather, *etc.*

Count
... This knave, *etc.*

Figaro
... He blusters in vain, *etc.*
(Marcellina, Basilio and Bartolo enter.)

Part VIII: Allegro Assai, E-flat Major

Marcellina, Basilio, Bartolo
Voi signor, che giusto siete, ci dovete or ascoltar.

Countess, Susanna, Figaro
Son venuti a sconsertarmi, ...

Count
Son venuti a vendicarmi, ...

Countess, Susanna, Figaro
... qual rimedio a ritrovar?

Count
... Io mi sento a consolar.

Figaro
(to Count)
Son tre stolidi,

Marcellina, Basilio, Bartolo
You, my lord, who are just, must listen to us now.

Countess, Susanna, Figaro
They've come to thwart my plan, ...

Count
They've come to avenge me ...

Countess, Susanna, Figaro
... what solution is there to be found?

Count
... How relieved I feel.

Figaro
(to Count)
These are three blockheads,

The Rise of Opera Buffa and Mozart's *The Marriage of Figaro*, I
Lecture 13—Transcript

Welcome to "How to Listen to and Understand Opera." This is Lecture 13, the first of a four-lecture set entitled "The Rise of Opera Buffa and Mozart's *The Marriage of Figaro*." First, we must deal with the birth of comic opera, what we call in Italy, opera buffa.

Some introductory statements, please. Comic opera—slapstick, satirical, often bawdy and almost always irreverent—has had a very different history than that of serious opera or what we call opera seria. For example, opera seria almost always enjoyed royal and aristocratic support, while comic opera had to rely for the most part on audience support. I would point out, and I would not be the first to point this out, that this pattern continues to this day. Grand opera, I mean the operas we would hear in our big opera houses, often receives government and foundation support, while musical theater must rely on ticket sales for its survival. The big difference between opera seria and opera buffa is that opera seria has its roots in aristocratic entertainment—the early court operas were for aristocrats—but comic opera has its roots in popular entertainment, and this is a huge and very enduring difference.

Since the Middle Ages, traveling musicians like the minstrels and the troubadours and the trouvères and the minnesingers provided comic musical entertainments for the lower classes. In Italy in the sixteenth century, that's the 1500s, these developed into more elaborate traveling companies and productions, which were called and which are called the "commedia dell'arte."

During the second half of the seventeenth century—that would be the period, that first phase of Baroque opera during which opera became in Italy a generally popular entertainment—during the second half, then, of the seventeenth century, comic interludes were introduced between the acts of Italian opera serie. These were called "intermezzi," and we shouldn't confuse these comic interludes with the intermezzi of the sixteenth century, which were part of the development of early opera. These late seventeenth-century intermezzi were actually comic interludes and scenes introduced within the acts of the larger and more dramatic opera serie. These comic interludes adopted many of the stock archetypal characters drawn from the Italian commedia dell'arte; and out of this mixture, Italian opera buffa came into being.

Donald Grout tells us that

> Comic opera grew up independently in each country, developing a number of very different national forms, such as the Italian opera buffa, the French opéra comique, the Italian ballad opera, the German singspiel, and the Spanish tonadilla. Certain features were common to all of these works in the early stages of their history. All of them showed signs of their humble origin in their choice of light or farcical subject matter and their preference for scenes, personages and dialogue taken from real life and common people. All of these comic opera genres were performed by comparatively unskilled singers, often very inferior singers about whom we could say that music was at best, a hobby. All occasionally parodied serious opera.

My friends, is there any topic more easy to parody than a grand, magnificent and serious opera? No, there is not.

> And many of these comic opera traditions used all kinds of everyday situations in place of the grand and overblown ones we would see in opera seria.

> Most importantly, all of these comic opera traditions underwent a gigantic change during the 1700s. They went from being low-class entertainment to middle-class comedy, acquiring in the process so many new features, both in terms of the libretto and the music; that by the end of the eighteenth century, by the end of the 1700s, the distinction between serious opera and comic opera had become almost insignificant. Comic opera in its beginning was lowbrow

entertainment, regarded by operagoers as something on about the level of a circus midway show. Within about 50 years, by 1750, comic opera had become the equal in terms of respectability and importance with serious opera. By the end of the eighteenth century, by the end of the 1700s, comic opera dominated the stage, having supplanted or absorbed the old opera seria almost completely.

The term "opera buffa" is used very loosely. It's a general distinction for Italian operas of the middle- and late-eighteenth century that don't come under the heading of opera seria. So, when we call something an opera buffa, it doesn't mean we're laughing in the aisles like idiots during every scene. It simply means that it's not one of these big, aristocratic, overblown, overly serious, formulaic opera seriae.

Back to the most important thing that I just read to you. By the end of the eighteenth century, the once lowbrow opera buffa dominated the stage, "having supplanted or absorbed the old opera seria almost completely." My friends, this statement begs the question, "How?" and the question, "Why?" How does a lowbrow entertainment completely supplant and overpower a highbrow one within a century? Well, we have to do some deep review, so please stay with me.

Musical style in the West, that is, in the European sphere, since the High Middle Ages has changed constantly in order to adapt to the societal and cultural environment of an ever-changing world. If you recall, we called this concept "music as a mirror," and I told you there were four basic tenets of music as a mirror. Western music has exhibited ongoing stylistic change since the High Middle Ages. That is tenet number one; constant change. Tenet number two; since the High Middle Ages composers have sought to express something of themselves, something of their world, in their music; the result being that, as the world around the composer changes, so does the style or the sound of their music. Tenet number three; what is considered expressive changes from era to era. The essential operatic expression of the early 1700s, the early eighteenth century, was the overblown and magnificent opera seria. The essential operatic style of the late 1700s, the late eighteenth century, was comic opera, opera buffa, a very different kettle of operatic fish altogether.

Fourth tenet of music as a mirror; as we move forward towards the present day the rate of change will increase exponentially.

The how and why behind opera buffa's rise from lowbrow, throw-away entertainment to high art has much to do with the historical, societal, and cultural conditions during the eighteenth century in Europe. Please, a little history. It's good for all of us; we know that. I mean history is like that medication that doesn't taste good in our youth, but as we grow up we don't mind at all. It's one of those marvelous things, and I'm always shocked by it—when you're a kid, history doesn't mean anything to you because you haven't lived long enough to understand that history is not dates and places; history is us—the way we behave. Until we've accumulated enough life experience to misbehave or at least to understand how the world really is, we can't sympathize one-on-one with dead people. Of course, as we get older history gets more fun because we realize this is just the family diary. We're basically looking back and seeing all the things everyone else has done, and it makes us feel better about ourselves and gives us a better understanding of this wonderful panoply that we call human activity. Anyway, back to a little history.

If we look at our history books, the eighteenth century, the mid-1700s, is called "the Enlightenment." The Enlightenment was the great revolution of the individual, circa 1730 to 1780 if we had to put dates on it. The Enlightenment was a period that saw the institutions of Europe—religious, political, social, educational, industrial, financial and artistic—slowly but inexorably lower their focus from the ruling aristocratic and clerical classes to a new class of people, rising from the depth of the new European mercantilism and trade and the very beginnings of the industrial revolution. For want of a better term, we call this new and rising class of people "the middle class," and the Enlightenment marks their entrance into the mainstream of European society.

Because of the weight and the financial buying power and the growing importance of this new class of people, a basic new philosophy emerges, a philosophy that takes them and their needs into account. We call that philosophy "universal humanism." Universal humanism, nineteenth- and eighteenth-century universal humanism, stated that all people are important, not just the representatives of church and state. Please, let me say that again. This is very important. Out of the Enlightenment—indeed, the Enlightenment is the emergence of a new worldview, a new philosophy that takes into account this new and growing class of moneyed and increasingly-educated people; and that philosophy is universal humanism, that recognizes the essential importance of every human being, whether they be born an aristocrat or not.

Concurrent with the rise of universal humanism is the growth of the vision, of the idea that, that institution that does the greatest good for the greatest number is good; this very populist vision of governmental and religious institutions. Now, we should understand that the spirit of the Enlightenment infused much of the aristocratic and ruling class as well, at least until the beginning of the French Revolution. Then of course, maybe some aristocrats were thinking, "This Enlightenment stuff's probably not such a good idea after all." My friends, the cat is out of the bag and will not be stuffed back in. There's that old plumber's adage; a bent pipe can never be righted. Indeed, an idea once it is abroad can never be removed and can never be stuffed back. Once a substantially large middle class says, "I'm okay and you're okay, and I want some control over my future;" once that happens it cannot be undone. But we must be fair. Without the support of the so-called "enlightened despots," many of the social and artistic reforms of the mid-eighteenth century could never have gotten off the ground. We should understand the Enlightenment is a gradual evolution, a change of vision of the role of all people in the Western society, rather than a middle-class revolution. It's a slow change in attitude; once begun it cannot be reversed.

Question; what sort of music resonates with this new idealized view of the common person that characterizes the Enlightenment? I mean, what sort of music, particularly what sort of vocal music, will our new aristocratic and non-aristocratic Enlightenment listeners prefer? I'm going to play you two pieces of music, kind of back-to-back, and I want us to think about this. Let's say you are one of these new middle-class burghers, who is now starting to consume music in a very large way. Which of these pieces is going to be more relevant to you both aesthetically—which one are you likely to like more and for what reasons—and which one seems to resonate more with the spirit of every person that is rampant during the eighteenth century?

First, I'm going to play you Antonio Vivaldi's "Siam navi all'onde algenti" from his opera *L'Olimpiade* of 1734. We listened to this in a previous lecture. This is that aria sung by the male soprano. I am going to play you the *da capo* portion, that is the return to the top of this aria, during which time our singer is singing this: "We are like ships on the silver waves, drifting out of control; like capricious winds are our affections, every pleasure is a rock, the whole of life a sea." I would remind you that these words, stiff and formal though they are, are by Pietro Metastasio, that great operatic reformer and key librettist of early eighteenth-century opera seria.

All right, my middle-class burghers, you, respond. Does this music appeal to you aesthetically, and does it seem to resonate with the spirit of every person and individuality of the Enlightenment?

(musical example)

All right, my Enlightenment listeners. I'm not saying that you didn't like this 50 years ago, but it's a different time now. Does this music resonate with the spirit of your age, the spirit of an idealized everyperson? Well, let's talk about it. We've got an incredibly complicated, ornamental, over-fussy melody, and a stiff, formal, over-fussy, metaphorical, allegorical set of words. "We are like ships on the silver waves, drifting out of control; like capricious winds are our affections, every pleasure is a rock, the whole of life a sea." Do people talk like that? Do you talk that way? I don't talk that way. If I talked that way, my wife would seriously wonder what cabinet I had been into as of late. Yes, and we also have a very unnatural sort of use of the voice. Whether we find the male soprano unnatural-sounding or not, this is also an unnatural way to use the voice. This is music of great artifice. It's music meant to show off the voice in its most extreme acrobatics and its most extreme display of virtuosity.

Let's take these comments and put them on the back burner for just a second, because now we've got to listen to another piece by comparison. The Vivaldi we just heard dates from 1734; let's listen to a piece of music written in 1786, 52 years later. This comes from Mozart's *The Marriage of Figaro*, and this is the beginning of Figaro's aria *"Non più andrai,"* "You'll go no more." Let me just tell you what we're hearing right now. Figaro is talking to the very,

very sexually promiscuous Cherubino, a 13-year-old boy who seems unable to control himself. Figaro is trying to frighten him to make him realize that if he has to go into the army, life's not going to be as easy as it's been flouncing around in women's boudoirs.

"You'll go no more, amorous butterfly, flitting about, night and day, disturbing ladies' rest, little Narcissus, Adonis of love. You'll wear no more these plumes, that smart and jaunty cap, those curls, that dashing air, that pink, effeminate complexion!" Ha, ha! "You'll wear no more," and so forth.

Let's listen to this music and let's compare it to the Vivaldi; and let's ask ourselves the same question. As a good middle-class audience, reveling in the new ideals of the Enlightenment, does this music resonate with those ideals or does it not?

Mozart's *"Non più andrai."* (musical example)

I would guess, without knowing any better, that our Enlightenment person is going to say—and it doesn't matter whether you're a member of the middle class or the ruling aristocratic class—you're going to say, "That's really nice. That's tuneful, that's memorable, it's engaging, it's accessible and that seems to resonate more with the spirit of our time, with its emphasis on a kind of idealized common person." This is common music, music for everyone. As I said before, it's music that also well reflects a specific dramatic moment. Figaro was trying to impress upon our 13-year-old horn-dog, Cherubino, his fate if he doesn't clean up his act very quickly.

Also, I would point out that this is entirely natural-sounding music, and natural is a buzzword. It's a buzzword coined by Jean-Jacques Rousseau, whom we will talk about in just a moment. It's natural use of the voice. We're not asking the voice to do anything that it really doesn't want to do, and it's naturally dramatic. The music and the words are about a dramatic situation. They're not going through some allegorical and metaphorical series of highfalutin' ideas. The artistic corollary to "that institution that does the greatest good for the greatest number" is that art, that music, that is accessible to the greatest number must be good. The Enlightenment sees, as a result, a whole new musical language evolve.

Now quickly, I've just got to make a differentiation so that things don't seem contradictory. We talked about the fact that since the 1650s opera in Italy has been a popular entertainment, but the kind of opera that was popular entertainment was opera that had grown out of aristocratic court opera, and had taken those aspects of court opera and blown them up tenfold. Despite the fact that opera in Italy is a popular entertainment at the end of the 1600s and the beginning of the 1700s, the nature of that opera grew out of aristocratic practice, and still tends to celebrate heroic, overblown, aristocratic-like characters. What changes, for example, in Italy in particular, in the 1750s and 60s is not necessarily the audience for opera; it's the kind of opera they want to consume. The reason why they're consuming this more frankly melodic and accessible opera is a function of the spirit of the times. Outside of Italy, opera is and remains an essentially aristocratic entertainment until the nineteenth century, the 1800s. The operatic revolution is of even greater import because, in those areas outside of Italy, only now are we beginning to get a middle-class audience for opera, and the opera they prefer is indeed this more melodic, accessible and Enlightenment-spirited opera.

The spirit of originality of every person and natural humanism that characterized the Enlightenment demanded, demanded, a musical style that would appeal to an idealized, average listener—a style which stressed beautiful melody and charm above everything and which avoided unnecessary complexity. The Enlightenment rejected what it considered the elitist, overblown, melodically-complex music of the Baroque. We call this new Enlightenment-inspired, accessible, melody-dominated musical style the Classical style. As this new style was brought to its state of highest development in and around the city of Vienna, circa 1770 to 1800, it's often referred to as the Viennese Classical style.

The reason why it's called the Classical style harkens back to Greek Classical art for which it is named. Greek art celebrates, above all, clarity of line. Clarity of line. Classical music celebrates clarity of melody—direct, accessible tunes. Greek art celebrates balance and proportion. Classical era music celebrates carefully wrought musical phrases and clear forms. Greek art celebrates aesthetic purity. Classical era music celebrates emotional restraint and elegance, and for our purposes, greater realism and naturalism in opera.

We should be coming to understand that the rise of opera buffa, the rise of comic opera, has most to do with a very changing world in the eighteenth century, a world in which music and politics were not two separate things but were considered one. Opera and politics; the rise of opera buffa. I would remind you of what the state of opera was around 1740, at what was the beginning of what we would now consider the Enlightenment; that is, what was the state of Baroque Metastasian opera seria. We have formulaic use of recitative and aria, predictable, one after the other. We have grandiose and expensive productions. Three, we have libretti based on bastardized versions of ancient history and mythology. Four, we have stiff, exaggerated, often overblown characters who suffer great emotional extremes. Five—and again, remember I'm going through the characters of Metastasian opera seria circa 1740—five, we have *da capo* arias, which are musically central to the operas. We have very few ensembles, almost no choruses. Basically, the musical interest is carried by these *da capo* arias, which, six, are abused profoundly by the singers, particularly the castrati.

This, then, is the state of Italian, which means essentially European, opera around 1740. To quote Samuel Johnson once again, the Italian opera is "an exotic and irrational entertainment." You know what? He's right, apropos of Metastasian opera seria. The relevance of this opera seria to the age of the Enlightenment was increasingly questioned by many contemporary artists, writers, philosophers and composers, which led inevitably to the political and aesthetic and musical rejection of Baroque opera seria by the real progressive philosophers and composers.

Chief among the critics of Baroque opera seria was Jean-Jacques Rousseau. Rousseau lived from 1712 to 1778. He was an anti-establishment French intellectual. He was an author, a philosopher, and a composer. In a future lecture, we're actually going to hear a bit of an opera composed by Mr. Rousseau. My friends, he was a beatnik, he was a hippie, he was a punk. Whatever the topic, he blasted the establishment. I mean, I could see Rousseau today in those baggy pants worn around his knees, on top of a skateboard with his hair shooting in various strange and unnatural directions, screaming about everything. He believed that the natural man was born pure, but was corrupted by civilization.

He had a major hand in writing the great French *Encyclopedia*, this virtual handbook of the Enlightenment, which was assembled between 1751 and 1765. For this *Encyclopedia*, Rousseau wrote two articles, which we might think of as being mutually exclusive but, of course, he thought of them as being absolutely related. He wrote the article on politics and he wrote the article on music. One of the greatest thinkers and authors of the Enlightenment, Jean-Jacques Rousseau launched a devastating attack on the aristocratic opera seria of the late Baroque. In attacking opera seria, the most important, substantial, and glamorous musical genre of its time, Rousseau was calling into question the basic aesthetic assumptions of the Baroque as well as attacking the aristocracy, which in France supported Baroque opera. Rousseau felt that Baroque opera seria plots and characters were as hopelessly artificial as their complicated music. Rousseau suggested that only an operatic genre that portrayed real people in actual life could be relevant to the humanistic spirit of the Enlightenment. For Rousseau, music equaled politics, equaled social structure, equaled opera.

Rousseau's influence and attitude sparked a huge controversy. His critical opposition to the old-fashioned, state-subsidized French opera erupted in 1752 in a verbal battle. It was actually a pamphlet battle, as one group wrote another tract and circulated it around and then the opposition wrote theirs and circulated it around. The good old days, my friends, the good old days. In any case, this pamphlet battle was known as the *guerre des buffons,* the "war of the buffoonists" or the "war of the comic actors," so-called because its immediate occasion was the presence in Paris of an Italian opera company which for two seasons had enjoyed sensational success in Paris performing new Italian comic operas or opera buffe.

Practically every intellectual or would-be intellectual in Paris, which means everyone, my friends, between the age of two and 102, had taken part in this debate; partisans of the Italian opera buffa on one side and the friends of traditional French and opera seria on the other. Rousseau was the leader of the pro-Italian faction, and he published an article, among the many published, in which he went so far as to argue that the French language was inherently unsuitable for operatic singing. These tracts and these pamphlets and these verbal arguments went to some wild extremes in their desires to make their points. Bottom line, Rousseau and his friends represented progressive and advanced opinion in Paris, and as a result of their campaign, traditional opera seria soon lost favor among French audiences. Rousseau and his followers embraced a new genre of opera, then emerging from Italy, particularly from the city of Naples, as the artistic solution for opera in the Enlightenment. Specifically, Rousseau and his clique embraced an opera entitled *La serva padrona, The Maid as Mistress*, composed by Giovanni Battista Pergolesi, and they celebrated this particular opera as the new ideal. Let's talk about it and listen to a little bit from *La serva padrona*.

Giovanni Battista Pergolesi lived a very short life, born in 1710, died in 1736, only 26 years; and *La serva padrona* was written when he was 23, in 1733. *La serva* began its life as one of these comic Italian intermezzi. It was originally written by Pergolesi to be performed along with his own opera seria, *Il prigioniero superbo,* and was premiered with *Il prigioniero* on September 5 of 1733 in Naples.

Let's just take a second and make a differentiation right now. Italy has been a country since the late nineteenth century. Italy was not a single country back in the early eighteenth century. We should understand that Naples and Venice—if we visit Naples and Venice, we realize how different they are even to this day—but while they had a common language back in 1733, they were not from a common country. So, let's see these as extremely distant cities with two very different aesthetic ideals. When we talk about Venetian opera, we talk about an opera that celebrates great complexity and ornamental virtuosity in the singing. For example, the Vivaldi we listened to is an example of Venetian opera, way overblown, way filled with display ornament in the voice writing. Neapolitan opera, which evolves later, is very different. Neapolitan opera celebrates arias, which are much more songlike, much more direct and much more tuneful. When we talk about the Venetian style, we're talking about a complex, highly-embellished, ornamental style. When we talk about the Neapolitan style, we're talking about a much more direct, songful style that, frankly, will have much more in common with the spirit of the Enlightenment than the Venetian style will.

Back to *La serva padrona*, a product of the Neapolitan style. It was performed in Paris as an opera unto itself, not as an intermezzo; and it represented the new attempt by young Italian composers and librettists to change the operatic language. Yes, another operatic reform. We talked about that constant pendulum swing of opera history. Around 1730 or so, certain young Italian composers began seriously trying to bring opera into harmony with the Enlightenment's changing ideals of music. Specifically, their efforts were directed towards making the entire design more natural—and there's that word "natural" again—that is, more flexible in structure, more deeply expressive in content, less laden with all that coloratura stuff, and more varied in other musical resources, such as duets, trios, and choruses if you could use them, and so forth. Don't be formulaic. Use what you have to use to make the drama work. Natural, natural, natural. Natural in all things, especially the music. Clean up the music and make it more direct and tuneful.

Typical of these early Enlightenment opera buffe was *La serva padrona*. *La serva padrona*, by example, features music that is lively and catchy. No formulas are followed; the music follows the necessities of the text. We have a small portable cast in *La serva padrona*, typical of opera buffa. In the case of *La serva,* we have a cast of only three singers, of which only two are singing parts. It's a cast of three with two singers, I should say. We have a soprano named Serpina. We have a bass named Uberto and then we have a third character named Vespone. But Vespone is a mute. He doesn't have to sing, so that will keep the payroll down. Just fill the opera stage with people who are playing mutes, and only have a couple of singers; and that indeed is what happens.

This opera, *La serva padrona,* is about a simple ruse by which a servant girl, Serpina (the serpent), tricks an old bachelor into marriage. We call this opera an opera buffa because it is less serious and lighter in plot content than an opera seria; we have familiar characters rather than heroic or mythological ones, people based in a common experience; thirdly, modest performing resources. A piece like this is only one step removed from commedia dell'arte. A piece with three players of which only two sing could be played almost anywhere a stage could be found.

Let me set the scene for you. Uberto is an old, or at least a rapidly aging, bachelor, financially well off. Serpina is his young, attractive maid who wants to become his wife. She wants to become the mistress of the casa. In order to make Uberto jealous and force him into asking for her hand, she claims to be engaged to Vespone, the mute. Uberto has been left with this information from Serpina, "Oh, I'd love you to meet my husband-to-be." Of course, Uberto can't believe she intends to marry this guy. She leaves, knowing that when she leaves, he's going to be mulling this over, and thinking this over, and some endless feedback loop in his mind is going to work him up into a frenzy. Indeed, he is confused as all get-go.

Here is the recitative that he sings at this moment of confusion:

> Now I can guess who it will be! Perhaps this will be her penance. He will do to her what she's done to me. If what she told me is true, a husband like him will keep her between the earth and a stick. Poor thing, she is! Otherwise I might think of…but she is a servant…but I wouldn't be the first…Would you marry her then? Enough…Oh no, no, it can't be. Irresponsible thoughts, get lost! Control yourself, I raised her myself. I know how she was born…Oh, Oh! How crazy you are! Easy now, easy now, please, please, think no more about it. Still, I feel a passion for her…that rotten creature…And yet, and yet, and yet...Oh God…here I go again…Oh…what confusion!"

All right, that's the recitative. No, these are not waves on the sea that mirror our allegorical emotions. This is the real thing. This guy doesn't know what to do. We can see one devil perched on the shoulder over here: "Don't marry her, don't marry her. Kick her out." The angel perched on the shoulder over there: "Yes; you wouldn't be the first. Show her happiness and joy, and leave her all you money." It's a back and forth, and then he begins the aria.

Here's the aria, "I'm all mixed up." "*Son imbrogliato io già,*" "I'm all mixed up." Isn't that a great name for an aria, not Hercules and Lydia. No, "I'm all mixed up."

> I have a certain ache in my heart. Honestly, I cannot tell whether it's love or pity. Common sense tells me: Uberto, think of yourself. I'm between yes and no, between wanting her and not wanting her, and I get more confused all the time, miserable fellow. What ever will become of me!

This aria is a *da capo* aria, but we hear no formula in it. When we listen to it now we're not going to hear the entire aria, we're only going to hear the first *A* section. We'll hear that long and wonderfully confused recitative; and then we'll hear the *A* section of the aria, and it will be enough for us to get the flavor and the spirit of this music into our ears. Uberto is a bass. It's not that he's a villain; it just means that he's an older man, because usually a bass will be either a villain or an older man, usually. Most importantly, and what I want you to notice, is how catchy and direct this music is. This is a great patter-style, lots-of-words, comic aria that perfectly fits the situation and perfectly fits the character. Please, let's sample it.

(musical example)

Can we identify with this guy? Well, of course we can. We don't have to have gone through his particular position to understand what he's feeling, because this is a common person dealing with common issues of love, lust, resistance, and everything else that we deal with in the reality of our everyday. Neither is this aria overblown; neither do we have some huge, coloratura, overstated version of these emotions. His confusion is enough, and that's exactly what Pergolesi is portraying. I would point out that in the recitative section we have the strings and the harpsichord playing. For the great bulk of the recitative, we hear an accompanied recitative. The beauty of this is that the sweeping strings can accentuate and render point to his confusion and emotions. I would also point out that it is a small band. It's basically a harpsichord with a small string section; so the orchestra is as portable as the singing cast is itself.

I think it's a most interesting point, my friends, that this flexible, tuneful, completely believable—that is, unartificial—aria was written in Naples one year before Vivaldi wrote the stagy and ornate *Siam navi all'onde algenti* in Venice. Indeed, these early opera buffe are contemporary with some of the most ornate and extreme opera seria. We should understand that in history nothing starts and stops in neat little packages, but ideas overlap and things grow in one region, only to take over later in other regions. Meanwhile, somewhere else, the old stuff might be popular for another 50 years. Things move in fits and starts, always overlapping, always cross-currenting with each other. The bottom line is, even as Metastasian opera seria reaches its highest level of ornateness, sophistication, and formula, the beginnings of opera buffa, which will ultimately replace that seria, are present and are growing.

When we return for our next lecture we are going to talk about the character types we experience in opera buffa and the general conventions of opera buffa. Until then, I thank you.

The Rise of Opera Buffa and Mozart's
The Marriage of Figaro, II
Lecture 14—Transcript

Welcome back to "How to Listen to and Understand Opera." This is Lecture 14, the second of a four-lecture set entitled "The Rise of Opera Buffa and Mozart's *The Marriage of Figaro*." We left off preparing ourselves to talk about opera buffa character types and conventions. Let us do so.

Even as it evolved and became more sophisticated, opera buffa continued to use archetypal characters drawn originally from the Italian commedia dell'arte. The largest and most significant character division in opera buffa, and this betrays its common roots, is between those savvy, street-smart servants and members of the lower class and, at the other extreme, the blundering, pompous professionals—aristocrats, doctors, lawyers and merchants. For example, some of the savvy, street-smart, underclass people we meet…well, we've met Serpina in *La serva padrona*. In *The Marriage of Figaro*, Susanna is such a street-smart servant; Figaro himself, is such a street-smart servant. If we were doing Mozart's *Così fan tutte* we would meet the servant, Despina, who was the oil that certainly lubricates the comedy and the drama in that particular opera, and Leporello does the same in Mozart's *Don Giovanni*. Blundering, pompous, aristocrats, doctors, lawyers and merchants include, in *The Marriage of Figaro*, Count Almaviva, Dr. Bartolo, Don Basilio; all of these titled people one could imagine all of these various degrees and titles after their names, but completely unable to deal with the reality of the real world. Uberto in *La serva padrona* was such a bumbling, rich person; and in *Don Giovanni*, Don Ottavio; and so forth and so on.

Opera buffa plots, almost by their very nature then, were highly politicized in an era when the relationship between the common, middle, and aristocratic classes was undergoing a profound reexamination. I mean, talk about the right genre of opera at the right time and the right place! No wonder Rousseau was so jazzed about *La serva padrona*. It was the right kind of music, the right kind of politics, at least Rousseau's kind of politics, all wrapped up in a neat little operatic package; a music and opera type made by the Enlightenment, for the Enlightenment, that celebrated common people both dramatically and musically. "Tres bon, tres bon," Mr. Rousseau might say.

Mozart's opera buffe. He wrote a few in his youth, indeed his first opera, written at the age of 12 in 1768, was an opera buffa, and that is *La finta semplice, The pretended simpleton*. His second opera buffa was *La finta giardiniera, The pretended gardener*, of 1775, at the age of 19. I would point out that the titles of both of these opera buffae indicate—*The pretended simpleton, The pretended gardener*—they indicate one of the central plot devices in opera buffa, and that is disguise and mistaken identity. Of course, the big opera buffe, the ones that put Mozart on the map and the ones that can never allow him to be removed from it, are the three opera buffe he did in conjunction with librettist Lorenzo da Ponte. Those operas are *The Marriage of Figaro* of 1786, when Mozart was 30, *Don Giovanni* in 1787, and *Così fan tutte* in 1789. Mozart wrote that one at the age of 33.

I've got to mention something about Mozart's age. We say he was 12 years old when he wrote his first opera buffa, he was 30 years old when he did a piece like *The Marriage of Figaro*; with Mozart I find it wise just to add 20 years. It's easier for us to deal with him and it's easier for us to absorb the masterwork level of these pieces, if we simply add 20 years to his age all the time. We could pretend that he wrote *La finta semplice* not at 12 but at 32; and that's about right! That makes us feel better. It makes us feel better to think that *The Marriage of Figaro* was written by someone who was 50, and not 30. Let's do that with Mozart. It's very handy, and it makes life easier for us. Let's just pretend he was born 20 years old; and then, the age that he was when he wrote these pieces is completely explicable, it's something we can better identify with.

Briefly, but importantly, let's take a quick diversion and talk about Lorenzo da Ponte, this marvelous librettist whose three comic libretti allowed Mozart to really transcend the entire genre with *Figaro*, *Giovanni*, and *Così fan tutte*. Lorenzo da Ponte was born Emanuele Conegliano, Jewish, March 1749, in Vittorio Veneto, Italy. At the age of 14, he was converted by his father to Catholicism. Yes, all the Conegliano *ragazzi* were converted to Catholicism. Their father, who was upwardly mobile and wanted good things for his family, knew that that was the only way his sons would have a chance to be educated, is if they were Catholic. Indeed, the following year, Lorenzo enters the seminary at Cenada at the age of 15. In 1773, at 24, he is ordained a priest. In 1779, six years later, at 30, Lorenzo da Ponte is run out of Venice for adultery. Yes, he was one of these creative priests. The priesthood lasted as long as the adultery charges lasted and that was the end of da Ponte, priest.

He flees Venice and heads almost straight north to Vienna, where he gets jobs writing poetry and libretti and develops this marvelous, marvelous literary gift very quickly. His first big success is his adaptation of Pierre Beaumarchais's controversial comedy, *The Marriage of Figaro*, for Mozart, which according to da Ponte had been suggested by Mozart. Da Ponte was nothing if not a *primo uomo* himself, very arrogant, very sure of himself. When he gives Mozart credit for anything—which is rare; I believe in da Ponte's memoirs the name of Mozart is mentioned four or five times maybe, so it's unusual for da Ponte to give Mozart credit for anything. It is significant that he would credit Mozart with having had the idea to do *The Marriage of Figaro*.

In 1792, having made many enemies—by the way, this is the year after Mozart dies—having made many enemies and deeply in debt, da Ponte leaves Vienna quickly, very quickly, and settles ultimately in London, where, among other things, he opens up an Italian language bookstore. In 1805, 13 years later, deeply in debt, one step ahead of his creditors, da Ponte and his family move—we should say, flee—to Elizabeth, New Jersey, where, among other things, he opens up a grocery store. The grocery store eventually fails, as did other business ventures in New York and Philadelphia. If da Ponte approached you with a scheme, asking for a loan, find a way to say "no." It would seem that he had the anti-Midas touch. He turned gold into lead.

Anyway, in 1825, 20 years after arriving in the United States, he became Professor of Italian Language and Literature at Columbia College in New York. He helps to build one of the first opera houses in the United States in New York City. The climax of his life in the United States is the production of *Don Giovanni* in New York in 1825. He dies in New York City, August 17, 1838, at the age of 89, having outlived Mozart by nearly 47 years. He was a brilliant poet, a brilliant dramatist, among the great librettists in opera history. Really, he ranks with the other three great ones as far as I'm concerned, we're talking about Metastasio, we're talking about Arrigo Boito, who was Verdi's librettist for *Otello* and *Falstaff*, and Hugo Hofmannsthal, who was Strauss's librettist for *Elektra* and *Der Rosenkavalier*.

Back to the Mozart/da Ponte *Marriage of Figaro*, with some background on the storyline. The characters and the basic storyline of *The Marriage of Figaro* grow out of two plays by the French dramatist, Pierre de Beaumarchais, who lived from 1732 to 1799. These two plays were *The Barber of Seville*, which was written in 1772, and then the sequel to *The Barber of Seville*, *The Marriage of Figaro*, which was written in 1784. More on the political and social implications of these plays in a moment.

First, *The Barber of Seville*, the first of these two plays. *The Barber of Seville* is a comedy; it contains very little social commentary or anything of that like. And *The Barber of Seville* has been set twice into an opera; once by Giovanni Paisello in 1782, and that's a piece that Mozart knew well, and then it was set again to become another opera by Gioacchino Rossini in 1816. We will talk about the controversy between the Paisello clique and the Rossini clique when we get to Rossini's *Barber of Seville*. The important characters we meet in this first play are as follows. We meet Count Almaviva. He's about 19 or 20 years old and he is in love with Rosina. She's about 15 or 16 years old. She is the ward of the evil, blowhard, and pompous Doctor Bartolo. The plot of this first play, of *The Barber of Seville*, sees Figaro, a former employee of Count Almaviva, join up with the count, and together they win Rosina for the count. There's lots of intrigue, there's lots of disguise and mistaken identity and a shaving scene. I mean, almost all of the stock scenes we'd expect in a commedia dell'arte we're going to get in the course of the play.

Here's the significant point, and I want you to remember this. At the conclusion of *The Barber of Seville*, Count Almaviva renounces his feudal *diritto di signore*, his right of the master, whereby the lord of each manor was entitled to deflower every maiden in his service on her wedding night. This is a renunciation that the count is later to regret.

The Marriage of Figaro is social commentary. Beaumarchais wrote it 12 years later. The action of *The Marriage of Figaro* takes place three years after

The Barber of Seville has concluded. We get to re-meet our characters three years later; we would hope three years wiser. Well, this is what we meet. We have a series of couples, two central couples. Count Almaviva has become, in the last three years, a shameless philanderer. Rosina, now the countess, not 20 years old yet, is old and wise and sad beyond her years. That's couple number one. Couple number two: Figaro is engaged to Rosina's maid, named Susanna. Of course, Susanna is that lovely young lady with whom Almaviva desperately wants to sleep. He intends to bed her despite the fact that he has renounced that right by which he might have been allowed to bed her. Then there's a third couple, Marcellina and Bartolo, and a fourth couple, Cherubino and Barbara. We'll meet these other two couples in due time. The action of this second play revolves around Almaviva's determination to sleep with Susanna, and Figaro and Susanna's equal if not greater determination to marry before he can force the issue.

Joseph Kerman tells us:

> For Mozart, *Figaro* was an initiation in theatric sophistication. His librettist was Lorenzo da Ponte, an experienced professional with wit, skill and polish to spare. An operatic version of *The Barber of Seville* had just made a success in Vienna, a bright, innocent play innocently composed by Giovanni Paisello, who was a leading opera buffa composer of the day. But Beaumarchais's sequel, *The Marriage of Figaro*, was politically and morally so suspect that it could not be staged at all without the sugar coat of music.
>
> Opera buffa at that time was gingerly turning towards adult themes, towards libertarianism, towards genuine wit and humanity. Mozart and da Ponte must have half-realized that they were creating living comedy out of the traditionally simple farce of Pergolesi and Paisello. Everything about Figaro was exceptional, advanced, brilliant and alarmingly real. It was much too clever to succeed in Vienna." As an aside, I would say the reason why it was too clever to succeed in Vienna is if you're going to make fun of aristocrats, the likelihood is that the greatest success will not occur where all the aristocrats live; and that was, of course, Vienna.

Mozart's sense of cleverness, power, and exhilaration remains an actual aesthetic quality of the piece, a quality that will always fascinate us.

Nicely said, Mr. Kerman. Let us move on, please. The politics of *The Marriage of Figaro*—and of course, we've already talked about the nature of opera and politics in the eighteenth century. They are inextricably entwined with one another. Despite the fact that the action ostensibly takes place in Spain, Beaumarchais's play is, of course, a scathing attack on the *ancien regime*, on the French aristocracy as it existed in 1784. The play was initially banned in France; initially banned in France, but I would tell you it was unequivocally, permanently, absolutely banned in Austria. It would seem that the Hapsburgs had much less a sense of humor than the Bourbon kings did in France about this sort of thing. Napoleon's comment, his famous comment regarding *The Marriage of Figaro,* is absolutely true. Napoleon said, "It is the revolution already in action." Indeed, five years before the French Revolution actually takes place, this play is looking very clearly forward to that revolution.

Da Ponte's libretto—and they had to get permission, they had to get permission from the censors, da Ponte and Mozart did, to even write this opera; of course, the libretto which was presented to them was pretty much stripped of the controversial aspects that were in the play. However, and this is the wonderful thing, Mozart put all of this back in with the music. The aristocrats tend to have pompous and measured music, music that rings of opera seria, music that rings of overblown and false characters. The common characters in this opera tend to have very modern music, very fluid, very real, very natural music. The distinction between the overblown aristocrats and the real, savvy, streetwise, common people is highlighted in the music in a way that no one could tell from just reading the libretto. I would tell you that after this piece was produced, the reaction was, "How did we let this happen?" Well, you couldn't tell until the music was written that this was going to happen. Mozart imbues his characters with an unbelievable degree of life, emotional depth, human legitimacy, and dramatic motivation. No one was ever better, and no one has been better since, in creating real people on the opera stage, strictly through music.

Here's our game plan; to meet the characters, observe the dramatic situation and finish our all-too-brief examination of this magnificent opera with the amazing, incredible, awe-inspiring and breath-taking Act Two finale. My friends, I am going to go to my adjectival palette constantly today. This is a stunning opera, and the Act Two finale is a stunning piece of work. There's no way I'm going to try to put on any kind of faux cynical mask of detachment when talking about Mozart; it's a waste of time. This is too good. We've got to wallow in it, and wallow it deserves to be.

Mozart, da Ponte, *The Marriage of Figaro,* Act One. The opera opens with a brilliant and bubbling and justly famous overture. Let's listen to the beginning.

(musical example)

It hurts to stop that. I know it does, I know it does. We must proceed. It's for you to buy the recording and wallow in this on your own. Put it on auto-play and listen to it 30 times. We never get tired of this music. It's really, really quite extraordinary. Mozart's control of harmony and form is so sophisticated that there's a tremendous sense of forward motion and variety, yet his melodic surfaces are so accessible and glow so brilliantly that it never loses its popular touch either. We have the perfect combination of great, great musical substance and great beauty at the same time. Often the beautiful face is not also the intelligent face, but in this case, in Mozart's case, it indeed is.

By the way, it was Mozart's habit to wait until the very last moment to write his overtures. This wasn't because he was lazy, there was nothing lazy about the man, it's because he felt that he didn't really know what kind of music should start an opera until the opera had gone through rehearsal and he really had a sense of its *Gestalt,* of its essential substance. It was not unusual for Mozart to write these overtures the night before the premiere, the day before the premiere. I guess he kind of liked the pressure of doing stuff like that. He was a little crazy that way, and of course, he had a facility the likes of which no one has ever had before or since. I would tell you—and it breaks my heart to tell you this because to speak it out loud, hurts—almost the entire *Marriage of Figaro* was written in six weeks, from beginning to end. Now, it should have taken a couple of years. Given the amount of music and the quality of the music, it should have taken a couple of years. Most of the opera was written in six weeks, that is, from start to finish. Done. That is impossible for me to conceive. It would take a copyist longer simply to copy out the parts than it took Mozart to compose this piece, finished, out of his mind. How he did that, no one knows. It's freaky. He was freaky. The music is amazing.

Let's proceed. Again, if we start stacking all this Mozart hyperbole on top of the music itself, this becomes almost superhuman. Let's avoid doing that, because Mozart was a person, and his insight into other people is what this is all about. Let's get some of that insight right away. Number One: We meet Figaro and his bride-to-be, Susanna. By the way, this is what we call a "numbers" opera, and this is a term I haven't used yet so I'd better use it now. Opera buffe, indeed even opera serie, are what we call "numbers" opera. The numbers are the arias; the duets; the trios; and the ensembles. These are the pieces within the opera that have the highest melodic profile. The recitatives are the connectors that connect these numbers together. If I say that this is Number One, it is the first substantial, vocal music in the piece. It is a duet, which tells us right away that we're not going to have that predictable series of arias and recitatives that we would have in an opera seria. Mozart is starting with a group sing, in this case two people. No formula. That's very important. Everything remains flexible to serve the drama.

Let me set the scene for you: We meet couple number one, that's Figaro and Susanna in a half-furnished room with a large armchair in the center. Figaro is measuring the floor and Susanna is trying on a hat in front of the mirror. Usually she's looping some ribbon on it and it trying to find just the right lay for the hat. We hear very chipper, upbeat, counting music, which sets the scene. Yes, Figaro is measuring the room for the wedding bed and he's excited about that. Susanna is trying on her wedding bonnet. They are a couple completely at ease with each other and we will hear that in this duet. They're accustomed to each other's company. They're accustomed to each other's presence. They would seem almost like happily married people already. This upbeat, bouncing number follows effortlessly that wonderful overture.

Figaro is counting "Cinque... dieci... venti...," "Five... ten... twenty... thirty... thirty-six... forty-three."

Susanna's not really listening to him, as married couples tend not to listen to each other. She's just looking at herself in the mirror saying, "Oh, now I'm pleased with it, yes, it seems just made for me." Figaro continues, "Five..." Susanna says, "Take a look, my dear Figaro..." "...Ten..." "Oh, oh. Take a look. Figaro, take a look." "...Twenty..." "Look at my hat now, please"

"...forty-three..."

She's getting annoyed. "Figaro, take a look, my dear Figaro, look at my hat, now." So finally, he stops what he's doing, "Oh, yes, sweetheart, now it's much prettier, it seems made just for you." Susanna says, "Take a look, really. Take a look." "Yes, yes, sweetheart." "*Si, mio cuore.*" Susanna goes back to the mirror, "Now I'm pleased with it, yes, yes."

The whole environment here is one of two people who love each other, who've spent a lot of time with each other already and are very at ease in each other's company. Finally, they sing together, "Ah, The wedding morn is nigh." Today's the day of the wedding. Here's another convention of opera buffa: All the action has to take place within a 24-hour period. It's the wedding day; it's the morning of the wedding day, so they think.

"How dear to my tender bridegroom is this charming little hat which Susanna made herself." As they sing together, they sing in what we call "thirds" and "sixths." They sing in intervals that trace these kinds of patterns. (piano example) In harmonizing together, the message to us, the audience, is clear; they are of a single mind, they are in complete harmony with each other.

Let's listen to this opening number. Let's be aware of the casual, easy nature of this music; the wonderful way that they exchange their pleasantries with each other, at first not being aware of each other, but finally, singing together and showing us the united front of their relationship.

(musical example)

What a fabulous introduction to this couple. We understand the relationship and we understand much about the individuals, too. They're people with whom we can immediately identify. I don't think any of us in the audience has trouble seeing parts of ourselves and our loved ones in Figaro and Susanna.

A spirited recitative ensues as Susanna finally notices—she's been so into this hat—she finally notices what Figaro's been doing. It's recitative secco, dry, accompanied by harpsichord only. Susanna says, "What are you measuring, my darling Figaro?" Figaro says, "I'm seeing if that bed which the Count is giving us will look well in this corner." Susanna's alarmed; "In this room?" Figaro says, "Well, of course, the master has generously given it to us." Susanna follows by saying, "Then you may have it all to yourself." "Well, what's your objection?" "I have my reasons." "Well, why won't you share them with me?"

Susanna has at once realized Count Almaviva's motive for giving them this particular room, and she'll have nothing to do with it. I'll tell you that motivation in a moment. Let's continue.

"Because I don't wish to share it with you. You are my humble servant, aren't you?" "But, I don't understand why you turn up your nose at the most comfortable room in the castle." "Because I am Susanna and you are an idiot!" "Oh, thank you very much. You're too kind; now tell me, do you know of any other room to suit us better?"

Right away, Susanna's mercurial temper and quick wit and intelligence are in evidence. She can go around calling anyone she wants an idiot and get away with it, because compared to her, they might be. Here's the problem. This lovely, big, wonderful and spacious room is located exactly between the countess's bedroom to one side and the count's bedroom to the other. Figaro figures that this is great, because they are right in between the two people they serve. Figaro is now again working for the count and Susanna is working for the countess. Susanna detects a greater problem here.

Number Two, another duet that immediately follows this recitative, represents at first Figaro's desire to explain to Susanna why this is such an optimum situation. An animated introduction indicates that the humdrum activity of Number One here gives way to increasing drama. Figaro attempts to explain the advantages of their new bedroom's location:

> Supposing one night my lady should call you ting, ting, ting, ting, why, you could go to her in a trice. Then it may happen that my master wants me dong, dong, dong, dong, and I'm with him in a hop, skip and a jump.

Susanna responds as if speaking to a child. We realize how savvy she is as she explains to Figaro the facts of life, gently mocking his naiveté as she goes. Susanna says,

> Oh, and suppose some morning your precious Count, ting, ting, ting, ting, should send you on an errand three miles away ting, ting, dong, dong, the devil brings him to my door and in a hop, skip, and a jump…

Of course, Figaro is scandalized. He can't believe she is saying this about his count. "Susanna, softly, softly, I pray you,…" Then Susanna says, "And in…" "…softly, softly…" "…a hop, skip, and a jump…" "…softly, softly…" "…ting, ting…" "…softly, softly…" "…dong, dong!" "…softly, softly."

"Listen to me!" Susanna says. And Figaro says, "Quickly, then!"

Susanna: "If you wish to hear the rest, dismiss your suspicions which do me wrong." Don't blame the messenger, buddy. I've got nothing to do with this. I'm just telling you what I know. Figaro says, "All right. I must hear the rest, though I am chilled with doubts and suspicions." Yes. Figaro can't believe that his count would have something in for his Susanna.

Let's listen to this marvelous duet, and then we'll proceed to find out what Susanna knows and Figaro does not. First, *"Se a caso madama."*

(musical example)

Poor, poor Figaro. Just when he thought life was about to get easy, his bride-to-be is telling him, "Not so fast, buster." Is this naive Figaro the clever and street-smart barber of Seville? He's about 30 now, and indeed, it would seem that he's a little slow on the uptake, unwilling to see his master's intrigue at a time when he's looking forward to the slower pace of a happily married life. He is Everyman, Figaro is; in one writer's words, "The first operatic hero with whom a modern audience can naturally identify." That is utterly true, I believe.

Susanna lays it out for Figaro in dry recitative:

"Now listen quietly." "All right. Tell me what is happening." "My lord, weary of pursuing beauties from far and near wishes to try his luck once again in the castle. But his appetite is not whetted by his wife, make no mistake."

Figaro says, "Well, well who is it, then?" "Well, it's your little Susanna." "You?" "Myself, and he hopes to further his noble plan by having us near him all the time." "Bravo! Tell me more." Yes, Figaro's starting to get mad.

"Hence the gracious concern which he lavishes on you and your bride-to-be." "Well, well, a sprat to catch a mackerel!" Susanna says, "Hush now, here comes the best part; Don Basilio, my singing teacher and his factotum, during lessons informs me daily of the Count's desire." So, Basilio is in cahoots with Almaviva, yes. In *The Barber of Seville,* he was the enemy of Almaviva.

Figaro, of course, says, "Who! Basilio? Why, that rogue!" Susanna responds sarcastically, "And did you believe that my dowry"—which is to be supplied by the count—that my dowry was the reward for your handsome face?" "I flattered myself that I deserved it." "No, no. His object is to claim from me those half-hours of pleasure which feudal privilege…"

"But what! Has not my lord abolished such rights on his estates?" "Oh, he regrets it now, it seems, and he's trying to redeem his right through me." "Bravo!" says Figaro. "I like that! How kind of my lord! We'll have some fun out of this! You've found…"

As Figaro speaks, we hear a bell ring from the countess's room. Figaro says, "Who rang? Why, it's the Countess." Yes, and now Figaro stands informed of Almaviva's intentions. Susanna says, "Goodbye, goodbye, sweet Figaro." Figaro says to Susanna, "*Coraggio, mio tesoro.* Courage, my treasure." And she says, "*E tu, cervello,*" "Use your brains, you big old guy, you."

So, she goes off, leaving Figaro by himself. Now, of course, the old Figaro comes out. He will use his brains, indeed. In a firm, almost heroic recitative, we witness Figaro's capacity for intrigue reborn before our very eyes. This is not a servant. This is a *mensch*.

> Bravo, my master! Now I'm beginning to understand the mystery, and see your plan quite plainly. We're off to London, are we? You as ambassador, and I as your courier, and Susanna as "secret attaché." Non sarà.—it will not be says Figaro here and now.

Yes, the superior underdog declares a quiet war on his employer. Figaro is determined, although he knows he must proceed quietly and with utmost stealth. We have a marvelous *da capo* aria, which I will read through quickly then we will listen to.

> If you wish to dance, *se vuol ballare*, my dear Count, I'll play the guitar, oh yes! And if you come to my school I'll teach you how to scheme I'll deal with you…but softly…by pretense I shall be better able to discover every secret.

> By parrying artfulness with artfulness, now pricking, now feinting jokingly I shall upset all his intrigues.

> If you wish to dance, my dear Count I'll play the guitar, oh yes!

Note the almost pop feel of this aria. It's very direct, immediate and accessible music. It matches Figaro well. It also matches the dance well. I would point out that the *A* sections are a galliard, a three-step, and the *B* section is a duple-meter dance. The point is, this is direct and earthy music that echoes a direct and earthy Figaro, now absolutely intent on taking charge of the intrigues that must ultimately lead to his marriage.

The recitative and aria "*Se vuol ballare*."

(musical example)

End of Scene One; Figaro exits. This, my friends, is trash talk, Travis Bickel, circa 1740, "You messin' with me? You messin' with me?" Yes, Figaro is armed and ready to do battle. Let us take a break. When we return, we will meet Bartolo and Marcellina. Thank you.

The Rise of Opera Buffa and Mozart's *The Marriage of Figaro*, III
Lecture 15—Transcript

Welcome back to "How to Listen to and Understand Opera." This is Lecture 15, the third of a four-lecture set entitled "The Rise of Opera Buffa and Mozart's *The Marriage of Figaro*." Where we have left off is, we are in Act One of the da Ponte/Mozart *The Marriage of Figaro*, and we've just heard the end of Scene One. Figaro has decided it's time for him to become the Figaro of old. He is determined to outfox Count Almaviva, who, he has been informed by Susanna, desires to bed Susanna before her soon and impending wedding with Figaro. The scene ends with Figaro confidently espousing his conviction that he will outwit the count on this one.

Thus, Scene Two begins and we meet another couple. This is couple number three. Couple number one was Figaro and Susanna, couple number two is the count and his wife the countess. This is couple number three, Doctor Bartolo and Marcellina. They are very interesting people, and they stand in stark contrast with the couple number one, Susanna and Figaro, we met in Scene One. Bartolo is the former guardian of Rosina, who is now, of course, the countess. His plans to marry her were squashed by Figaro and Count Almaviva in *The Barber of Seville*, the action of which took place three years ago.

Marcellina is Bartolo's former maid. She's about 48 or 50 years old. She has lent Figaro a sizeable sum of money, which has now come due. Figaro and Susanna plan to pay back this loan with the money they receive as a dowry from the count. But Marcellina happens to know that if Susanna spurns the count, he will withdraw the dowry. Figaro, unfortunately, secured the loan by promising to marry Marcellina if he could not pay her back in time. This gets more interesting by the minute, I think. Both Bartolo and Marcellina want to see the impending wedding fail, each for their own reasons; Bartolo out of pure nastiness and revenge, and Marcellina because she's liable to come up with a very young, spry, nimble and, one would hope, virile husband.

Offstage, before they've entered, Marcellina has just told Bartolo about Figaro's debt. This is the recitative that begins Scene Two.

Bartolo says, "And you wait till the day fixed for the marriage to speak to me of this?" Marcellina responds,

> I'll not lose heart, doctor. To break up a planned marriage at an even more advanced stage than this is a mere pretext which has sufficed before now. And besides this contract he has obligations to me, never fear! But we must frighten Susanna and artfully induce her to refuse the Count; he, out of spite, will take my part and so Figaro shall be my husband.

Bartolo responds, "Very well. I'll do all I can. Tell me all without reserve." Then he says aside, "I should relish marrying off my former servant," that's Marcellina, "to the man who, that time, engineered my ward's elopement." Yes, indeed. Vengeance is a dish best served cold. Dr. Bartolo's hatred for Figaro boils over.

While I read this, let's realize that the music that Mozart has supplied for Bartolo is pompous, loud, old-style, opera seria music. We're going to hear sweeping strings and dotted rhythms, the stuff of the old-style French overture, that music that was used in the French court to welcome the king to the theater, the king being Louis XIV back in the seventeenth century. This is music that stinks of age, pomposity, of an age that has passed; and Doctor Bartolo, we know right away, is just a big old humbug.

> Vengeance, ah, vengeance is a pleasure reserved for the wise; to forget affronts and outrage is ever base and cowardly. With cunning and acumen, with common sense and discretion, it can be satisfied. A difficult matter. But believe me, it shall be done. If I have to turn inside out the legal code, if I have to read the entire index with some ambiguity, some synonym, I'll find a way to confound him. All Seville knows Bartolo. That knave Figaro shall be outwitted.

Do we really for a second believe that this blowhard can outfox our Figaro? No, not for a second do we. Again, I want us to note while we listen to this marvelous comic aria *"La vendetta,"* "the vendetta," vengeance. How old and dated and pompous this music is, perfectly suited to this character. This is what I meant before when I said that whatever da Ponte took out by way of offensive characterizations of the wealthier people, Mozart plugs right back in with the music. Let's listen and let's smile. It's most comic and most true to the character.

(musical example)

That's marvelous. Please notice that Bartolo is a bass, and that's the kind of voice that we would expect of an older man of villainy. It stands counter to Figaro who is, of course, a tenor, the typical star, the typical hero of an Italian opera. I should add that Susanna is generally a part sung by a lyric soprano, and Rosina, the countess, whom we will meet soon enough, is a part generally sung by a more dramatic soprano.

Let's move on, please. We have to take a quick break and talk about the character archetypes that da Ponte is drawing on for his characters, really that Beaumarchais is drawing on for his characters here. Now that we've met enough of them, it behooves us to observe the Italian commedia dell'arte archetypes from which the French playwright, Beaumarchais, and then, of course, the Italian-born librettist, da Ponte, draw their characters.

Dr. Bartolo, who we've just heard from, comes from a stock character named Pantalone. He's a rich, miserly, old clod. He's a merchant from Venice, always being robbed, always being cuckolded. We never find out, by the way, what he's a doctor of. It's more an officious title, more than anything else, that just shows us that he prides himself as an expert on many things but really knows very little.

Figaro comes from the archetype of Arlecchino, Harlequin; a valet, athletic and graceful, a ladies' man, cunning, claiming noble birth. These again are stereotypical characters that if you went to see a commedia dell'arte play and someone was called "Pantalone," you would know right away what kind of person, what kind of character they were. If someone was called "Arlecchino," you would know what kind of person they were. Well, Bartolo is a Pantalone and Figaro is an Arlecchino.

Rosina in *The Barber of Seville* is a Colombina. Here in *The Marriage of Figaro,* Colombina is Susanna. Colombina is a pretty, young girl, loved by everybody though feared for her sharp and acidic tongue and wit. Often the action of the story revolves around her desire to marry. Indeed, the only character regularly involved in opera buffa who does not figure in the cast list of the commedia dell'arte, is the old hag, whether nursemaid confidante or rapacious spinster. She was a stock character in classical Roman comedy. In *The Barber of Seville* the old hag was Berta, and here in *The Marriage of Figaro,* it is of course, Marcellina, with all of her desire to marry the young Figaro. Following Bartolo's paean to vengeance, Marcellina and Susanna run into each other and indulge in a wonderfully catty recitative and duet. Yes, Marcellina keeps saying, "I will get your Figaro," and Susanna keeps saying, "But your age, your age." Every time Susanna brings up Marcellina's age, Marcellina compresses a little further, kind of like a prune under the midday sun, until finally the victor is clear, and that is Susanna.

We move forward to the entrance of Cherubino. Cherubino is a young nobleman, although at the age of 13 we really should call him a young nobleboy, who has been sent to court to complete his education. Now properly named, he is Leon de Astorga, and he lusts after every woman he sees everywhere, at court, in the fields, everyone. It's said that Beaumarchais created Cherubino out of his own adolescent memories. I think almost every man would create a Cherubino out of his own adolescent memories. I would add that this part is written for a soprano, a female soprano not a male soprano, and indeed this part will be sung by a woman in performance today. That's to indicate that Cherubino, for all of his crazed sexuality, still has not had his voice change. So he is 13 and sounds 13. Again, the part of Cherubino would be most likely sung by a lyric soprano, a soprano with a light and flexible voice.

Let me read. We're back in Susanna's bedroom and Cherubino enters. Now a quick word. A mature, sexually mature, male will not generally enter a woman's bedroom who is not his wife. I think I can make that statement with some fair security. But children wander in and out of bedrooms without thinking twice about it, flopping down on the bed or the floor, and twirling their legs, and so forth. All right, that's our Cherubino. He's a half-man and he's a half-boy; and he's used to wandering in wherever he wants. There's that moment at which all of us have to face the facts that we cannot take, if we're a man, our daughter into the men's room with us anymore and our wives can't take our sons in to the women's room anymore. Well, Cherubino would seem not quite to have gotten to that point yet.

Anyway, he walks into Susanna's bedroom, plops himself down and says, "Dear Susanna, is it you?" Susanna says, "'Tis I. What do you want?" Cherubino is already waxing, "Ah, my sweetheart, what a misfortune!" Susanna, "Your sweetheart? What's happened?"

So Cherubino tells Susanna his woes: "Yesterday, because the Count found me alone with Barbarina"—that's the daughter of Antonio, the drunken gardener—"he decided to send me away; and if my beautiful godmother the Countess does not intercede on my behalf I shall go away and never see you again, my dear Susanna."

Of course, Susanna says, "You won't see me again. Bravo!" Too bad! "But does your heart sigh no more in secret for the Countess?" Yes, the countess. Cherubino's face flames, "Ah. She inspires me with too much respect! Happy you, you who can see her when you wish, you dress her in the morning, help her to undress at night, busy yourself with her pins and her lace…ah! If I were in your place…" This guy's out of control, out of control.

Let's sample the opening of the enduring aria, "*Non so più cosa son.*" Testosterone-crazed, his voice as of yet unchanged, Cherubino blurts out his confusion at his own developing sexuality. I want to point this out, and I'll point this out in the manner by which I read the text. Mozart has brilliantly set these words. He keeps having rests in inconvenient places. He keeps forcing the singer to breathe when the singer doesn't want to breathe; and this creates a mock despair, kind of gasping; a kind of heavy breathing that is necessary to get this song out. Of course, it's a heavy breathing that corresponds exactly with this unrestrained, uncontrolled, and unhampered sexuality that poor Cherubino is suffering right now. The throes of male adolescence. Would any of us willingly teach in a junior high school? No, no indeed not.

Cherubino says,

> I no longer know what I am, or what I'm doing, now I'm feverish, now I'm chilled; every woman makes me change color, or makes me tremble with emotion. The very words "love" and "delight" excite me and make my heart race. And I am forced to speak of love by a desire that I can't explain. I speak of love waking, I speak of love dreaming, to the water, to the shadows, to the mountains, to the flowers, the grass, the fountains, to the echo, the air, the winds which waft away with them the sound of my fruitless words...And if no one is there to listen, I speak of love to myself.

Of course, this "speak of love" really should be, properly put, "fantasize" of love, but then we would enter into a different reality and da Ponte and Mozart aren't going to touch that one, if you'll excuse me.

Let's listen to the first minute or so of *"Non so più cosa son,"* a superb and effective setting by Mozart. Now, we meet the character of Cherubino.

(musical example)

All right, my friends, it's time for some action. The count, uninvited, suddenly enters Susanna's room. Susanna was right on the button on this one. Of course, Cherubino is terrified that the count is going to find him alone with Susanna. Yesterday, the count found him alone with Barbarina and is now ready to send him away.

Cherubino says, "Ah, I'm lost...the count!" Susanna says, "Oh, poor me!" The count comes in and as he does so, Cherubino hides behind that big chair that's in the center of the room.

Count Almaviva: "Susanna, how agitated and confused you seem." Susanna: "My lord, I beg pardon, but if we were to be surprised here...Go, go I beg you." "Oh, a moment and I'll leave you." Then he walks around fingering things and being sleazy. "Listen." Susanna says, "I cannot." "Two words. You know that the King has appointed me ambassador to London. I have decided to take Figaro with me." "My lord, if I dared..." "Oh, speak, my dear, and with that right which you have from me, while you live, ask, command and dispose of me."

Susanna: "Leave me, my lord, I claim no rights, nor wish nor understand them." Yes, Susanna's trying to brazen this one out, trying to dumb it out. "How unhappy I am."

"Ah, no, Susanna. I want to make you happy! You know how much I love you, Basilio has already told you." Yes, her music teacher, who's been pimping for the count. "If you would only, for a few moments meet me in the garden at dusk, Oh, I would pay for such a favor." He gets slimier and sleazier by the moment.

Let's just listen to this dry recitative, the count's entrance.

(musical example)

The count is not a likeable fellow. He's a bully, he uses his position to get what he wants; and we don't like him from the start.

I confess, as you are aware, this is the first recitative dialogue I've played for you from this opera, and I apologize for this. Recitative, especially in Mozart, is not just that half-spoken stuff that occurs between the arias, especially not in Mozart's recitatives. They are an intrinsic and essential part of the drama, during which the singers truly become actors. Mozart's recitatives, with their unexpected harmonic twists, their extraordinary character, their interaction and dramatic thrust, are as brilliant in their own way as the arias; and I apologize for not having played more of the recitatives. Of course, we are victims of the limited time we have together, so I've made choices. When you're sitting and listening to this opera with your libretti, you'll revel in these wonderful recitatives where, as I say, the singers become actors and the comic and dramatic exchanges are as good as anything you will find on the stage anywhere in a theater.

Act One continues: Following Count Almaviva's unsolicited entrance to Susanna's room, more and more people start to show up. The place eventually begins looking like a bus station outside of a military base. Figaro, incidentally, has also entered by now and he has witnessed the count's presence, very unhappily realizing, of course, that Susanna was absolutely right. The count will let himself in whenever he damn pleases.

Eventually, a furious count discovers Cherubino, who, of course, has been hidden and witness to the count's attempt to buy Susanna. Cherubino has seen and known everything and the count realizes it.

Cherubino begs forgiveness. Cherubino says, "Forgive me, forgive me, my lord." The count responds, "You don't deserve it." Susanna says, "He's only a child." The count, who knows, "Less so than you think." Cherubino, "I was at fault; but never from my lips…" Cherubino is about to say, "Never from my lips will I say how you tried to buy Susanna's body with money." No. He doesn't get that far, because the count immediately cuts him off.

The count realizes that the best way to deal with Cherubino is not to deal with him at all—"I've got to get this guy out of the castle and off my stage as quickly as possible."

The count hastily interrupts Cherubino, "All right, all right, I pardon you; I'll do more: there is a vacancy for an officer in my regiment: it is yours. You leave at once. Goodbye." Susanna and Figaro say, "Oh, let him at least stay until tomorrow." The count responds, "No, he leaves at once." Cherubino is glad to be alive at this point and he says, "My lord, I am ready to obey your command." The count says, "Come on, for the last time kiss Susanna." He says, aside, "An unexpected blow for them"—because the count sees Cherubino in cahoots, as Cherubino will soon be, with Figaro and Susanna. The count leaves thinking, really believing, that he's gotten rid of Cherubino, leaving Figaro, Cherubino and Susanna onstage.

Figaro says to Cherubino, still quite annoyed, "Well, captain, give me your hand. I want to speak to you before you go. Goodbye, little Cherubino! How your destiny changes in a mere moment." Yes, clearly Figaro is none too happy to have found Cherubino in his wife-to-be's bedroom. The following aria is intended to scare the living daylights out of Cherubino, and it works. This aria is structured as a rondo; that means we're going to have a refrain that will keep coming back, a sung refrain, not an instrumental *ritornello* in the style of Monteverdi, but rather a sung refrain that will return periodically after other contrasting refrains. The sung refrain that keeps coming back is this, it's the one that represents Cherubino in his present state: a randy little dandy.

Figaro says, "You'll go no more, amorous butterfly, flitting around, night and day, disturbing ladies' rest, little Narcissus, Adonis of love." Now verse two, the first contrasting verse, Figaro describes Cherubino's present wardrobe, "You'll wear no more these plumes, that smart and jaunty cap, those curls, that dashing air, that pink, effeminate complexion!" Then we go back to that original verse, "You'll go no more, amorous butterfly, flitting about, night and day, disturbing ladies' rest, little Narcissus, Adonis of love."

Then verse *C*:

> Among warriors, by Jingo! Bushy mustaches, tight tunic, shoulder arms, saber at your side, neck straight, serious-faced, a big helmet or a big turban, much honor, but little money. And instead of the fandango, a forced march through the mud, over hill and dale, in snow and scorching sun, to the accompaniment of trombones, mortars and cannons, and cannonballs whistling and whining in your ears.

And so forth and so on. This martial and explosive episode describes a life that is increasingly unattractive to our 13-year-old Cherubino. Figaro's ulterior motive becomes clear: to dissuade Cherubino from leaving at all. Figaro needs allies, and he knows he can make Cherubino an ally very easily at this point, given the relationship between Cherubino and the count. Once again, Figaro sings, "You'll go no more, amorous butterfly," and then concludes this wonderful aria, "Cherubino, march to victory and military glory!"

This is that "*Non più andrai*" that we sampled in a previous lecture as an example of classical era melody and directness in opera. This will conclude Act One, so it's got to be a big moment, and indeed, the ending of this aria is a big moment. Let's listen to Figaro's "Non più andrai." It is Number 9 and concludes Act One of *The Marriage of Figaro*.

(musical example)

William Mann tells us that it was *"Non più andrai"* which first won the Viennese to *The Marriage of Figaro*, and *"Non piu andrai,"* which became an almost international success. Mozart, by the way, quoted this very tune of his in the finale of *Don Giovanni*, his next great opera done with Lorenzo da Ponte, in the last act and the final scene, and even arranged it as a contradance. It was quickly adopted as the official slow march for the English regiment of the Coldstream Guard, regimental tradition claims, since 1787. One year after it was premiered, this tune was already being played by the Coldstream Guard. Last year, I was in London and I witnessed the changing of the guard at Buckingham Palace to this music, to *"Non più andrai,"* so it is still in that repertoire to the present day.

Let's move on to Act Two. That was a stirring and wonderful end of Act One. The sides have been defined, we have met most of the characters, and indeed, the dramatic moment, the oil on which the drama lubes, is present. Susanna is the object, and whether she can be married off to Figaro before she is seduced or taken by the count is the essential issue of this opera.

There's one character we have not met. Mozart has saved one main character for the signal moment of the beginning of Act Two, and that is, of course, the countess, Rosina. Now she makes her entrance. I'll set the scene. The countess's boudoir; at the right is a door and a closet is on the left. At the back, a door leads to the servants' rooms, and of course, that would be the room where Figaro and Susanna are. At one side is a window. Susanna is with the countess and appears to have told her something painful. The countess makes a gesture of disgust and resignation, and Susanna goes to her room.

My friends, the countess is depressed. She's only 18 or 19 years old, but her marriage has not turned out to be anything of what she had hoped and expected. She is disillusioned and sadly world-wise beyond her years. Susanna, of course, has come to tell the countess what's been going on. Again, as William Mann points out, Susanna has come to the countess, not out of spite, because she loves the countess; nor out of goody-goody self-protection, let alone hope of remuneration; but simply because she, Susanna, is a practical, level-headed young woman. The count is preparing an assault on the happiness of his wife, his valet and her personal maid, that is Susanna herself. Susanna must collect allies. Figaro has just collected an ally in Cherubino. Well, Susanna is collecting allies also, and the best are those most closely implicated, her mistress and her intended bridegroom; she, with authority, he with cunning. Figaro has already made some plans; Susanna has told the countess, and will shortly tell her about those plans. But first, the countess needs to have a good cry.

The act opens with a wonderful weeping aria, "*Porgi amor*," "Grant, oh love." We have a longish instrumental introduction, which at once sets the lyric melancholy mood and acts as an entr'acte for Act Two. It also lends Rosina's, or the countess's, entrance great gravity and dignity. Let's just hear the very beginning of Act Two and the beginning of this longish aria, "Grant, o Love, a cure for my grief and sighing! Bring my darling back to me, or at least let me die."

Beginning of Act Two, "*Porgi amor*," the countess's entrance.

(musical example)

The countess has her cry and Susanna reenters to finish telling her the story in secco recitative. Countess: "Come, dear Susanna, finish your story." Susanna says, "It's already finished." The countess responds, "So he wanted to seduce you?" Susanna says, "Oh, my lord does not pay such compliments to women of my station; he made me a business proposition." The countess: "Ah! The cruel wretch no longer loves me." Susanna says, "Why, then, is he jealous of you?" The countess responds, "He is like all modern husbands, willfully unfaithful, naturally capricious, and yet proudly jealous. But if Figaro loves you, he alone could…" Enters Figaro, singing, "La la la la la la la …" Susanna says, "Here he is."

Yes, Figaro has arrived and he describes this half-baked plan of his, in two parts. This is how they're going to get the count. First, he suggests that Cherubino be dressed as Susanna in order to lay a trap for the count. Then Part Two; make the count jealous by sending him an anonymous letter describing a tryst between the countess and an imagined lover—make the count really jealous. This is a really bad idea, and the countess and Susanna are not terribly impressed with it. But you know what? They don't have anything else to offer; so they figure, it's the best we've got, let's run with it.

Time to engage Part One of the plan, and that is to get Cherubino in there and to dress him up as Susanna and use him for bait. The ladies call for Cherubino, now dressed, of course, in his military garb, prepared to depart. Cherubino enters and sings a very famous aria called, *"Voi che sapete,"* as a serenade, as a goodbye to the countess. For the interest of time, we are going to move past *"Voi che sapete,"* but it's a very famous tune and it's one that most, if not all, of you would recognize. It's a lilting serenade, which again, ably describes our child-man, our would-be lover. We move past it.

The ladies respond to this lovely serenade. The countess says, "Bravo, you've an attractive voice, I never knew you could sing so well." Susanna says, "Oh, truly, everything he attempts he does well." Yes, she's trying to butter him up. "Come, brave soldier, I imagine Figaro has told you…" Cherubino says, "He told me all." Now, of course, Cherubino is in on everything.

Susanna, measuring herself by Cherubino, "Let's see; it will be just right; we're exactly the same height—off with that coat." The countess says to Susanna, "What are you doing?" Susanna says, "No need to worry." The countess says, "But what if someone should come in…" Susanna responds, "Let them, what harm are we doing? I'll close the door. But what can we do about his hair?" These two women are stripping down the 13-year-old boy. He must be in hog heaven, of course; but this is a potentially delicate situation.

The countess says, "Fetch one of my bonnets from the closet. Quickly!" Susanna goes out. The countess says to Cherubino, looking in one of his pockets of the coat which he's just taken off, "What is that document?" Cherubino says, "What? It's my commission." The countess says, "They're in a great hurry!" Cherubino says, "Well, I just now received it from Basilio."

Then the countess points out, "In their hurry, they've forgotten to put the seal on it." Cherubino's commission is incomplete and non-binding without the seal—how very, very convenient. Susanna comes back in. "What seal?" she asks. The countess says, "The one on the commission." Susanna says,

"Mercy! What haste! Here's the bonnet." The countess responds, "Hurry; yes, that's right; what a plight we should be in if my lord should come in now!" They continue the act of undressing and partially dressing Cherubino.

Imagine the scene: We've got a half-cross-dressed Cherubino, half- cross-dressed to look like Susanna. Susanna leaves the room, leaving the lovelorn 13-year-old, half-dressed as a woman, in the boudoir of the object of his desire, the countess. Does this all sound familiar, Cherubino being in the wrong bedroom at the wrong time? Indeed. Guess who's about to come to the door?

(Knocking sounds) The countess says, "Who can be knocking on my door?" The count from outside, "Why is this door locked?" The countess says, "My husband! Heavens! I'm lost! You here in this state of undress. He's received the note; he'll be madly jealous…" Of course, the count is shrieking, "Why the delay?" A bad spot.

(musical example)

Now listen good, and listen very tight. Cherubino runs and hides in the closet dressing room, locking the door behind him. The countess unlocks the front door to the room and the count enters, filled with piss, vinegar, anger, and jealousy, holding the note that Figaro sent him to do this very thing, and that is, fill him with jealousy. The count hears a noise in the closet, of course. Cherubino is trying to plant himself in the wall and knocks something over, and the countess tells him that it's Susanna in the closet. Meanwhile, Susanna slips back into the boudoir via another entrance and observes how close to disaster everything has become. Are you with me? Are you with me? Good. A little more before we take our break.

The count is convinced that the countess's lover, the one represented by this fraudulent note, is in the closet. He decides to get a crowbar in order to pry open the closet door, and he takes the countess with him, meanwhile locking all the doors to the bedroom to prevent any escape. Susanna leaps from her hiding spot, runs to the wardrobe, accompanied by nimble, scurrying strings, and has to do something quickly to get Cherubino out and away. My goodness, we have to stop. When we return, the rescue of Cherubino, the re-arrival of the count, and the Act Two finale. Thank you.

The Rise of Opera Buffa and Mozart's *The Marriage of Figaro*, IV
Lecture 16—Transcript

Welcome back to "How to Listen to and Understand Opera." This is Lecture 16, the fourth in a four-lecture set entitled "The Rise of Opera Buffa and Mozart's *The Marriage of Figaro*." My friends, here is where we left off: The count is convinced that the countess's lover—because of the note, he thinks she has a lover—is in the closet in her boudoir. He decides to get a crowbar in order to pry open this closet. Remember, Cherubino is hiding in this closet, terrified to be found half-dressed in another woman's bedroom. Another woman that the count has a relationship with will mean, not just his banishment, but his inevitable death and perhaps, God forbid, his emasculation. He has locked the door behind him. The count determines to go get a crowbar to pry the door open. He takes the countess with him and locks the door behind him.

Here's the scene; Susanna has been hiding in the countess's bedroom, and now she comes out of hiding. Cherubino has locked himself in the closet, the count has locked the front door, thinking no one can get out and no one can get in. Susanna leaps from her hiding spot, runs to the wardrobe closet, accompanied by nimble, scurrying strings. She starts banging on the door. "Open quickly, open—it's Susanna. Come out and away with you."

Cherubino comes out from the dressing room, half-dressed, with his eyes the size of dinner plates, a little drool coming down from the side of his mouth, completely terrified. "Alas, What a horrid scene, what a disaster!" Susanna says, "This way…that way…" She doesn't know what she's doing.

Cherubino says again, "What a disaster!" He's breathless, he's confused; and in panic, our dynamic duo seems unable to come up with a plan of action. Susanna goes to the doors, "The doors are locked"—both Susanna and Cherubino say together, "The doors are locked, what is there to be done?" Cherubino gets even more panicked, "I've got to find a way out." Susanna says, "He'll kill you if he finds you." Wonderful. Thanks, Susanna.

Cherubino's panic ratchets up even further, "What about the window? What about the window? It looks out on the garden." This window is way up.

Susanna says, "Stop, Cherubino, stop, for pity's sake." Cherubino walks to the window, "I must find a way out." "Stop, Cherubino!" "He'll kill me if he finds me." "It's too high to jump," yells Susanna. Cherubino responds, "Leave me alone." He starts putting his leg over the windowsill. Susanna says, "Stop, for pity's sake!" Cherubino says, "Leave me alone! Before I'd harm her, I'd leap into the fire. Give her this kiss from me." He kisses Susanna. "Goodbye! That's how it's done." He jumps off, out of the window. Susanna says, "He'll kill himself. O heavens! Stop for pity's sake! Stop, stop!" Usually, typically in performance, a little shriek from Susanna—Aahhh!—will accompany Cherubino's bolt through the window. Then, of course, we usually hear some smashing sounds as he hits below.

Let's listen to this marvelous No. 14, the rescue of Cherubino.

(musical example)

Again, the setting by Mozart is absolutely brilliant. We have a continuous patter in the orchestra, and then of course, in fits and starts as would reflect the panicky language of Susanna and Cherubino, they layer their words on top of the orchestral continuity. We have that sense of constant panic and the sense of breathless panic from our players, provided both by orchestra and by their words.

All right. Susanna runs to the window and looks out after Cherubino and says, "O, look at the little rogue, how he runs!" Yes, look at that sucker motor! He was scared. "He's a mile off already; but there's no time to lose; into the closet; then let the braggart come, I'm waiting here for him." Susanna now locks herself into the closet. The count and the countess reenter. The countess, of course, has not a clue that Susanna and Cherubino have switched places, and as a result, she has admitted to the count that Cherubino is in the closet. The count is beside himself with rage. Who knows where this anger will lead. That brings us to the Act Two finale, No. 15, and a very quick timeout, please.

The following exchange comes from the film version of Peter Shaffer's *Amadeus*. While there's no evidence that such an exchange actually took place, it has the marvelous ring of truth to it, so I would read it for you. Mozart: "I had a scene in the second act; it starts as a duet, just a man and his wife quarreling. Suddenly, the wife's scheming little maid comes in, duet turns into trio; then the husband's valet, quartet. Then a stupid old gardener—quintet, sextet, septet, octet! How long do you think I can sustain that?" Emperor Joseph II: "Well, six or seven minutes, eight?" Mozart: "Twenty, sire. How about 20. Twenty minutes of continuous music." That is indeed what we will get, 20 minutes of continual music. All the time, more and more people, entering the stage and entering the group, sing.

The finale had become an integral part of the opera buffa tradition by the mid-eighteenth century, by 1750. It is one of the essential elements that so sets opera buffa apart from opera seria; the finale. In his memoirs, Lorenzo da Ponte described a recipe for an opera buffa finale, and now I quote Lorenzo da Ponte:

> The finale is a sort of little comedy in itself and requires a fresh plot and special interest of its very own. Recitative is excluded from it. Everything is sung and all the singers should appear on the stage, even if there were 300 of them, one by one, by twos, by threes, by sixes, by tens, by sixties; to sing solos, duets, trios, sextets, thirteenets, sixtyets. And if the plot of the play does not allow of it, the poet must find some way of making the plot allow it.

As writer Michael Knott points out,

> Da Ponte reports also in his memoirs that he was in direct contact with Mozart during the course of writing the libretto. Considering that none of the text da Ponte wrote for any other composer entails anything remotely approaching the ambitions of this finale, perhaps Mozart deserves much of the credit here as well.

I would echo that.

Each of the finale scenes hinges on a point of conflict between the characters on stage. No sooner is one dispute resolved, then another character enters, bringing a fresh element of conflict, and so it goes.

Let's dive into this extraordinary finale. Part One; the count is standing before the closet door, he's got his sword in one hand, the crowbar in the other; and he's going absolutely bonkers, screaming at the closet door. "Out you come, you ill-bred brat, quickly now, you little wretch!" Homicidal rage! We will hear that well-portrayed by these harsh and absolute accents in the orchestra. The countess, of course, is trembling, vainly trying to calm him down, his macho gone bananas. "Ah, my lord, your rage makes my heart tremble for him." The count says, "And do you dare still oppose me?" The countess says, "No, but hear me." The count says, "Speak up quickly." Yes, he's sputtering with indignation. The count cannot believe that Rosina is trying to defend herself, or Cherubino.

The countess says quickly, "I swear before heaven that any suspicion and the state in which you find him, his collar undone and his chest bare"—it's sounding worse and worse as she describes our half-naked Cherubino. The count says, "Collar undone! Chest bare! Go on." The countess responds, "To dress him up as a young woman…"The count says, "Ah, I understand, unworthy wife, I will soon be revenged." His wife is having an affair with a 13-year-old, which she has been cross-dressing as a woman. Yes, I could see where his macho would get up in a little bit of a dander.

"Give me the key," he demands. The countess says, "He is innocent!" "Give me the key!" "He is innocent! You know he is." The count says, "I know nothing of the sort! Away out of my sight. You are faithless and wicked, and seek to disgrace me." The countess says, "I'll go, yes, but…" "I don't hear you." "But…" "I'll not hear you." "I'm not guilty!" cries the countess. And the count says, "I can read it in your face! Die, die!" My goodness! We should hear the octave drop in the orchestra at that moment as if the blade has fallen upon her neck.

Of course, the count draws his sword; opens the door because he has been given the key; and who do they find standing there but Susanna. The count is astonished. "Susanna?" The countess equally astonished, "Susanna?" Both count and countess are rendered speechless.

Finale, Part I. (musical example)

What a surprise.

Finale, Part II. I don't know how they did it, but they "done" it. A gentle introductory rhythm indicates Susanna's careful but playful words. She must brazen this out without raising any new suspicious from the count.

Susanna, "My lord! Why so dumbfounded? Take your sword, and put the page to death, that ill-bred page, you see him here before you." The count says, "What sly minxes!" The countess says, aside, "What a fantasy…how can this be?" The count meanwhile says, "My head…is reeling." Susanna says, "They are so bewildered, they're quite at a loss." Countess is staring at her and saying, "Susanna is here!"

The count, of course, is starting to look around Susanna. He can't be kept quiet for long. "Are you alone?" Susanna says, "Oh, look. Perhaps he's hidden in here." She points inside the closet. Really, she should keep her mouth shut at this point, but she can't resist giving it to the count.

The count says, "Let's see," and the count and Susanna go in. Susanna says, "Look!" The count thrashes around the wardrobe momentarily, looking for Cherubino.

Finale, Part II, trio. (musical example)

Part I of the finale was a duet, Part II of the finale, a trio. There's a marvelous moment halfway through that part we just listened to where each of the characters is standing on stage, the countess, the count, and Susanna, each saying their own thing, each reflecting their own worldview; three different strands of music. Only in opera, my friends, can you have three different people singing three different things, reflecting three different visions, and it melds and works together.

Finale, Part III, allegro; everything starts speeding up again. A brighter, chattering melody would depict Rosina's relief and her rapidly beating heart. She starts, "Susanna, I'm half dead, I can hardly breathe." Susanna says, aside to the countess, "Put your mind at ease and be happy, Cherubino's safe by now."

The count says to the countess, "I think I made such a mistake. And to think of it, I can scarcely believe it. If I wronged you, I ask your pardon, but to play such a trick was cruel." He's filled with remorse and he desperately wants to be forgiven. Of course, the countess and Susanna have no pity for him at all. "Your follies do not deserve forgiveness."

The count says, "But I love you!" The countess says, "Don't say it!" "I swear I do!" The countess says, "You're lying! I am the faithless, wicked wife who is always deceiving you." The count says, "Susanna, help me to calm her anger."

Of course, Susanna says, "Thus are punished those who are suspicious." The countess responds, "Must the constancy of a loving heart such harsh reward expect?" I mean, do I really have to be treated this way, buster? The count says, "Oh come on, Rosina!"

Now the countess gets mad. Her anger does comes out, "Cruel one! I'm no longer your Rosina, but the miserable object of your abandon whom you have been pleased to make suffer."

The count says, "Confused, repentant, I've been punished enough…" Have pity, have pity. Then the count starts thinking again, "But you said the page was shut in there." The countess says, "Well, I was only trying to test you." "But your trembling, your anxiety?" "It was only a joke." "But such a heartless note?"

Oh, yes, the note. Susanna and the countess say, "That note was from Figaro, and Basilio delivered it." So much for plan A; it's completely shot. The count says, "Ah, those villains. I'll…" Susanna and the countess remind him, "He deserves not forgiveness who forgives not others."

"Well then," says the count, "if you wish, let us make peace all round. Rosina will not be adamant with me." Rosina says, "Ah, Susanna, how softhearted I am! How can a woman's wrath ever be taken seriously?" Susanna responds, "With men, my lady, whatever you do, and wherever you turn, you will see that always you end up like that." The count says, "Look at me!" The countess says, "For shame, sir!" Finally, he says, "Look at me, I was wrong, and I'm sorry." Susanna, the countess, and the count all sing, "From this moment, I will be able to learn to appreciate her."

All right, the first crisis has been averted. Let's listen to a portion of this Part III of the finale.

(musical example)

We move on to the finale, Part IV. Figaro enters. Now, my friends, there are four on stage. We're up to quartet. Figaro has attempted to time his entrance just so. Perhaps the count at this moment, quite remorseful, can be rushed into marrying Susanna and Figaro; this would seem to be a good moment. Note please, the jolly, cheerful, entry music quickly gives way to increasingly quiet music as the count is determined to ask Figaro some questions. What was Figaro's role in this note, and what is this all about with him?

Figaro says, "My lord, the musicians are ready outside; hear the trumpets and the pipes. Mid the singing and dancing of your retainers, let us run, let us haste to the wedding." Let's get this show on the road! The count says, "Hush, hush, less hurry." Figaro says, "The crowd awaits me." The count says, "Hush, hush, less hurry; relieve me of a doubt before you go."

Susanna, countess, and Figaro say, "A delicate situation,…" The count asks, "I must…ask you. And of course, I must play my cards carefully. Do you know, Master Figaro, who wrote this letter?" The interrogation begins, at first quietly and not too powerfully, but with a slightly accusatory tone, the count asks Figaro about the letter. Remember the letter. Now, please, Figaro doesn't know that the ladies already admitted that he, Figaro, wrote the letter. Figaro doesn't know that anyone knows his part in this, so he's going to act like he doesn't know anything, which is going to create a real problem, obviously.

"Do you know, Master Figaro, who wrote this letter?" Figaro says, "I do not." Susanna says, "You don't know?" Figaro says, "No!" The countess says, "You don't know?" Figaro says, "No!" The count says, "You don't know?" Figaro says, "No!" Then they all say, "You don't know?" Figaro says, "No! No! No!"

Susanna says, "Didn't you give it to Don Basilio?" I mean, "Come on, Fig. I'm settin' you up here." Figaro says, "No." The countess says, "To deliver it." The count says, "You remember?" Figaro says, "Oh dear, oh dear!" Susanna: "And what about the page..." Countess: "...Who tonight in the garden...?" The count says, "Do you understand now?" Figaro says, "No, I don't." He's going to admit nothing.

The count says, "You look in vain for defense and excuse, your face is giving you away. I can see you are lying." Figaro says, "My face, then, is lying, I am not." Susanna and the countess are beginning to get worried, of course, "In vain you sharpen your wits,...we've told everything...You've nothing left to repeat." Again, the count says, "What's your answer?" And Figaro says, "Nothing, nothing!"

Now we must ask ourselves, "Why is he being so adamant?" It's clear the women are setting him up to admit that he did it. It's clear also that the count knows that Figaro did it. Why will he not admit to it? Because he hates the count. Because the count is trying to ruin his life, and Figaro doesn't care whether he is the servant or the master. It makes no difference. He doesn't care who he's talking to. He will not give the count any bit of satisfaction here. At once, my friends, the class war is joined. Figaro is not the servant. He is the equal, and he will give the count nothing unless he chooses to. The count is not used to this—this kind of obstinacy, this kind of attitude in his own castle; unheard of. My friends, it is the revolution already in action.

"What is your answer?" "Nothing, nothing!" "You confess, then?" "No, I don't!"

Susanna and the countess to Figaro, "Hey, hold your tongue, you simpleton. The joke has got to finish." Figaro says, "To end it happily as is usual in the theater, with a wedding, we should now round it off." "Yes," Figaro's saying, "you want me to admit something? First, we get married and then I'll admit."

Susanna, Countess, and Figaro, "Oh my lord. Don't oppose it, pray, meet our desire."

The count says, "Marcellina!" He's praying for his trump card. Whatever's going on now, he feels like he's being pushed toward the wedding. He says, "Marcellina, it's high time for your appearance."

Let's sample Parts IV and V of the finale so we can hear what the quartet sounds like before moving on.

(musical example)

We move forward to finale, Part VI. Antonio the gardener staggers in drunk and now we have a quintet, five people on stage. My friends, we also have trouble, big trouble. Antonio, the drunken gardener, the uncle of Susanna and the father of Barbarina, has seen something or someone fall out the window.

Antonio says, "Ah, my lord, my lord!" The count says, "What's the matter?" Antonio, "What insolence! Who did this? Who was it?" Yes, he's usually holding a handful of crushed carnations in his hand. Susanna, countess, count, Figaro: "What do you say? What ails you? What's happened?" Antonio says, "Listen, listen." They all say, "Speak up then."

He says, "From the balcony overlooking the garden, I see a thousand things thrown every day; and just now, maybe worse, I saw a man, my lord, thrown down." The count says, "From the balcony?" Antonio says, "Yes, look at my carnations!" Cherubino landed on the flowers. The count says, "Into the garden?" Antonio says, "Yes!"

The women say, "Figaro, help us now!" The count says, "What do I hear?" Susanna, countess, Figaro: "That fellow disconcerts us, that old drunk. What's he doing here?" Meanwhile, the count continues talking to Antonio, "A man you said. But where's he gone?" "Ah, the rascal was off in a flash, and out of my sight."

Susanna: "You know that the page..." Figaro says, "I know everything. I saw it happen." Figaro laughs, "Ha, ha, ha, ha." "Hold your tongue there," says the count. Antonio says, "What's so funny?" Figaro says, "You're drunk from dawn every day. Meanwhile, the count wants the story. Now repeat to me, a man from the balcony, from the balcony, into the garden, yes, into the garden..." Susanna, countess, and Figaro, still trying to distract him, "But my lord, it's the wine talking."

The count says, "Go on just the same. Did you see his face?" Antonio says, "No, I didn't." The count says, "You didn't?" Antonio says, "I didn't see him!" So Figaro steps in, "You maudlin old fool. Keep quiet a moment, making such a fuss about nothing. I can't keep my secret any longer." All right. He goes for it. "It was I who jumped into the garden."

The count says, "You? Who?" Antonio says, "Who? You?" Figaro says, "That surprised them, didn't it?" The count of course, says, "I cannot believe it." And Antonio says, "When did you get so big?" Uh, oh. Count says, "I don't believe it." Antonio says, "After you jumped, you weren't that big." Who'da thought? Figaro says, "Well, that's what always happens when people jump."

Anyway, as we keep going through this section, and time forces us to skip through this section and move on to the next, Figaro is trying to convince everyone there during this quintet that it wasn't him, that it wasn't anyone else but him, and he manages to do that. At one point, Cherubino's name comes up and, of course, the count jumps at that. But then Figaro says, "Well, then he would have had to ride back from Seville, because he's already away. He's been sent to the garrison." Antonio says, "That can't be because I didn't see a horse jump down." So, Antonio gets all confused. By the end of this section, it sounds as if Figaro is on the verge of victory. He claims that shut in the closet, waiting for his love Susanna, he panicked when he heard the count screaming and that it was he who jumped out.

Now we move to Part VII and Part VIII, the conclusion of this extraordinary Act Two finale. And again, I beg your forgiveness for rushing so quickly through so much text and for skipping so much music. We simply are limited by my time with you, but I would ask you, please, to listen to the opera on your own with the translation of the libretto. Nothing can replace the quietude and singularity of your personal experience of this thing in its entirety, without the interruptions that I'm providing. Let's go on to Parts VII and VIII and finish up.

We still have quintet; it looks for all the world like Figaro's talked his way out until Antonio says, "These, then, will be your papers that you lost." Now, we don't know yet what these papers are, but we know Cherubino dropped them and we fear the worst. Figaro has not a clue what papers this could be.

The count says, "Here, give them to me." Figaro says, "I'm trapped." Susanna and the countess say, "Figaro, beware!" The count says, "Tell me Figaro. What are these papers?" Figaro, of course, is going to stall, "Just a moment, just a moment, I have so many, wait." The amazing Figaro will now try to figure out what these papers are. The music is slow and deliberate as the count smells an opportunity to trap Figaro, and Figaro must slow the action so he has time to think.

Antonio says, "Perhaps it's a list of your debts." And Figaro says back, "No, it's a list of innkeepers, more likely." The count says to Figaro, "Speak up! Well." The countess, "Heavens, it's the page's commission!" She's the first to see that it's the seal-less commission. The count says, "Well?" Susanna says aside to Figaro, "It's the commission!" The count says, "Come now!"

Figaro says, "Oh, what a head! It's the commission that the boy gave me a while ago." Count: "Why did he do that?" Figaro: "It needs…" The count says, "It needs…" The countess says, "The seal." Susanna says, "The seal." The count says, "Answer!" Figaro says, "It's usual…it's usual to seal the document."

Thank goodness this kind of word of mouth across the stage has finally gotten to Figaro, and he's answered properly. A gentle cadence would seem to confirm that the problems are over; but they're not, because a sudden burst from the orchestra accompanies the unceremonious entrance of Marcellina, Basilio and Bartolo.

During this whole caper that we just read through, Antonio had exited, so we'd been back down to quartet; now we're up to septet, with three more people onstage. Of course, Marcellina is just what the count ordered. Marcellina, Basilio and Bartolo reveal the debt that Figaro owes to Marcellina. Figaro does not want to have to pay this debt. The count says, "We're going to have to have a court case and we're going to have to try this," and so a whole new series of dialogues go on. Of course, Susanna, the countess, and Figaro are saying, "Why listen to these blockheads? They are fools." Of course, Marcellina, Basilio and Bartolo make their case. The finale ends with Marcellina, Basilio, the count and Bartolo saying, "What a fine stroke, how wonderful!" It would seem that the marriage is undoing itself right now because Marcellina will insist, will insist on having her day in court, and, if Figaro loses, on having Figaro.

Let's at least start section VII and perhaps hear all of VIII.

(musical example)

This is miraculous music, balancing this number of forces, having all of these different world views expressed simultaneously, giving everyone their say and making it all come together as a holistic entity. It's impossible, and yet Mozart pulls it off. Really extraordinary.

This continuous sequence of solos and duets, trios, quartets, quintets, ultimately septets, that comprise this finale offered Mozart the sort of opportunity for melodic and harmonic development ordinarily associated with symphonies and concerti and string quartets. Truly, for its speed, its degree of contrast, the continuous dramatic line and development and harmonic plan, only a great symphonist or a great composer of concerti or string quartets could have written something like this finale.

Joseph Kerman writes, "It should be emphasized that the drama of *The Marriage of Figaro* is Mozart's, not Beaumarchais's and not da Ponte's. Music here does not merely decorate what the playwright or librettist has designed. Mozart's music creates a drama that they never suspected." That's a wonderful and pointed point.

William Mann wrote,

> In this finale Mozart and da Ponte invented genuine music drama, something that Peri, Monteverdi, Vivaldi, and Handel and the rest, including Gluck,

—from whom, of course, Mozart had learned so much,

> had not achieved at this level. The characters and the situations are credible as well as amusing, sometimes even touching. The words are worth hearing and we can understand them. The music goes on revealing new subtleties, new truth; the more frequent it is heard and the more frequently we study it. Granted, to play favorites is infantile when works of art are concerned; however, when people insist on playing favorites about music, the second act finale of Figaro claims a prior place on the list. It is second to nothing.

In the remainder of the opera, one glory follows another. It's during the third act trial, when Maracellina wants her contract honored, that it's discovered that Figaro is actually the long-lost illegitimate son of Marcellina and Dr. Bartolo. It's such a kick. The look on the count's face—you could knock him down with a feather. In the fourth act finale, we have a chunk of music that stands second only to the second act finale. In it, the count's intrigues are exposed and in as magical a passage as has ever been created, he begs forgiveness from the countess and she grants it. It's a moment of profound redemption. It's as if we've all been forgiven our sins and reconciled to our loved ones.

In conclusion I would point out something. Mozart's operas are not "easy listening". They require our total involvement, just as the dramas and comedies of Shakespeare, Ibsen, and Stoppard require our total involvement. In Mozart's time, his operas were not considered easy listening. They were, for many, too long, too melodically varied, and too harmonically complex. One recalls that famous conversation between the Emperor Franz Joseph and Mozart, following the Vienna premiere of Mozart's *The Abduction from the Harem,* in 1782. Emperor Franz Joseph said, "Too fine for our ears and an immense number of notes, my dear Mozart." And Mozart's famous response, "Just as many notes, your majesty, as are required."

Mozart's characters live and breathe. They're never mere archetypes. Mozart's operas seem quite modern to our ears today because he imbues his characters with such an incredible range of moods, emotions, subtlety, unconscious motivation; in a word, he gives his characters humanity.

Brahms wrote of *The Marriage of Figaro*, "Every number in Figaro is a marvel. I simply can't understand how anyone could create anything so perfect. Such a thing has never been done before, not even by Beethoven." Joseph Kerman wrote that it's difficult to discuss Mozart's great operas without lapsing into platitudes. "The vindication of opera as drama comes in occasional, unique triumphs, and among these Mozart has left our most precious examples."

We save our last word, our last Mozartian platitude, for Gioacchino Rossini, whose own *Barber of Seville* we'll meet in our next lectures. Rossini wrote this, "The Germans have always been at all times the greatest harmonists, and the Italians the greatest melodists. But the moment the North produced Mozart, we of the South were beaten on our own ground, because this man rises above all nations, uniting in himself the charm of Italian melody and all the profundity of German harmony. Mozart is the only musician who had as much knowledge as genius and as much genius as knowledge."

Thank you very much.

Timeline

c. 1440 .... Josquin des Prez born (d. 1521).

c. 1546 .... Giulio Caccini born (d. 1618).

1561 .... Jacopo Peri born (d. c.1633).

1562 .... Ottavio Rinuccini born (d.1621).

1567 .... Claudio Monteverdi born (d. 1643).

1573–1592 .... Florentine Camerata.

1588 .... English defeat Spanish Armada.

1598 .... *Daphne*, considered first opera, by Peri and Corsi.

1600 .... Peri's *Euridice*.

1604 .... Shakespeare's *Othello*.

1607 .... Monteverdi's *Orfeo*.

1618 .... Beginning of Thirty Years' War.

1630 .... Boston founded by Puritans.

1632 .... Jean-Baptiste Lully born (d. 1687).

1649 .... King Charles I of England beheaded.

1660 .... Alessandro Scarlatti born (d. 1725).

1661	Louis XIV becomes King of France.
1675	Antonio Vivaldi born (d. 1741).
1683	Jean-Philippe Rameau born (d. 1764).
1685	Revocation of Edict of Nantes in France.
1687	Isaac Newton's *Principia Mathematica*.
1688	England's Glorious Revolution.
1698	Pietro Metastasio born (d. 1782).
1710	Giovanni Battista Pergolesi born (d. 1736).
1712	Jean-Jacques Rousseau born (d. 1778).
1714	Christoph Willibald von Gluck born (d. 1787).
1715	Scarlatti's *Tigrane*.
1719	Rediscovery of Pompeii.
1733	Pergolesi's *La serva padrona*.
1751	First volumes of French Encyclopedia.
1756	Wolfgang Amadeus Mozart born (d.1791).
1776	Declaration of Independence.
1781	Mozart's *Idomeneo*.

1786	Mozart's *Marriage of Figaro;* Carl Maria von Weber born (d. 1826).
1788	Arthur Schopenhauer born (d. 1860).
1789	French Revolution begins.
1791	Mozart's *The Magic Flute;* Giacomo Meyerbeer born (d. 1864).
1792	Gioacchino Antonio Rossini born (d. 1868).
1797	Gaetano Donizetti born (d. 1848).
1801	Vincenzo Bellini born (d. 1835).
1804	Mikhail Glinka born (d. 1857).
1808	Goethe's *Faust.*
1813	Giuseppe Verdi born (d. 1901); Richard Wagner born (d. 1883).
1815	Battle of Waterloo.
1833	Aleksandr Borodin born (d. 1887).
1835	Cesar Cui born (d. 1918).
1837	Mili Balakirev born (d. 1910).
1838	Queen Victoria crowned; George Bizet born (d. 1875).
1839	Modest Mussorgsky born (d. 1881).

1841	Saxophone invented.
1842	Glinka's *Russlan and Lyudmila*.
1844	Nicolai Rimsky-Korsakov born (d. 1908).
1848	*Communist Manifesto* by Marx and Engels.
1853	Crimean War begins.
1858	Giacomo Puccini born (d. 1924).
1859	Wagner's *Tristan und Isolde*.
1861	Russian serfs emancipated.
1863	Lincoln's Gettysburg Address.
1864	Richard Strauss born (d. 1949).
1868–1869	Mussorgsky's *Boris Godunov*.
1869	Opening of Suez Canal.
1870	Franco-Prussian War.
1877	Invention of phonograph.
1900	Freud's *The Interpretation of Dreams*; Puccini's *Tosca*.
1901	Boer War.
1905	Einstein's special theory of relativity.

1918 .... Armistice ending the First World War.

1920 .... League of Nations formed.

1939 .... Beginning of World War II.

1941 .... Strauss's *Capriccio*.

Glossary

aria: The general term for an extended solo in opera—the equivalent of a soliloquy—which brings the action and "real time" to a temporary halt, and in which the character expresses his or her feelings about the action and events just described. Arias generally have a high melodic profile and are typically accompanied by the full orchestra.

aria da capo: A baroque aria form schematized as A-B-A´. An initial musical phrase (A) is followed by a contrasting passage (B). The initial phrase is then recapitulated but now embellished and ornamented by the singer.

arioso: A sung passage with enough melodic contour to sound aria-like, but which has a syllabic sort of setting and the narrative quality of a recitative.

baritone: The middle category of male voice, higher in range and lighter in timbre than bass, but lower and heavier than tenor.

bass: The lowest category male voice—rich, dark, heavy, and powerful.

basso profundo: An unusually deep bass voice.

bel canto opera: A style of early-19th-century Italian opera that stresses simple, songlike melodies and harmonic accompaniment and that cultivates a highly decorous style of singing.

cadenza: A florid, improvised passage to be performed by singers before the final bars of an aria or movement.

castrato: A male soprano whose soprano voice has been preserved by castration prior to puberty.

cavatina: A slow and lyric aria meant to display the singer's breath control, line, and beauty of tone.

coloratura: Literally, "coloration" or "coloring." As used in music, the term refers to brilliantly ornamented writing for the voice, or to the type of voice agile enough to specialize in such music.

coloratura soprano: The highest of the soprano voices, characterized by broad range, clear quality, and exceptional agility.

comic opera: An expression sometimes used in English either as a translation of the French opéra comique or the Italian opera buffa.

commedia dell'arte: Traveling musical companies that originated in 16th-century Italy. Their performances led eventually to comic opera.

contralto: The lowest category of female voice.

countertenor: An exceptionally high male voice, comparable to the female contralto.

dramatic voice: A heavier, darker, and more forceful voice than a lyric voice; used in reference to soprano, tenor, and baritone voices.

ensemble: Continuously sung passages in which any number of singers may participate. Ensembles were typically used to end acts. They reached their highest state of development in opera buffa.

Gesamtkunstwerk: "The all-inclusive art form," Richard Wagner's term for his all-encompassing music dramas.

grand opera: A spectacular and dramatic genre of opera, developed in early-19th-century France and designed to appeal especially to the middle class. This term is often used to refer to 19th-century opera in general.

homophony: A melodic texture in which one melody line predominates with all other musical material heard as secondary or as accompaniment.

intermezzo: A comic interlude inserted between the acts of Italian opera seria during the second half of the 17th century and the first half of the 18th century.

intermezzo/Intermedio: Musical prologues and interludes inserted into the spoken Italian dramas of the late 16th century.

leitmotif: A theme or motive associated with a particular person, thing, or dramatic idea.

libretto: Literally "little book." The verbal text of an opera, written for the composer to set to music.

lyric opera: An operatic genre that combines opéra comique's use of spoken dialogue and direct, appealing melodies with grand opera's tendency toward numerous performers and grandiose singing.

lyric voice: A fairly light, warm, clear, and flexible voice; used in reference to soprano, tenor, and baritone voices.

madrigal: A work for four to six voices that freely mixes polyphonic and homophonic textures and uses word-painting.

melodrama: A genre of musical theater that combines spoken dialogue with background music.

mezzo-soprano: The middle category of female voice, between contralto and soprano.

monophony: A melodic texture consisting of a single unaccompanied melody line.

music drama: An operatic form created by Richard Wagner. Refers to a through-composed operatic work which stresses dramatic and psychological content and in which voices and orchestra are completely intertwined and of equal importance.

opera: A drama which combines soliloquy, dialogue, scenery, action, and continuous (or nearly continuous) music, the whole greater than the parts.

opera buffa: A general designation for Italian operas of the middle and late 18th century that do not come under the heading of opera seria. These productions were melodically simpler and more "popular" than Baroque opera seria.

opéra comique: A popular French operatic genre that developed concurrently with grand opera in the early 19th century but employed spoken dialogue rather than recitative and featured somewhat less pretentious productions than grand opera.

opera seria: "Serious" opera of the Baroque era—elaborate and grandiose productions typically based on subjects from ancient history and/or mythology.

operetta: Literally, "little opera." During the 19th century, the term came to mean a lighter type of opera, usually with spoken dialogue separating the musical numbers.

overture: An instrumental prelude to an opera.

parlante: Literally, "talking"; a compositional technique used by Giuseppe Verdi and other late-19th-century operatic composers in which recitative-like vocal lines were underlaid with continuous thematic music played by the orchestra.

pastorale: The style of dramatic poetry that dominated Italian theater in the late 16th and early 17th centuries, featuring sylvan settings and mild love adventures and usually ending happily.

polyphony: A melodic texture consisting of two or more simultaneous melody lines of equal importance.

recitative: A style of writing for the voice in which the rhythms and inflections of speech are retained. In opera, it is used for action, dialogue, and narrative. Recitatives are most typically *secco* or "dry" (i.e., accompanied only by *basso continuo*).

ritornello: An instrumental refrain.

sinfonia: An independent musical piece that acts as an introduction or a postlude.

singspiel: German for "sing-play." Refers to a partly sung, partly spoken German theatrical genre with its roots in popular culture.

soprano: The highest category of female voice.

spinto soprano: The soprano voice lying between the lyric and dramatic soprano voices and having qualities of both.

tenor: The highest category of male voice.

tone poem: A purely instrumental work that tells a specific story and invokes explicit imagery; a term created by Richard Strauss.

verismo opera: A genre of opera characterized by dramatic and expressive realism and naturalism, especially in the portrayal of people, events, and emotions. This genre was popular among Italian and French opera composers in the late 19th and early 20th centuries.

voci bianchi: Literally, "white voices," referring to those of the *castrati*.

word-painting: A compositional technique that seeks to form an expressive syntax by matching literary descriptions with corresponding musical events; this technique is characteristic of madrigals.

Biographical Notes

Bernard de Ventadorn (c. 1150–1180): Important French troubadour poet and composer of the second half of the 12th century.

Bizet, Georges (1838–1875): French opera composer famous for *Carmen*, his greatest work and the most popular opera of all time. A master dramatist, Bizet deftly establishes character and mood through his music.

Boito, Arrigo (1842–1918): Italian librettist and composer. Boito's libretti for Verdi's *Otello* and *Falstaff* are considered among the greatest in all Italian opera.

Da Ponte, Lorenzo (1749–1838): Italian librettist and poet. Da Ponte rose to the peak of his achievement with his libretti for Mozart's operas *The Marriage of Figaro*, *Don Giovanni* and *Così fan tutte*.

Caccini, Giulio (1551–1618): One of the earliest Italian opera composers and a member of the Florentine Camerata.

Gesualdo, Carlo, Prince of Venosa (c. 1560–1613): Italian lutenist and composer, famous for his innovations of harmonic progressions and dissonance.

Glinka, Mikhail (1804–1857): Russian composer regarded as the founder of Russian musical nationalism. His operatic masterpiece is *Ruslan and Lyudmila* of 1836.

Gluck, Christoph Willibald (1714–1787): Major composer who effected a synthesis of elements of Italian opera and traditional French opera. Essential features of his operatic style include melodically simple and emotionally direct arias; recitatives that demonstrate a high melodic content; the use of dance as integral to the dramatic action; strong reliance on choruses, and a high degree of integration of dance, chorus and solos.

Hofmannsthal, Hugo von (1874–1929): Great Austrian librettist who wrote the libretti for many of Richard Strauss's operas.

Josquin des Prez (c. 1440–1521): Preeminent composer of the Renaissance who used both polyphonic and homophonic styles. His madrigals represent the Renaissance ideal of emotional and character expressivity.

Leonin (Magister Leoninus) (c. 1135–c. 1201): Composer and poet of the Notre Dame school and greatest exponent of florid organum.

Lully, Jean-Baptiste (1632–1687): Major French composer, who laid the foundation for the French operatic tradition. Lully created a national style that focused on magnificence, tragic drama and dance. He designed a type of recitative that was modeled on spoken drama, using one pitch per syllable and reflecting the flexibility of the French language, with its continuous changes of meter. His arias tend to be short and limited in vocal range, with an emphasis on clear enunciation.

Machaut, Guillaume de (c. 1300–1377): Important composer of sacred and secular music; master of polyphonic technique and musical eloquence.

Mahler, Gustav (1860–1911): Great Austrian composer and opera conductor of the late romantic era. Although he never wrote an opera, Mahler was a master of smaller-scale vocal music and his orchestral music has deep affinities with vocal music in its expressive content.

Metastasio, Pietro (1698–1782): Greatest librettist of the first half of the 18th century. Metastasio standardized his libretti into a formulaic dramatic procedure and formularized arias into a structure known as the "da capo" aria. His reforms influenced the development of opera seria.

Meyerbeer, Giacomo (1791–1864): German-born composer who almost single-handedly established French grand opera. Meyerbeer was famous for his ability to manage enormous forces on stage. His most famous opera is *Les Huguenots* of 1836. His operas have fallen into obscurity because they lack musical and dramatic substance.

Monteverdi, Claudio (1567–1643): Italian composer credited with the creation of the first opera, *Orfeo* of 1607. Monteverdi did not invent opera, but elevated it to a level of artistic viability and substance it had not previously enjoyed. His most important contribution to the genre was an elevated form of recitative: *arioso*. He was the first composer to use purely instrumental passages in ensemble numbers in opera. He was in advance of his time in his use of dissonance and chromatic harmonies and in his ability to express fundamental emotions through music. Many of his operas are still performed today.

Mozart, Wolfgang Amadeus (1756–1791): Great Austrian composer of the classical era. His operas are widely regarded as his greatest contribution to musical history. A major aspect of Mozart's significance as an opera composer is his unprecedented genius for musical characterization and dramatic momentum. He is a consummate master of complex and subtle vocal and orchestral manipulation. Mozart's music does not just decorate the libretto. It creates a whole new drama, revealing subtleties and truths that go beyond the libretto. It energizes the dramatic action and fleshes out his characters, imbuing them with an extraordinary range of moods, emotions, subtlety, unconscious motivation and humanity.

Mussorgsky, Modest (1839–1881): Great Russian composer and member of the so-called Russian Five, a group of composers who established the Russian national style of the mid to late 19th century. His opera *Boris Godunov* is the pinnacle of Russian opera.

Pergolesi, Giovanni (1710–1736): Italian composer of *La serva padrona* (1733), the first important opera buffa that laid the foundation for subsequent contributions to the genre.

Peri, Jacopo (1561–1633): One of the earliest Italian opera composers and member of the Florentine Camerata. Peri is known for his operas *Daphne* and *Euridice*.

Puccini, Giacomo (1858–1924): Great Italian composer of universally popular operas. Puccini was the greatest exponent of the opera verismo style, which found inspiration in the dark side of human nature. He was a superb lyricist and consummate dramatist. Among his best-loved and renowned operas are *Madam Butterfly*, *Tosca* and *La Bohème*.

Rameau, Jean-Philippe (1683–1764): Foremost French composer of the 18th century. Rameau's operas display much less contrast between aria and recitative than contemporary Italian operas. Although Rameau's operas are rarely heard outside France because they are tailored to particular French tastes, they are worth seeking out for their musical value.

Rinuccini, Ottavio (1562–1621): Italian poet/librettist and member of the Florentine Camerata. Rinuccini wrote the libretti for the earliest operas: Caccini's *Euridice* and Peri's *Daphne*.

Rossini, Gioacchino (1792–1868): Greatest Italian composer of the bel canto style. Rossini had a great gift for wit, comedy and compositional innovation. He pioneered the use of strings instead of harpsichord or piano to accompany recitative. He invented the long, orchestral type of crescendo known as the "Rossini crescendo." He was a master of orchestral color and musical characterization. His opera, *The Barber of Seville* remains one of the best-loved and greatest comic operas of all time. Its most famous aria, "Largo al factotum," introduces the character of Figaro and is a brilliant example of musical characterization.

Rousseau, Jean-Jacques (1712–1778): Swiss-born French philosopher and composer who embraced the Italian opera buffa genre as an example of opera appropriate to the Enlightenment. His *Le Devin du village* (1752) is very close to the popular French tradition of opéra comique.

Scarlatti, Alessandro (1660–1725): Founder of the Neapolitan school of opera, Scarlatti's operas exerted substantial influence on other opera composers.

Strauss, Richard (1864–1949): Brilliant German composer, whose music stretches Wagnerian concepts to further limits. Strauss's psychopathological and erotic masterpiece *Salome* represents experimental, post-Victorian trends at the turn of the 20th century.

Verdi, Giuseppe (1813–1901): Greatest Italian opera composer of the second half of the 19th century. Verdi's operas endure because of their use of well-written libretti, their melodic beauty, their focus on human emotions, their psychological insight, and their unsurpassed dramatic power. Among Verdi's greatest operas are *Rigoletto*, *La Traviata* and *Otello*.

Wagner, Richard (1813–1883): Great German composer whose operas revolutionized music and whose opera, *Tristan and Isolde* is considered, along with Beethoven's Ninth Symphony, the most influential composition of the 19th century. Wagner developed the concept of the music drama (*Gesamtkunstwerk*) as an artistic genre that encompasses all types of art: drama, music, poetry, dance, etc. He created the leitmotif whereby musical motives are assigned to characters, things or concepts and he gave the orchestra unprecedented power as the purveyor of inner meanings and unspoken truths.

Weber, Carl Maria von (1786–1826): German composer whose opera *Der Freischütz* became the definitive work that established 19th-century German opera, characterized by the use of spoken dialogue, and plots that hinge on the supernatural as found in German medieval legend.

Weelkes, Thomas (c. 1575–1623): One of the great English madrigal composers. Weelkes was a master of word painting.

Bibliography

General Sources

Donington, Robert. *Opera and its Symbols*. Yale University Press, 1990.

Grout, Donald. *A Short History of Opera*. 2d ed. Columbia University Press, 1965.

Grout, Donald, and Claude Palisca. *A History of Western Music*. 5th ed. W.W. Norton, 1996.

Hamm, Charles. *Opera*. Allyn and Bacon, 1966.

Kerman, Joseph. *Opera as Drama*. University of California Press, 1988.

Mordden, Ethan. *Opera Anecdotes*. 1985. Reprint, Norton, 1996.

New Grove Dictionary of Music, The. Macmillan Publishers, 1980.

Palisca, Claude, ed. *Norton Anthology of Western Music*. 3d ed. W. W. Norton, 1980.

Plaut, Eric. *Grand Opera—Mirror of the Western Mind*. Ivan R. Dee, 1993.

Schonberg, Harold. *The Lives of the Great Composers*. Norton, 1970.

Weiss, Piero, and Richard Taruskin. *Music in the Western World*. Schirmer, 1984.

Italian Opera

Kimbell, David. *Italian Opera*. Cambridge University Press, 1991.

Mozart

Dent, Edward. *Mozart's Operas*. Clarendon/Oxford University Press, 1991.

Heartz, Daniel. *Mozart's Operas*. University of California Press, 1990.

Mann, William. *The Operas of Mozart*. Oxford University Press, 1977.

Puccini

Osborne, Charles. *The Complete Operas of Puccini*. Atheneum, 1982.

Strauss

Del Mar, Normen. *Richard Strauss—A Critical Commentary of His Life and Works*. Cornell University Press, 1986.

Verdi

Budden, Julien. *The Operas of Verdi*. Cassell, 1973.

Hepokoski, James. *Otello*. Cambridge University Press, 1987.

Phillips-Matz. *Verdi*. Oxford University Press, 1993.

Wagner

Magee, Brian. *Aspects of Wagner*. Oxford University Press, 1988.

Millington, Barry. *Wagner*. Princeton University Press, 1984.

Notes

Notes

Notes

Notes

Notes

Notes

Notes

Notes

Notes